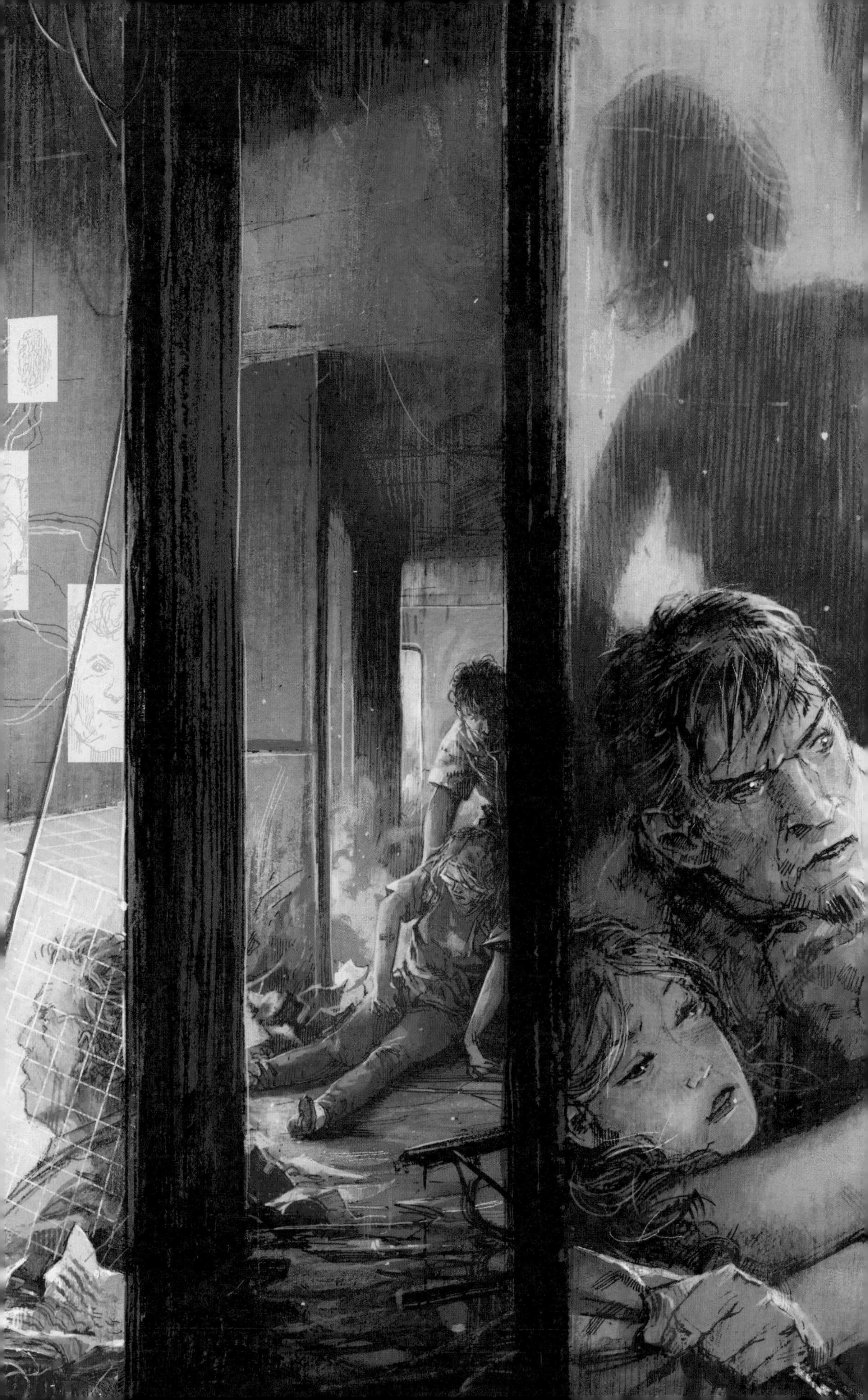

THE BUNKER

VOLUME 3

Written by
Joshua Hale Fialkov

Chapters 10-13 Illustrated and Colored by
Joe Infurnari

Chapter 14 Illustrated by
Brahm Revel

Chapter 14 Colored by
Jason Fischer

Lettered by
Joe Infurnari

Edited by
James Lucas Jones and Robin Herrera

Designed by
Jason Storey

PUBLISHED BY ONI PRESS, INC.

Publisher, Joe Nozemack
Editor In Chief, James Lucas Jones
Director of Sales, Cheyenne Allott
Director of Publicity, Fred Reckling
Production Manager, Troy Look
Graphic Designer, Hilary Thompson
Production Assistant, Jared Jones
Senior Editor, Charlie Chu
Editor, Robin Herrera
Associate Editor, Ari Yarwood
Inventory Coordinator, Brad Rooks
Office Assistant, Jung Lee

VOLUME 3

This volume collects issues 10-14 of the
Oni Press series *The Bunker*

ONIPRESS.COM
FACEBOOK.COM/ONIPRESS • TWITTER.COM/ONIPRESS
ONIPRESS.TUMBLR.COM • INSTAGRAM.COM/ONIPRESS
THEFIALKOV.COM/@JOSHFIALKOV • JOEINFURNARI.COM/@INFURNARI

FIRST EDITION:
DECEMBER 2015

LIBRARY OF CONGRESS CONTROL NUMBER:
2015944013

ISBN 978-1-62010-274-9
eISBN 978-1-62010-275-6

10 8 6 4 2 1 3 5 7 9

PRINTED IN CHINA

CHAPTER
10

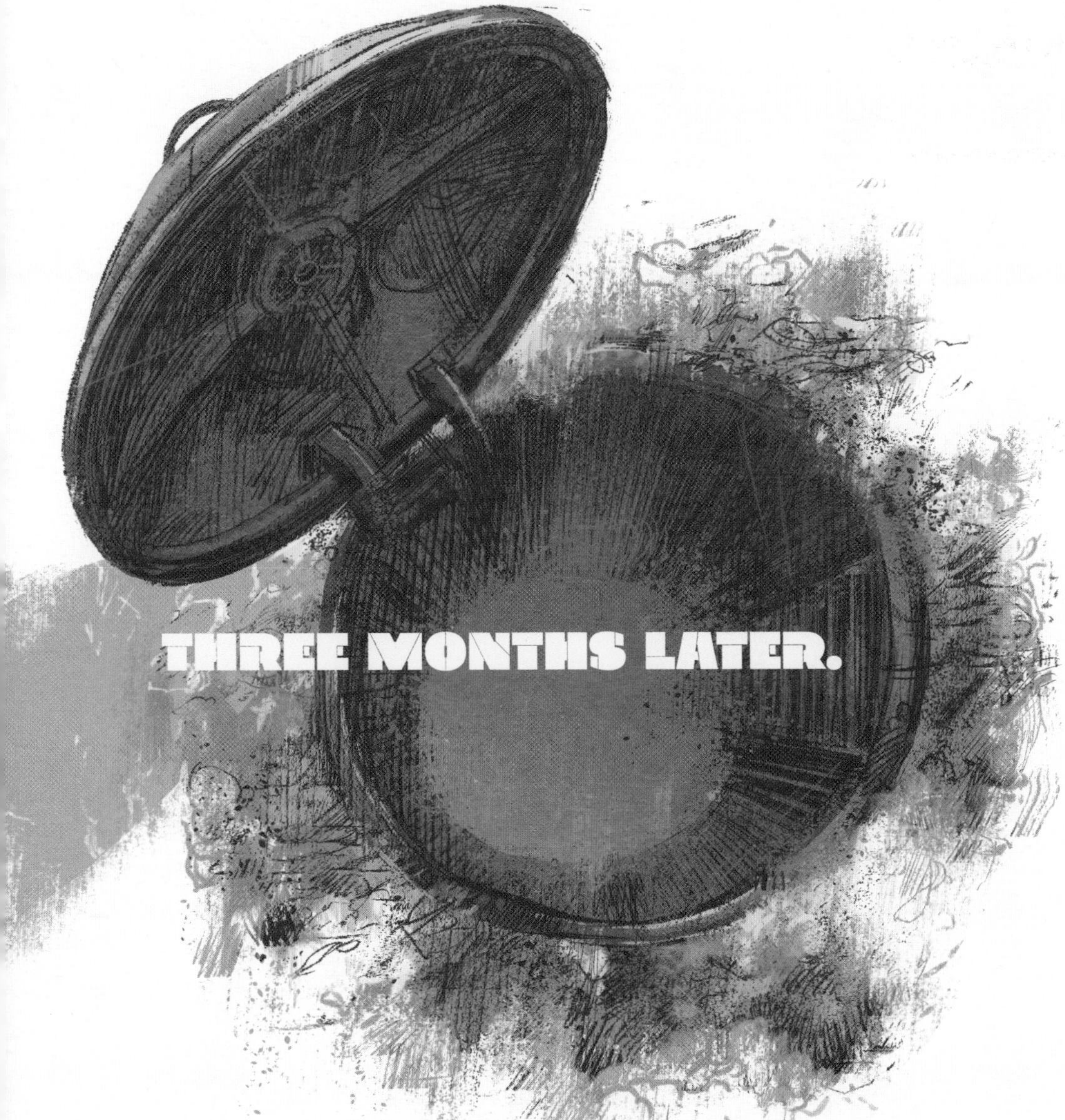
THREE MONTHS LATER.

BZZZ

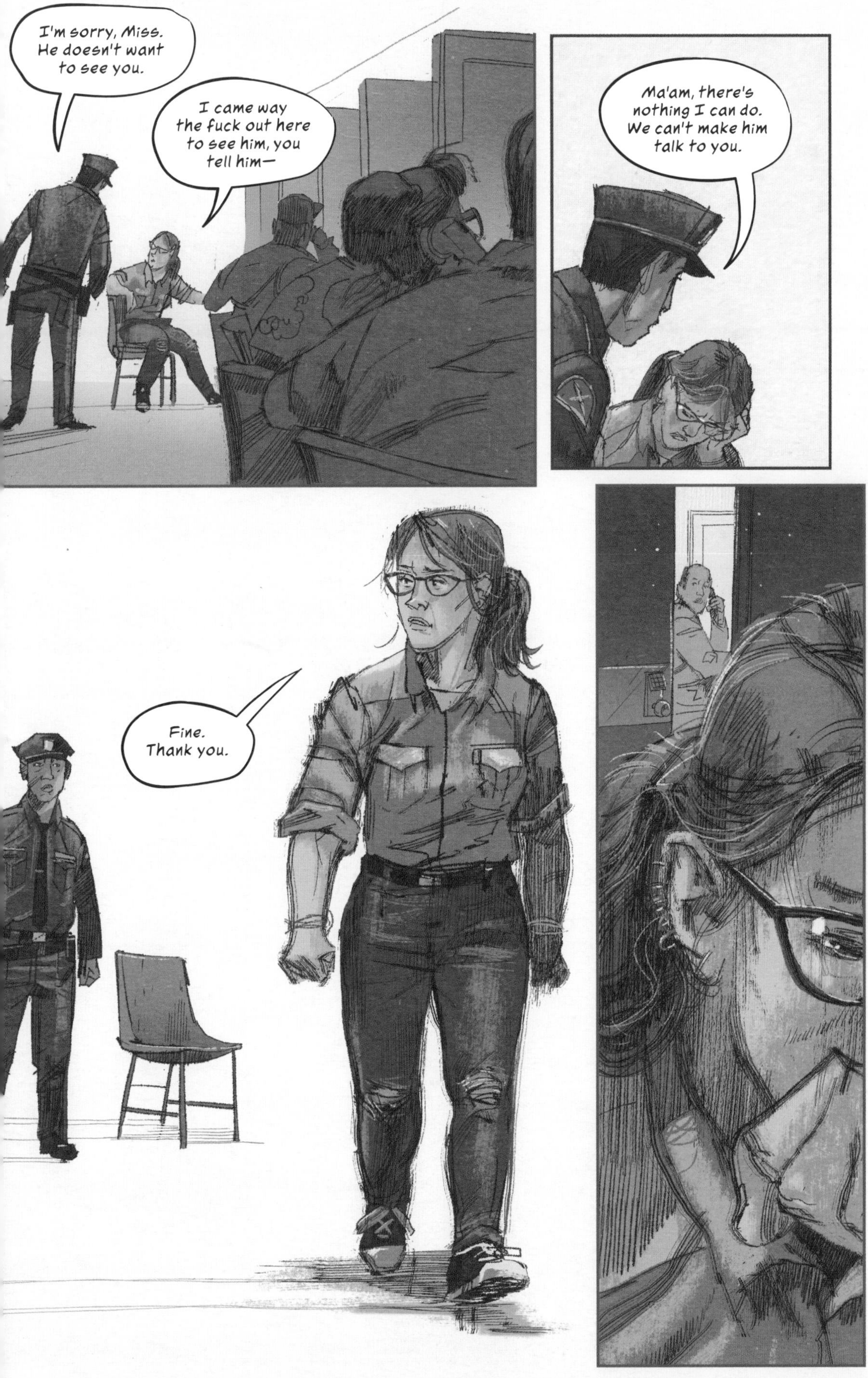
I'm sorry, Miss. He doesn't want to see you.
I came way the fuck out here to see him, you tell him—
Ma'am, there's nothing I can do. We can't make him talk to you.
Fine. Thank you.

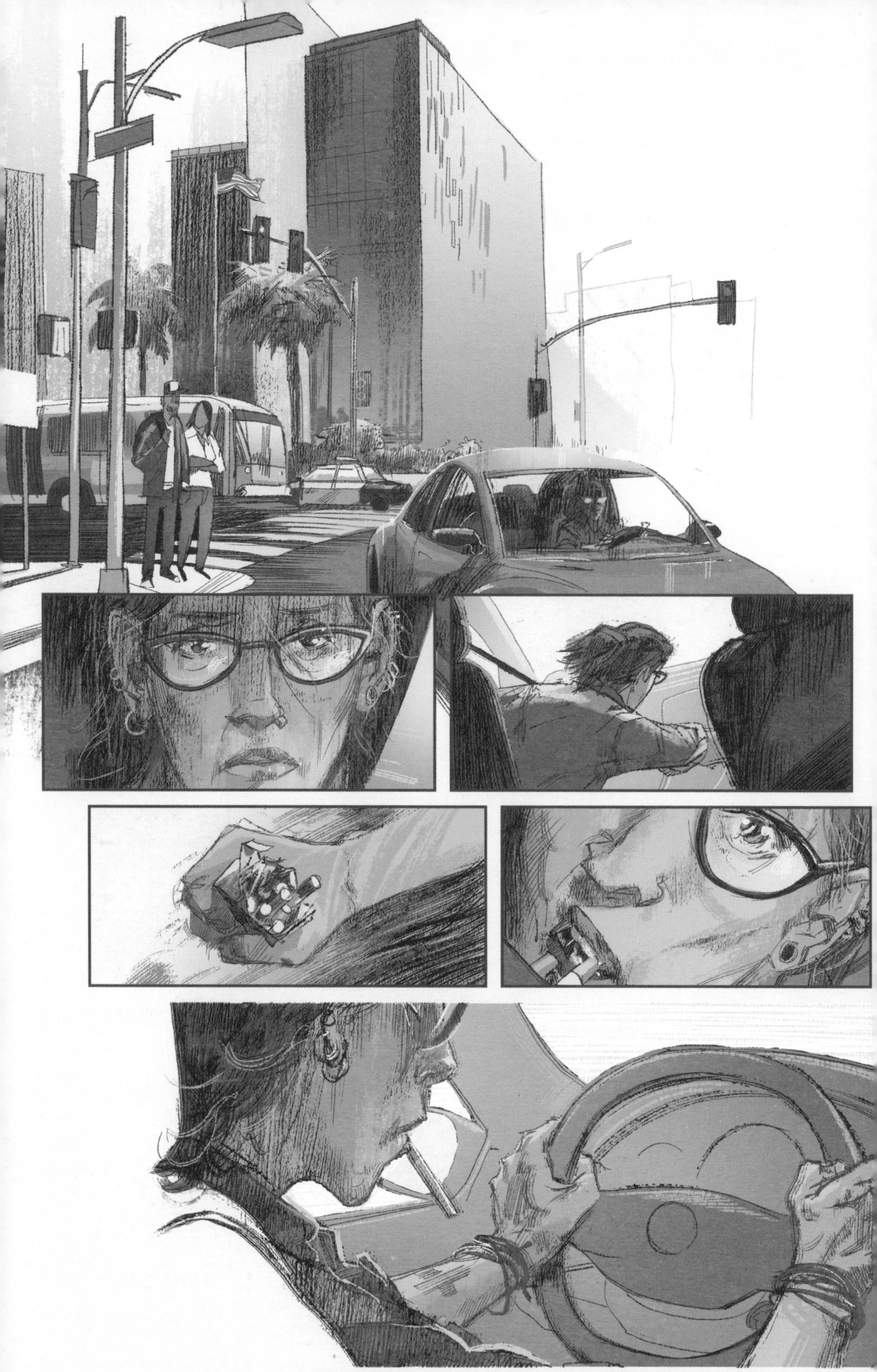

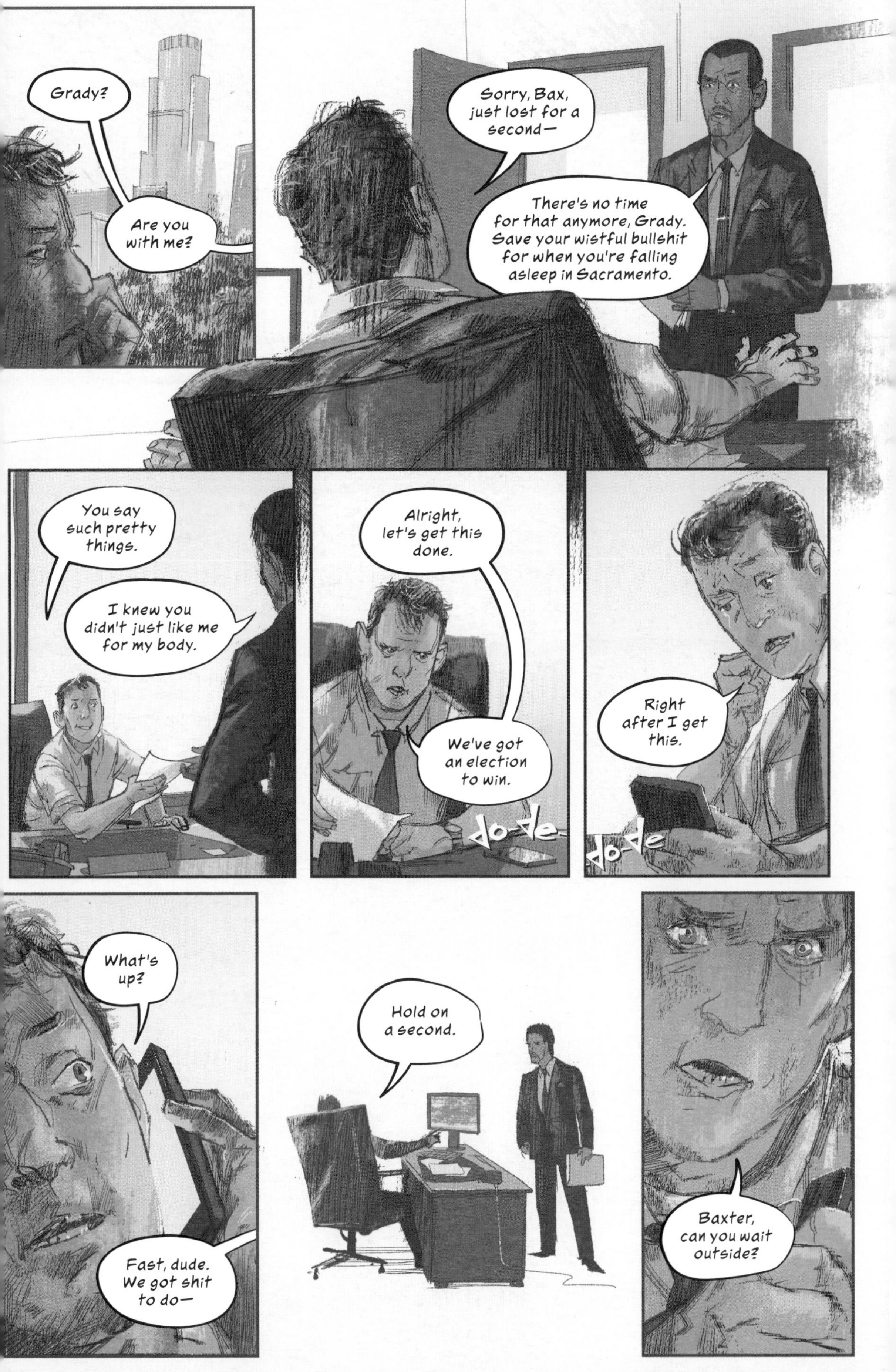
Grady?
Are you with me?
Sorry, Bax, just lost for a second—
There's no time for that anymore, Grady. Save your wistful bullshit for when you're falling asleep in Sacramento.
You say such pretty things.
I knew you didn't just like me for my body.
Alright, let's get this done.
We've got an election to win.
do-de-
do-de
Right after I get this.
What's up?
Fast, dude. We got shit to do—
Hold on a second.
Baxter, can you wait outside?

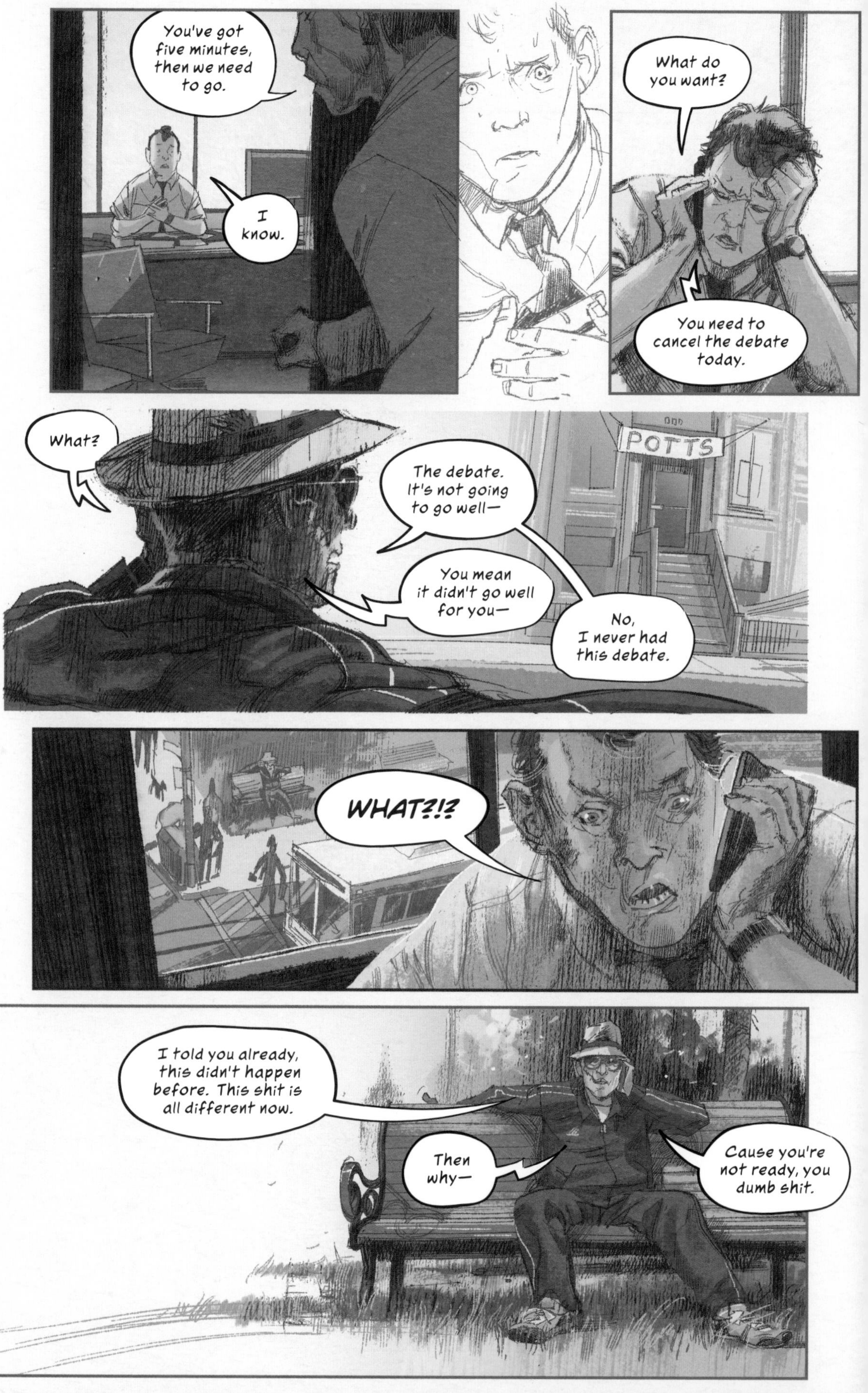
You've got five minutes, then we need to go.
I know.
What do you want?
You need to cancel the debate today.
What?
The debate. It's not going to go well—
You mean it didn't go well for you—
No, I never had this debate.
POTTS
WHAT?!?
I told you already, this didn't happen before. This shit is all different now.
Then why—
Cause you're not ready, you dumb shit.

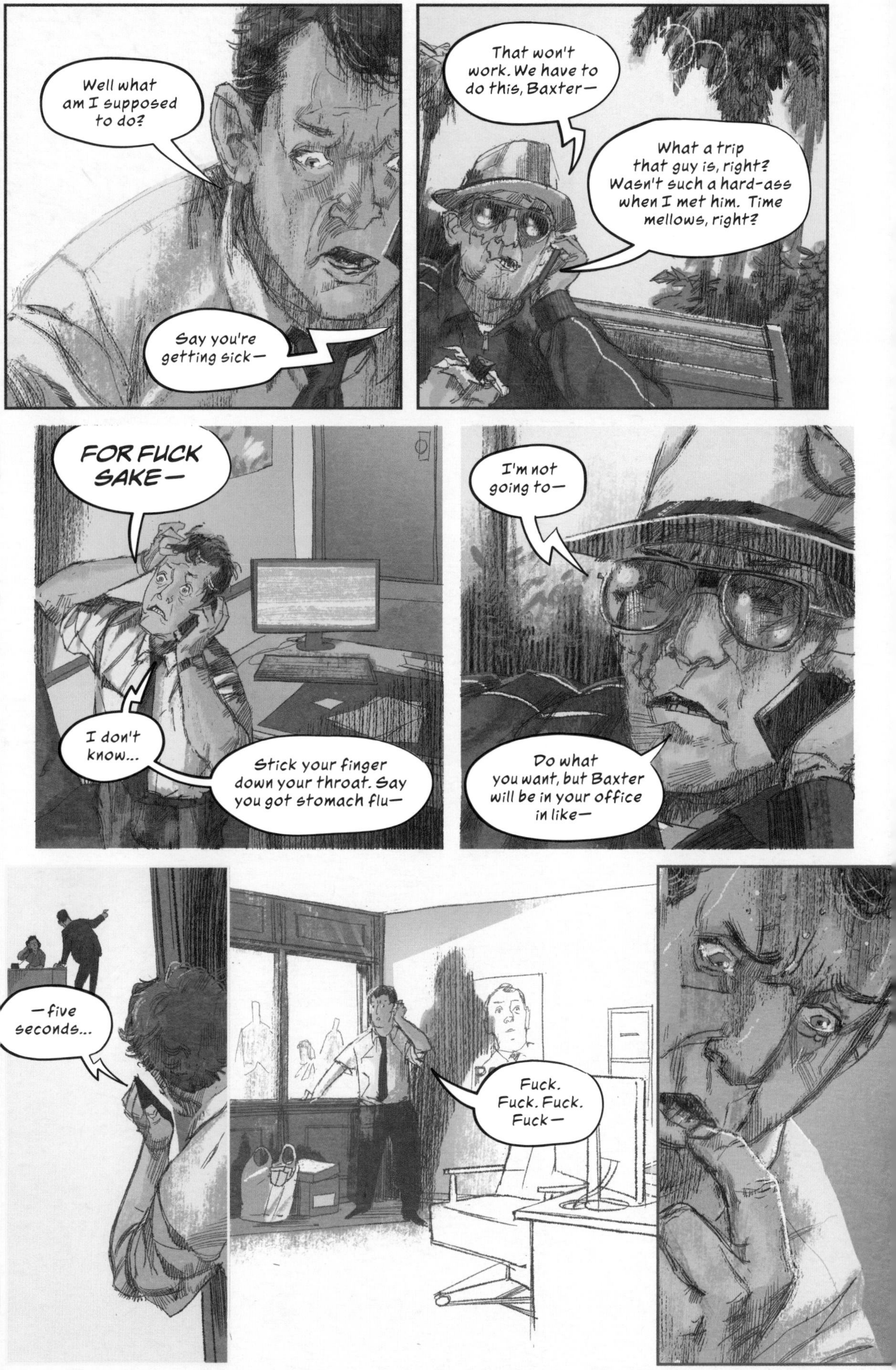
Well what am I supposed to do?
Say you're getting sick—
That won't work. We have to do this, Baxter—
What a trip that guy is, right? Wasn't such a hard-ass when I met him. Time mellows, right?
FOR FUCK SAKE—
I don't know...
Stick your finger down your throat. Say you got stomach flu—
I'm not going to—
Do what you want, but Baxter will be in your office in like—
—five seconds...
Fuck. Fuck. Fuck. Fuck—

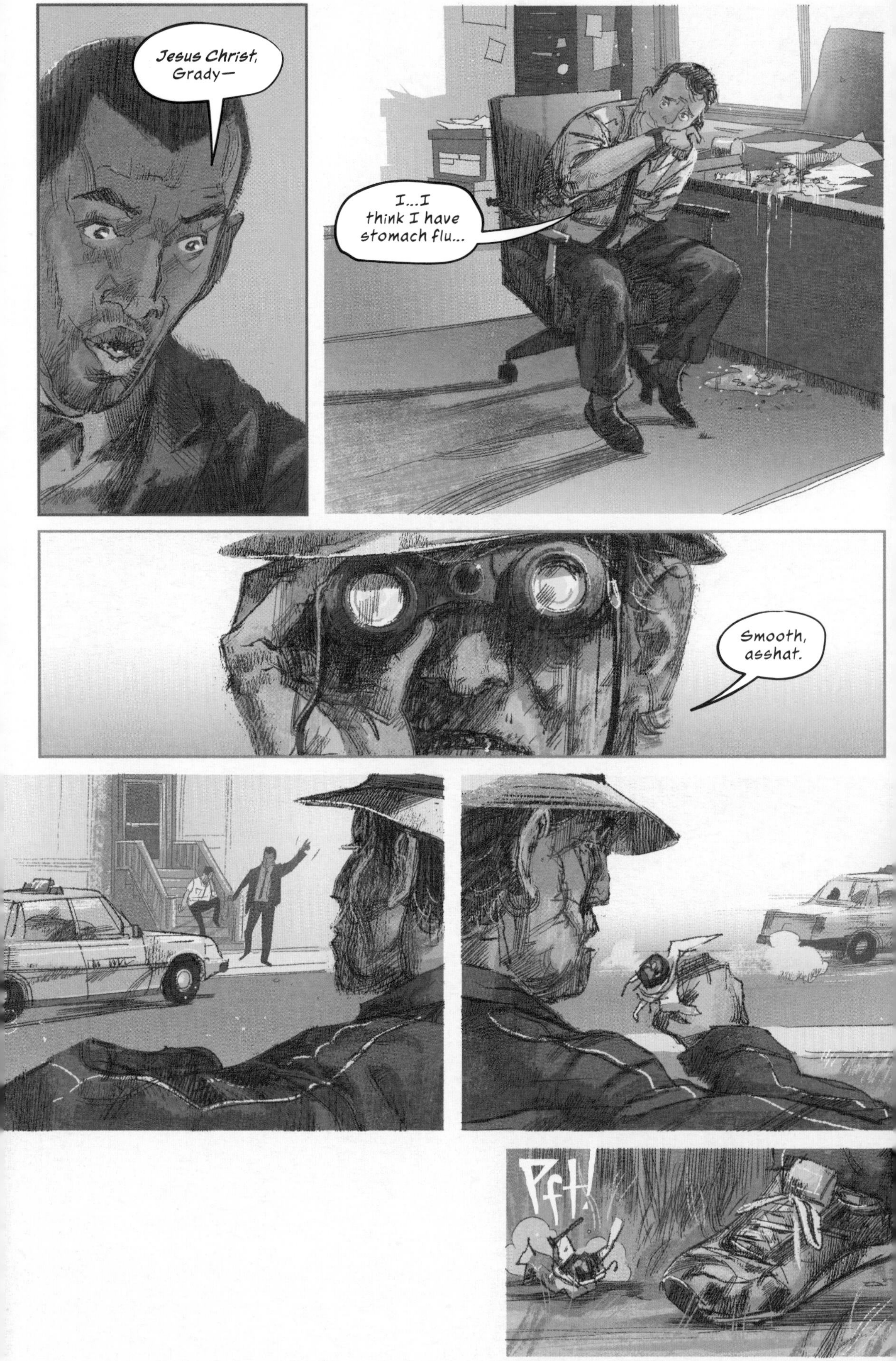

Jesus Christ, Grady—
I...I think I have stomach flu...
Smooth, asshat.
Pft!

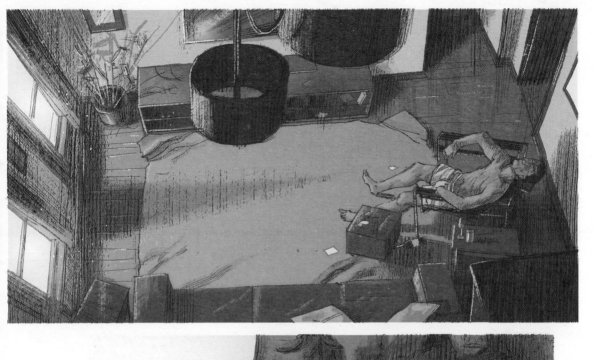

Fuck.

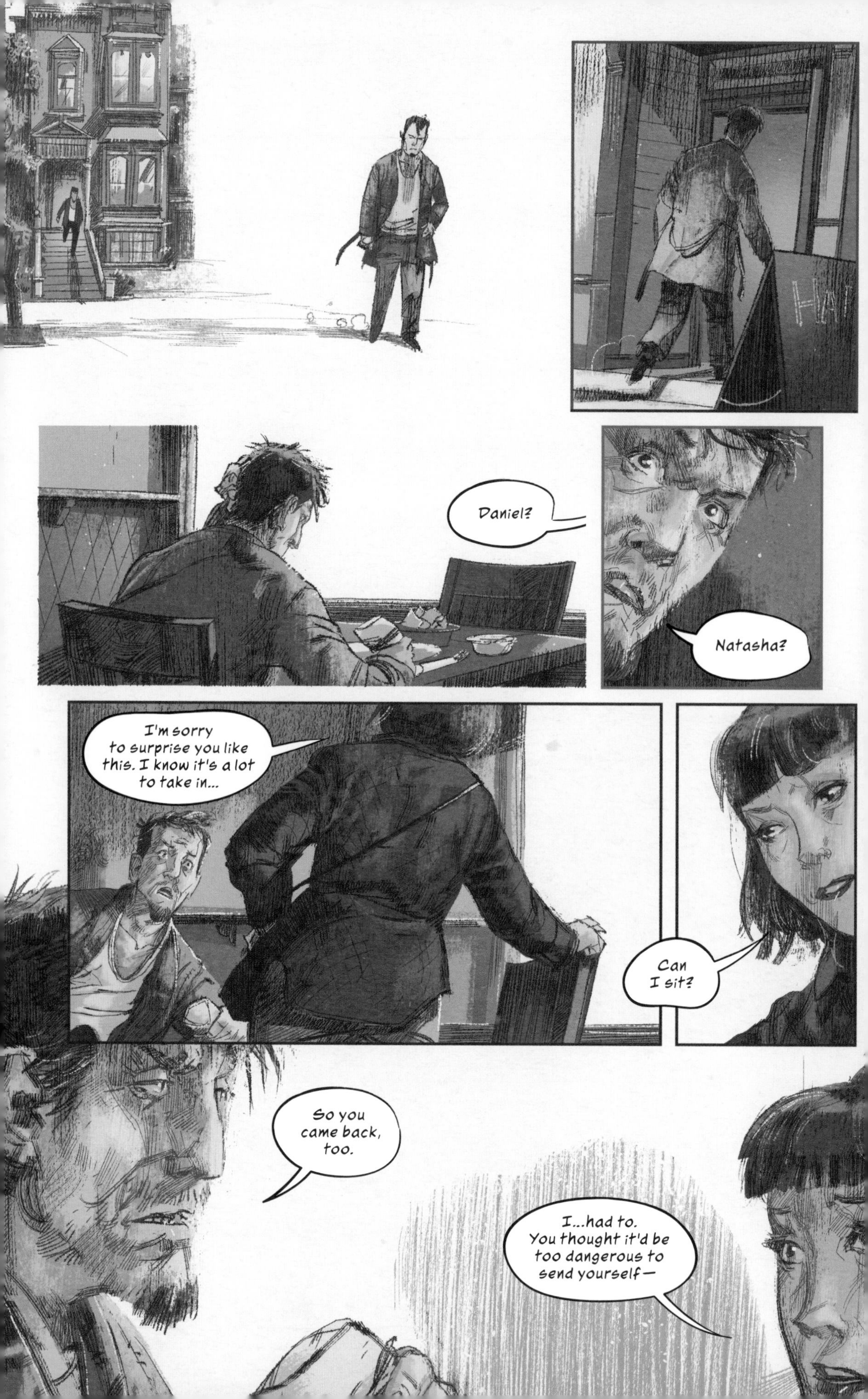
Daniel?
Natasha?
I'm sorry to surprise you like this. I know it's a lot to take in...
Can I sit?
So you came back, too.
I...had to. You thought it'd be too dangerous to send yourself—

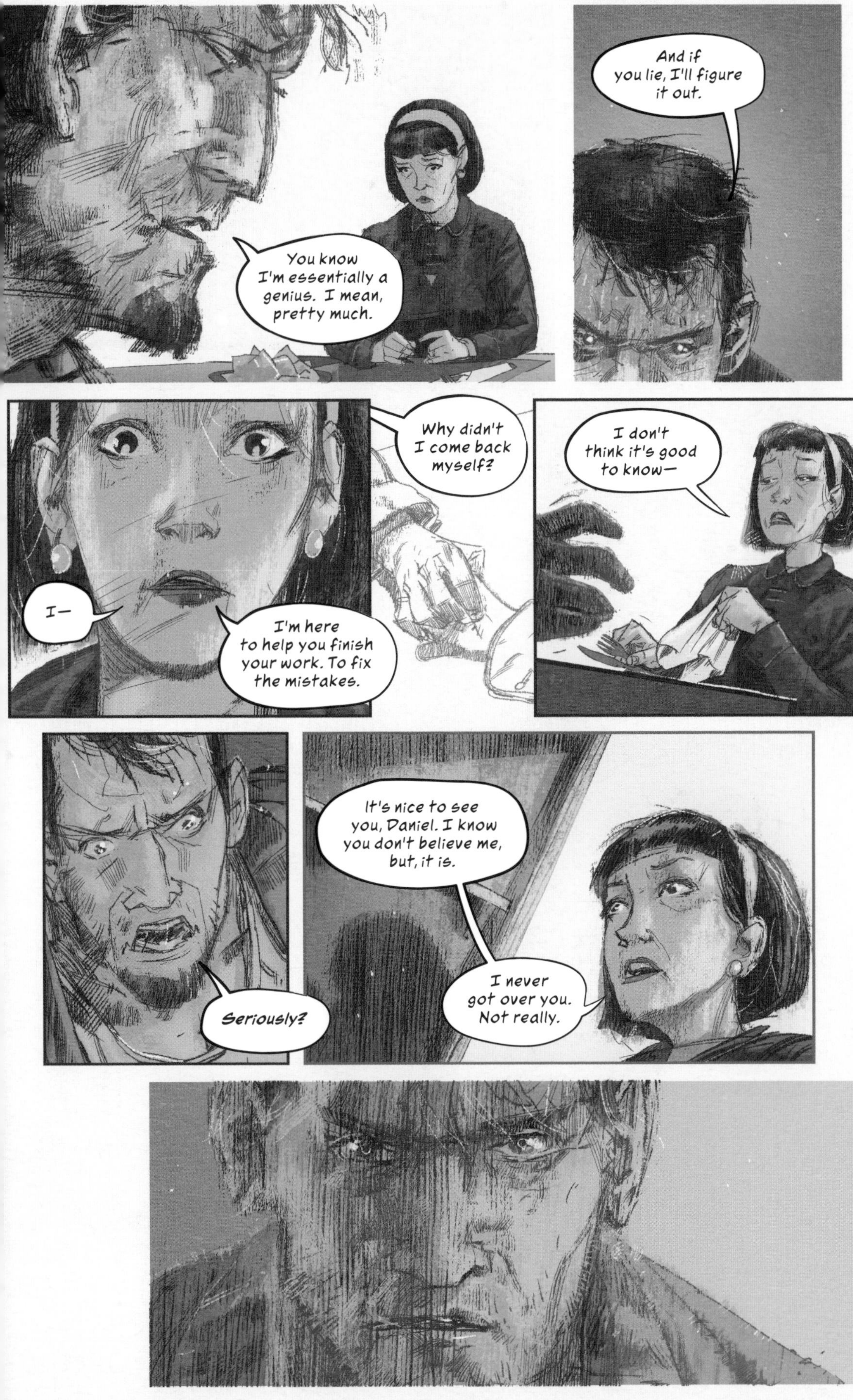
You know I'm essentially a genius. I mean, pretty much.
And if you lie, I'll figure it out.
I—
I'm here to help you finish your work. To fix the mistakes.
Why didn't I come back myself?
I don't think it's good to know—
Seriously?
It's nice to see you, Daniel. I know you don't believe me, but, it is.
I never got over you. Not really.

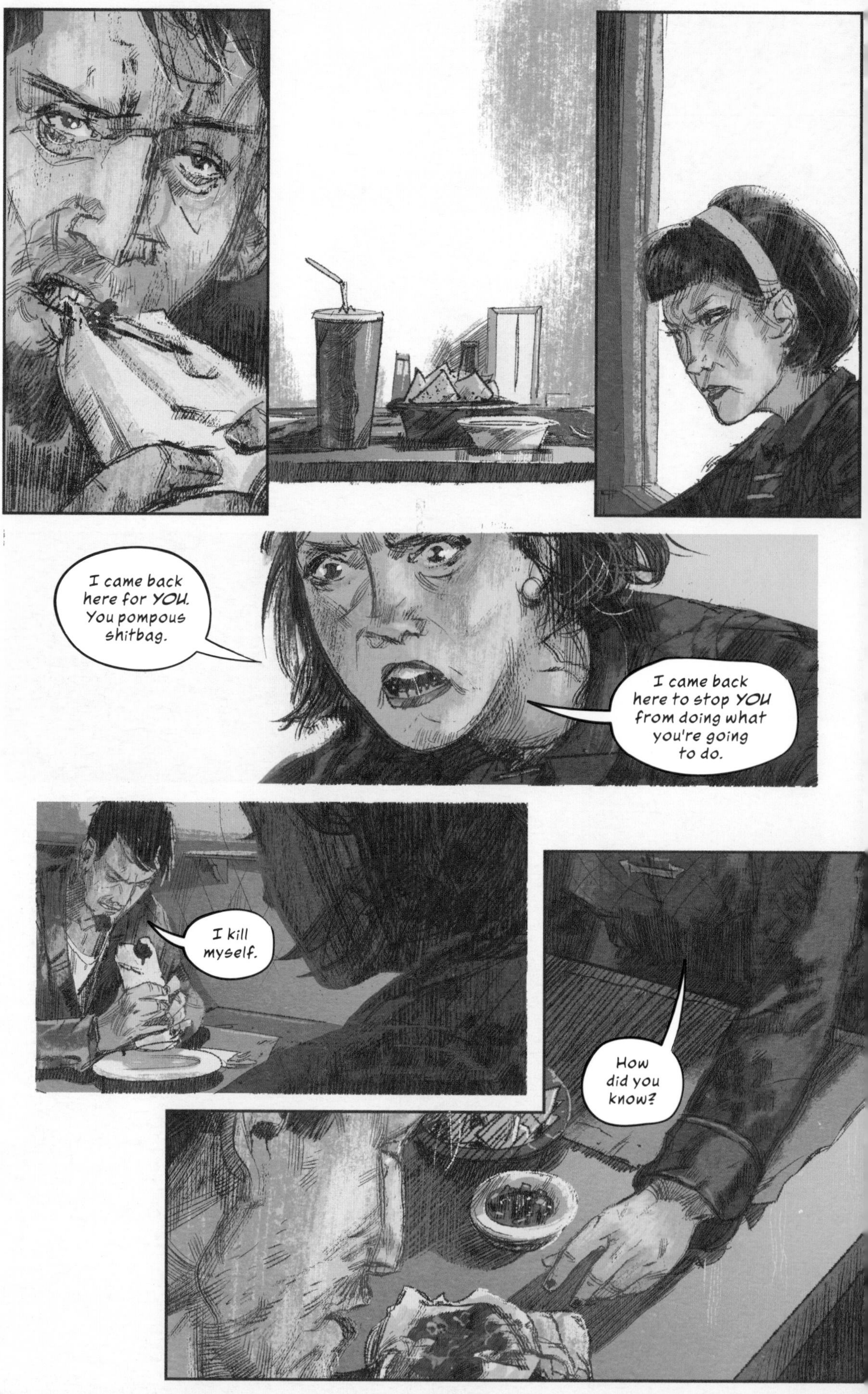
I came back here for YOU. You pompous shitbag.
I came back here to stop YOU from doing what you're going to do.
I kill myself.
How did you know?

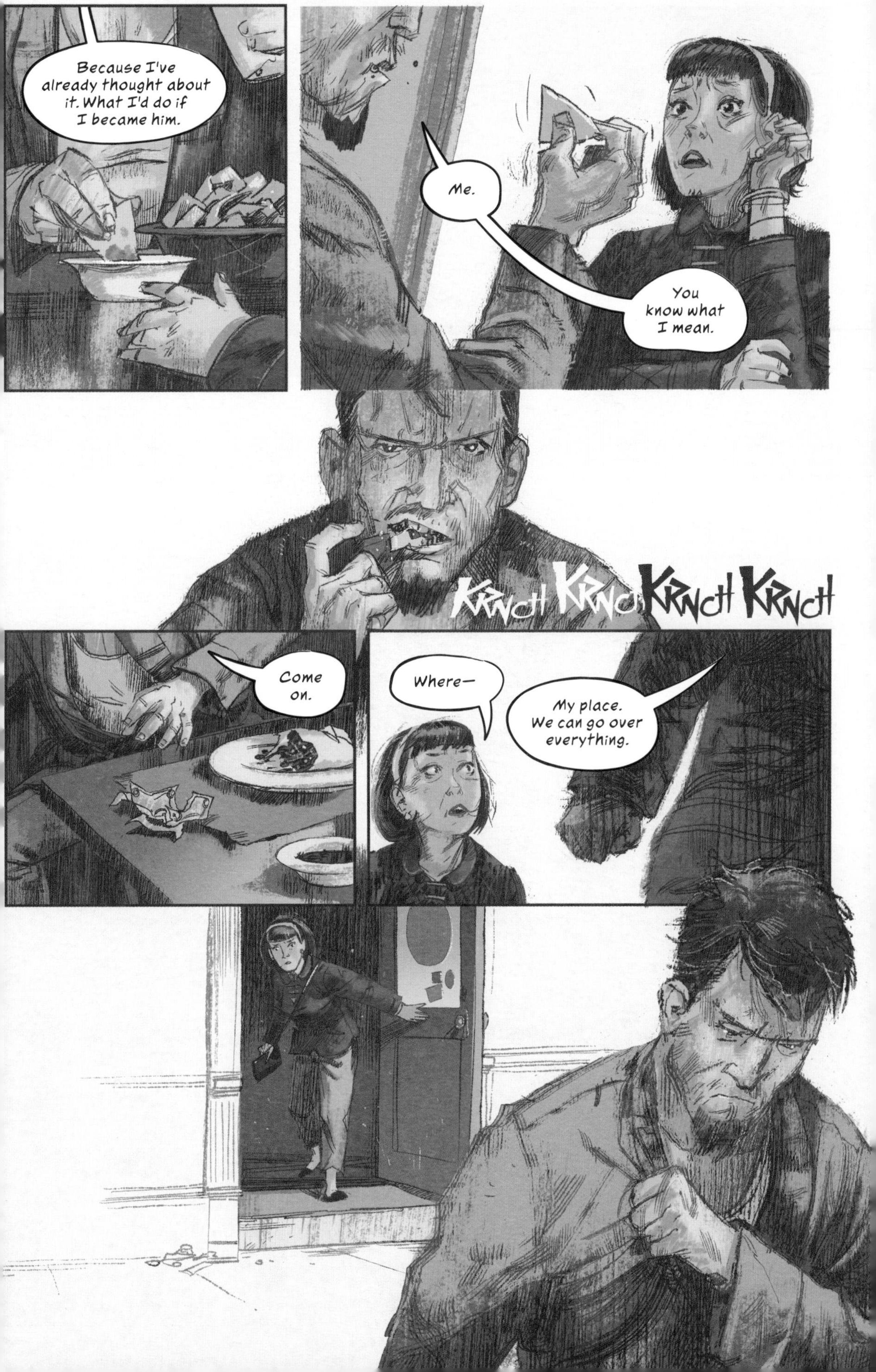
Because I've already thought about it. What I'd do if I became him.
Me.
You know what I mean.
KRNCH KRNCH KRNCH KRNCH
Come on.
Where—
My place. We can go over everything.

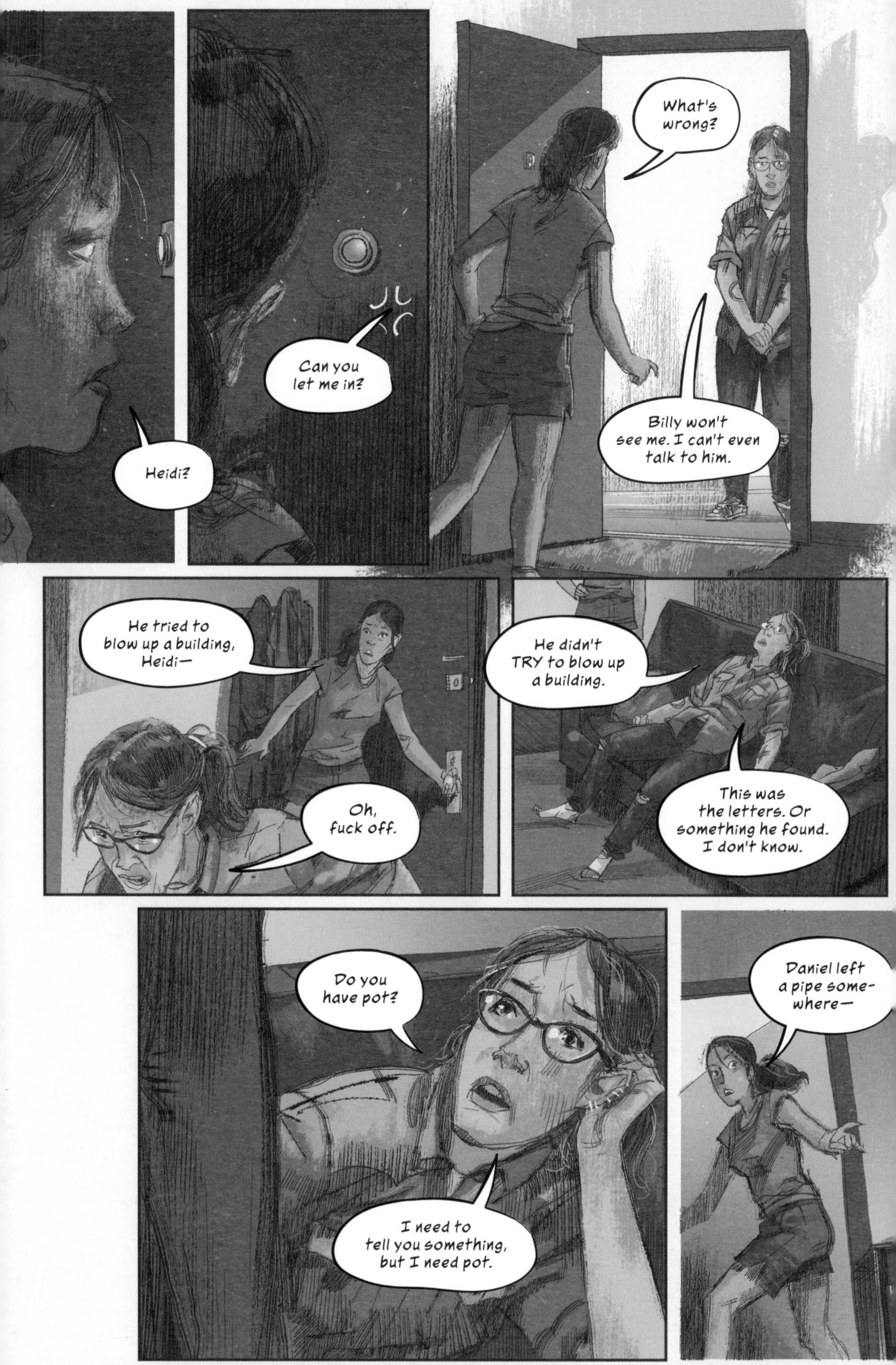
Heidi?
Can you let me in?
What's wrong?
Billy won't see me. I can't even talk to him.
He tried to blow up a building, Heidi—
Oh, fuck off.
He didn't TRY to blow up a building.
This was the letters. Or something he found. I don't know.
Do you have pot?
I need to tell you something, but I need pot.
Daniel left a pipe some-where—

Here.

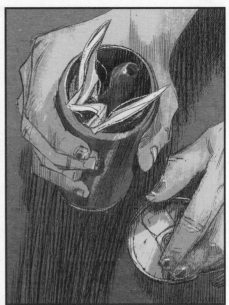

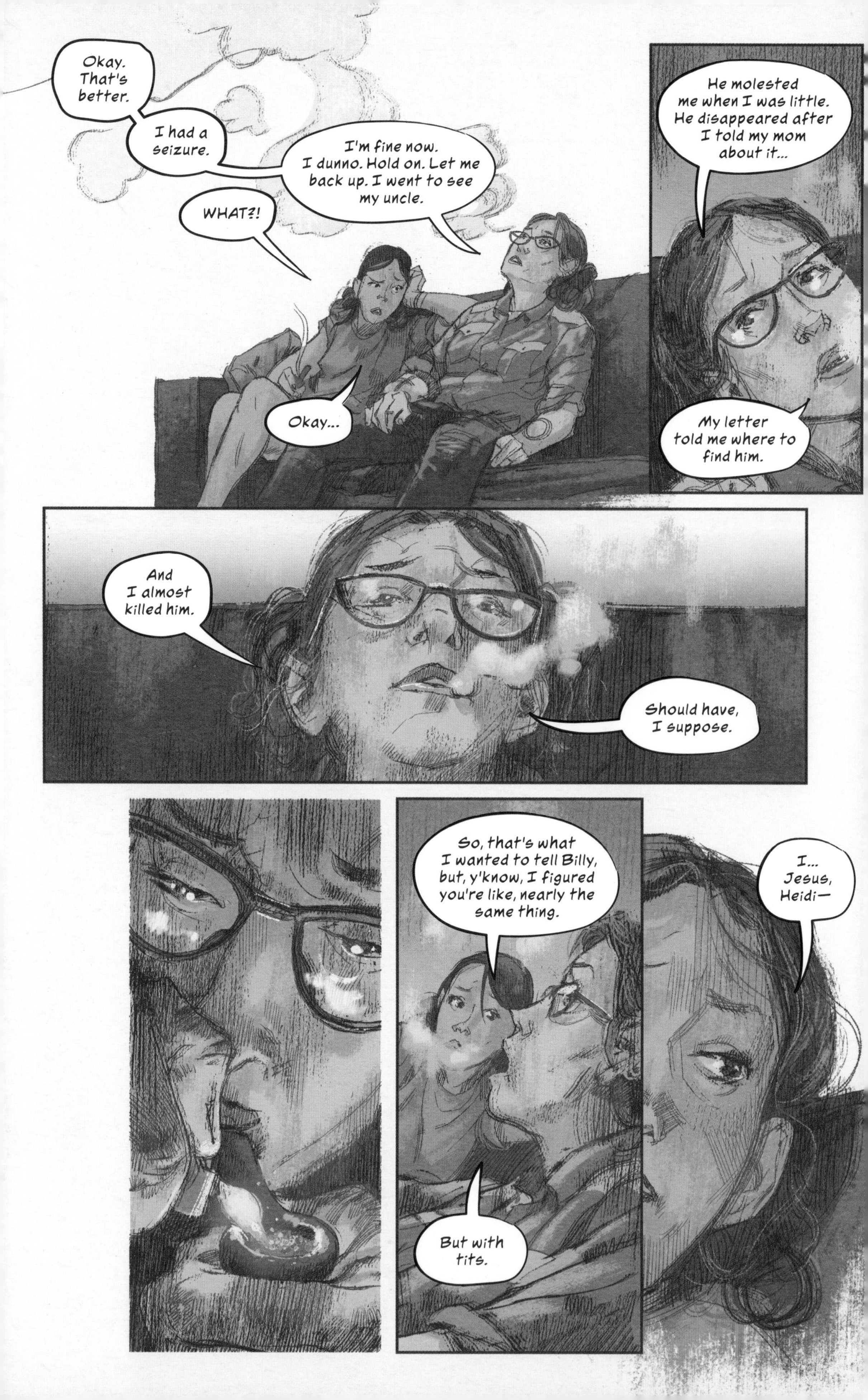
Okay. That's better.
I had a seizure.
I'm fine now. I dunno. Hold on. Let me back up. I went to see my uncle.
WHAT?!
Okay...
He molested me when I was little. He disappeared after I told my mom about it...
My letter told me where to find him.
And I almost killed him.
Should have, I suppose.
So, that's what I wanted to tell Billy, but, y'know, I figured you're like, nearly the same thing.
But with tits.
I... Jesus, Heidi—

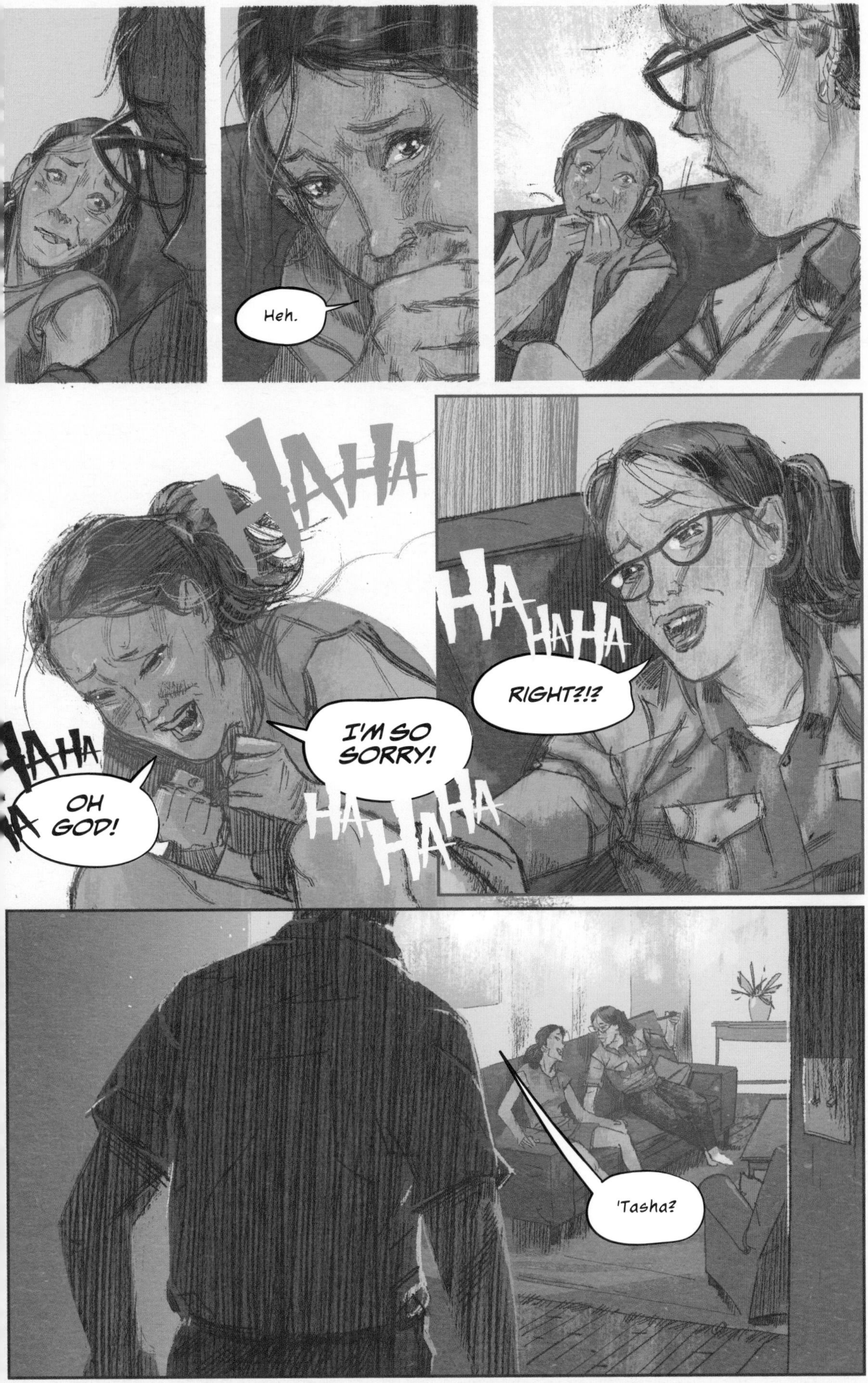
Heh.
HAHA
HA HAHA
RIGHT?!?
HAHA
HA
OH GOD!
I'M SO SORRY!
HAHAHAHA
'Tasha?

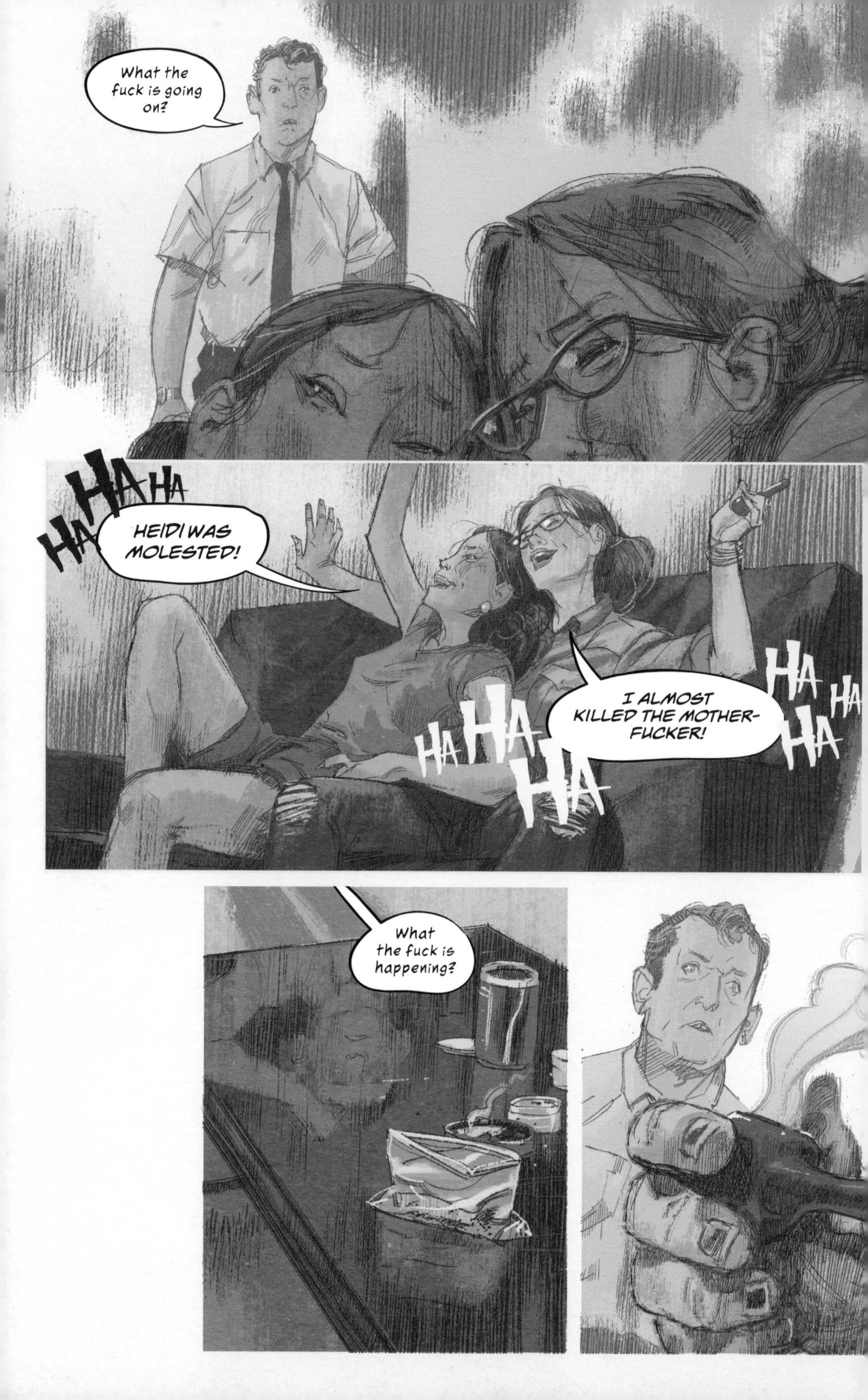
What the fuck is going on?
HA HA HA HA
HEIDI WAS MOLESTED!
I ALMOST KILLED THE MOTHER-FUCKER!
HA HA HA HA
HA HA HA
What the fuck is happening?

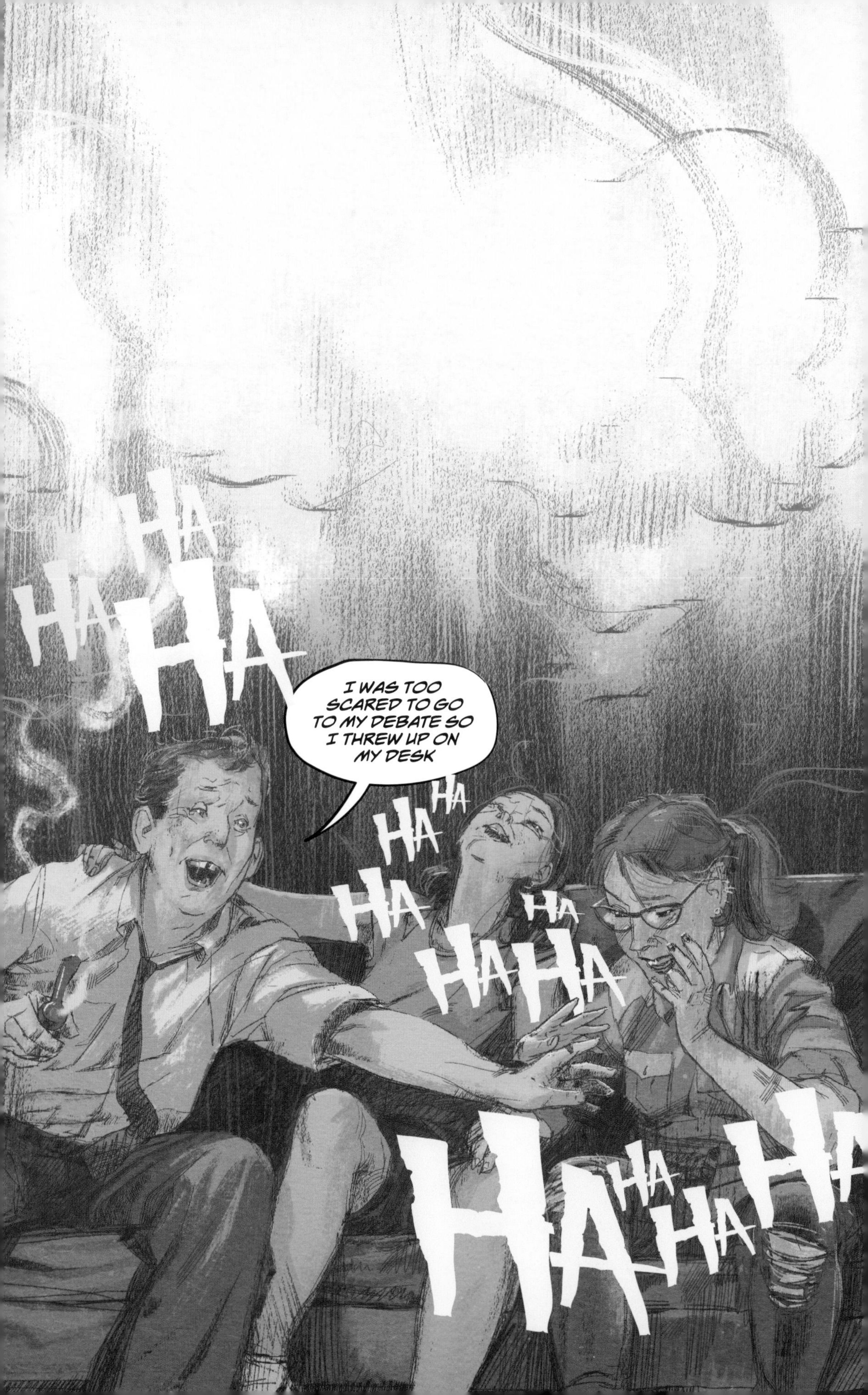

HA HA HA HA
I WAS TOO SCARED TO GO TO MY DEBATE SO I THREW UP ON MY DESK
HA HA HA
HA HA HA
HA HA HA HA HA

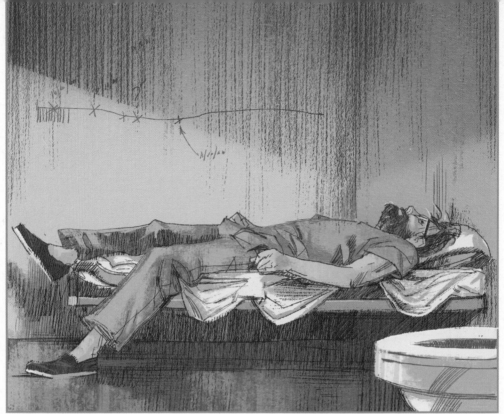

Prisoner, eat up.

No.

This is day 7 without food or water, prisoner. Tomorrow we do an IV.

Whatever.

You have another visitor.

Tell my sister I don't want to see her.

It's not her. It's some guy.

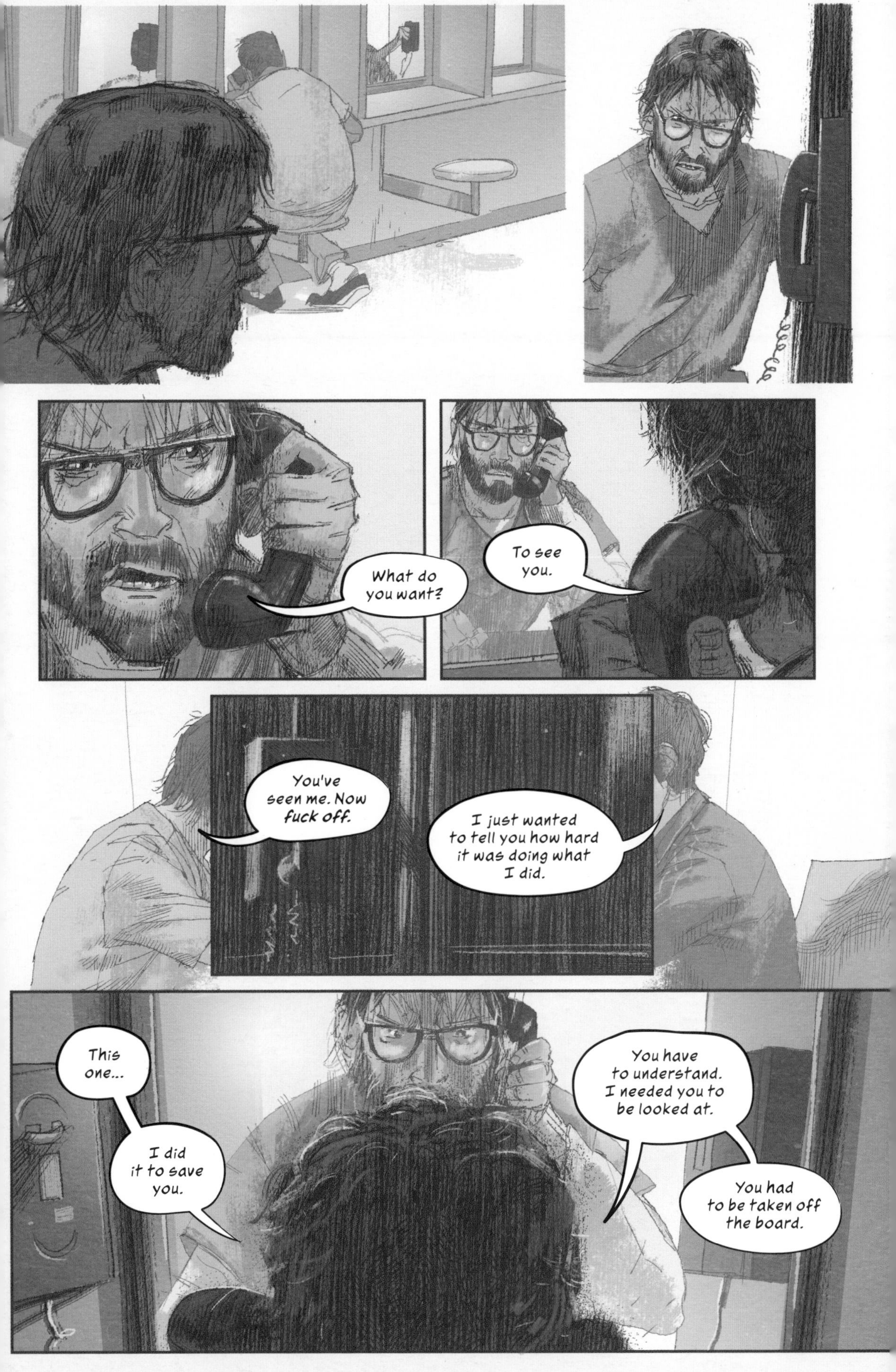
What do you want?
To see you.
You've seen me. Now *fuck off.*
I just wanted to tell you how hard it was doing what I did.
This one...
I did it to save you.
You have to understand. I needed you to be looked at.
You had to be taken off the board.

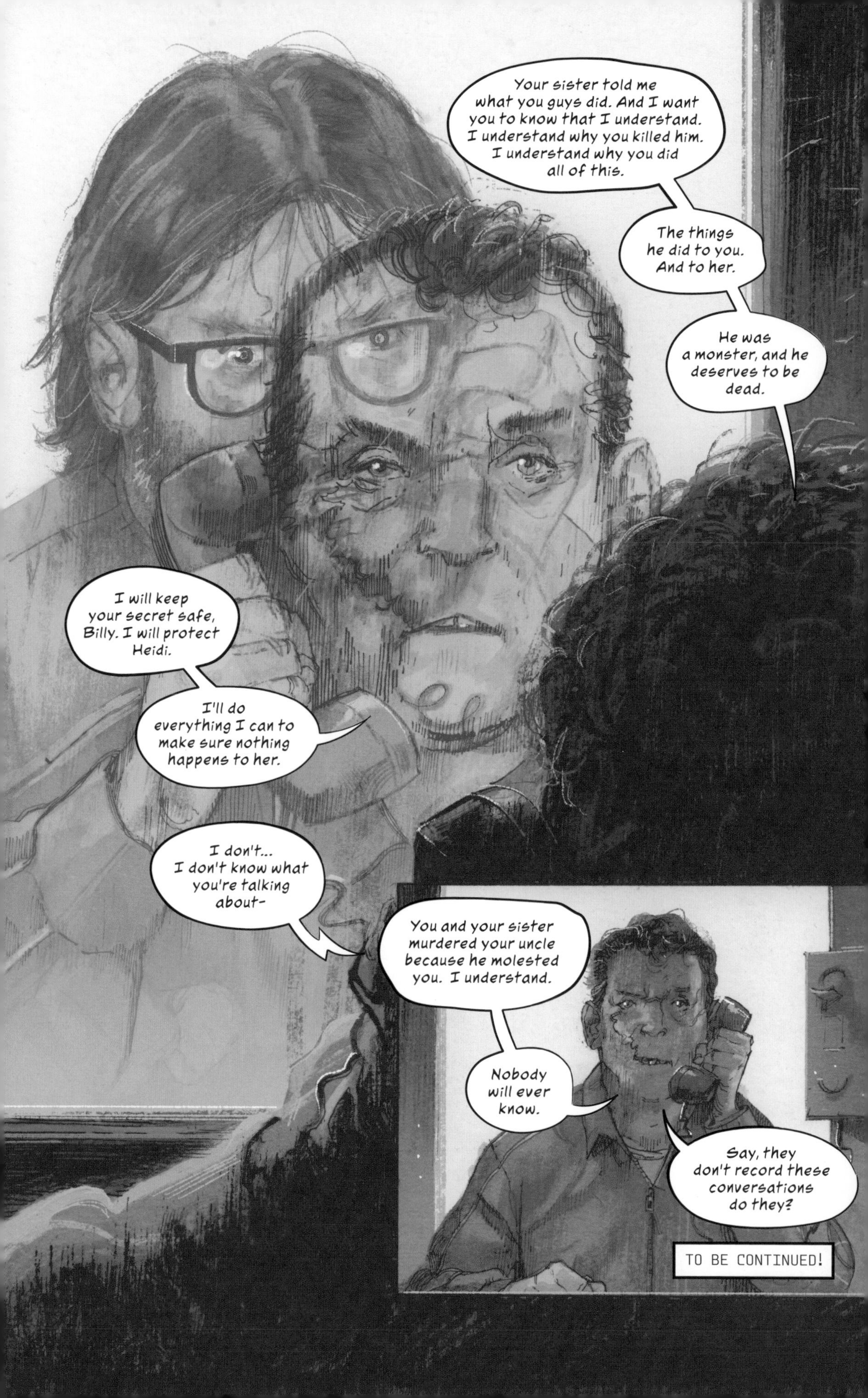
Your sister told me what you guys did. And I want you to know that I understand. I understand why you killed him. I understand why you did all of this.
The things he did to you. And to her.
He was a monster, and he deserves to be dead.
I will keep your secret safe, Billy. I will protect Heidi.
I'll do everything I can to make sure nothing happens to her.
I don't... I don't know what you're talking about-
You and your sister murdered your uncle because he molested you. I understand.
Nobody will ever know.
Say, they don't record these conversations do they?
TO BE CONTINUED!

CHAPTER
11

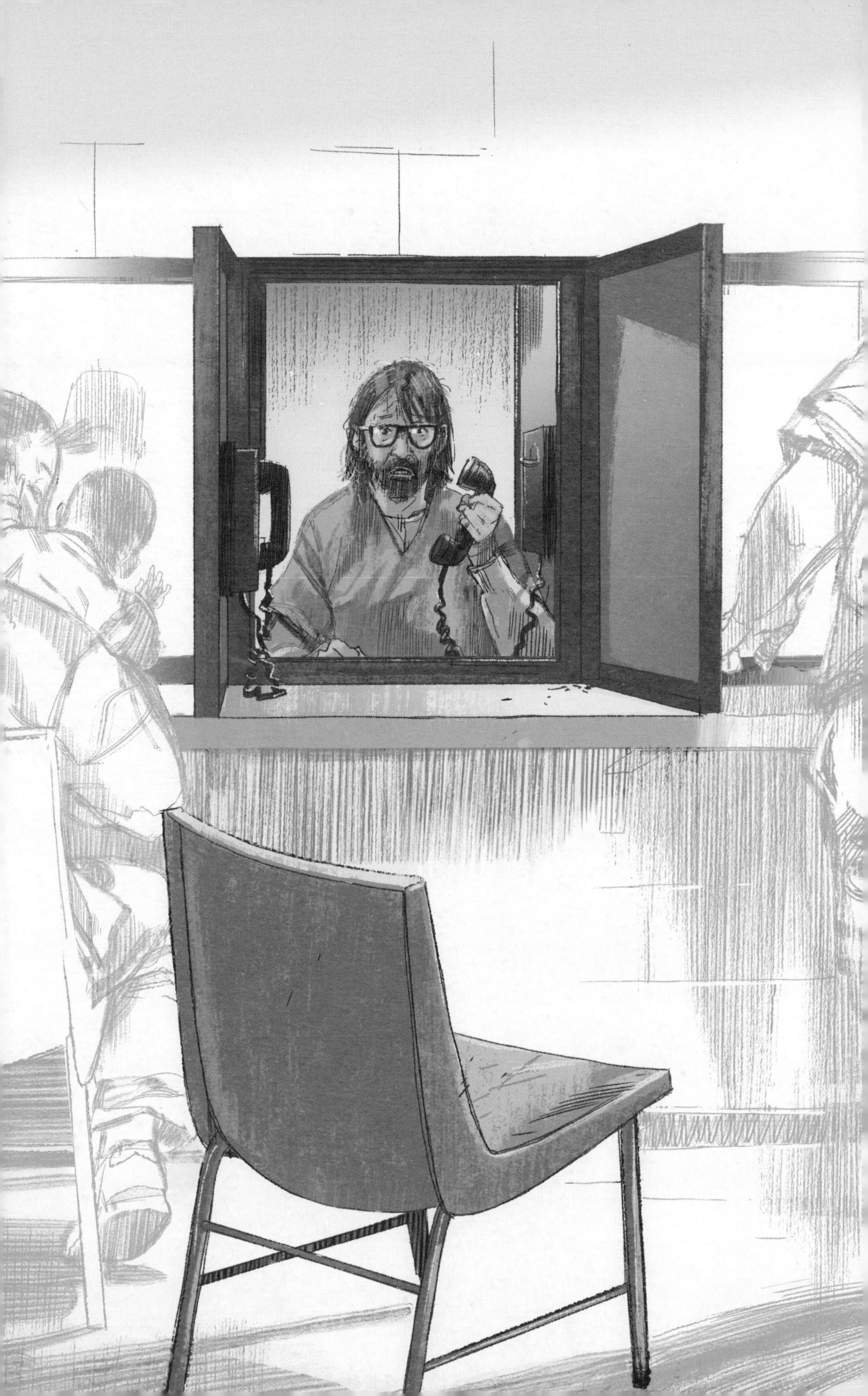

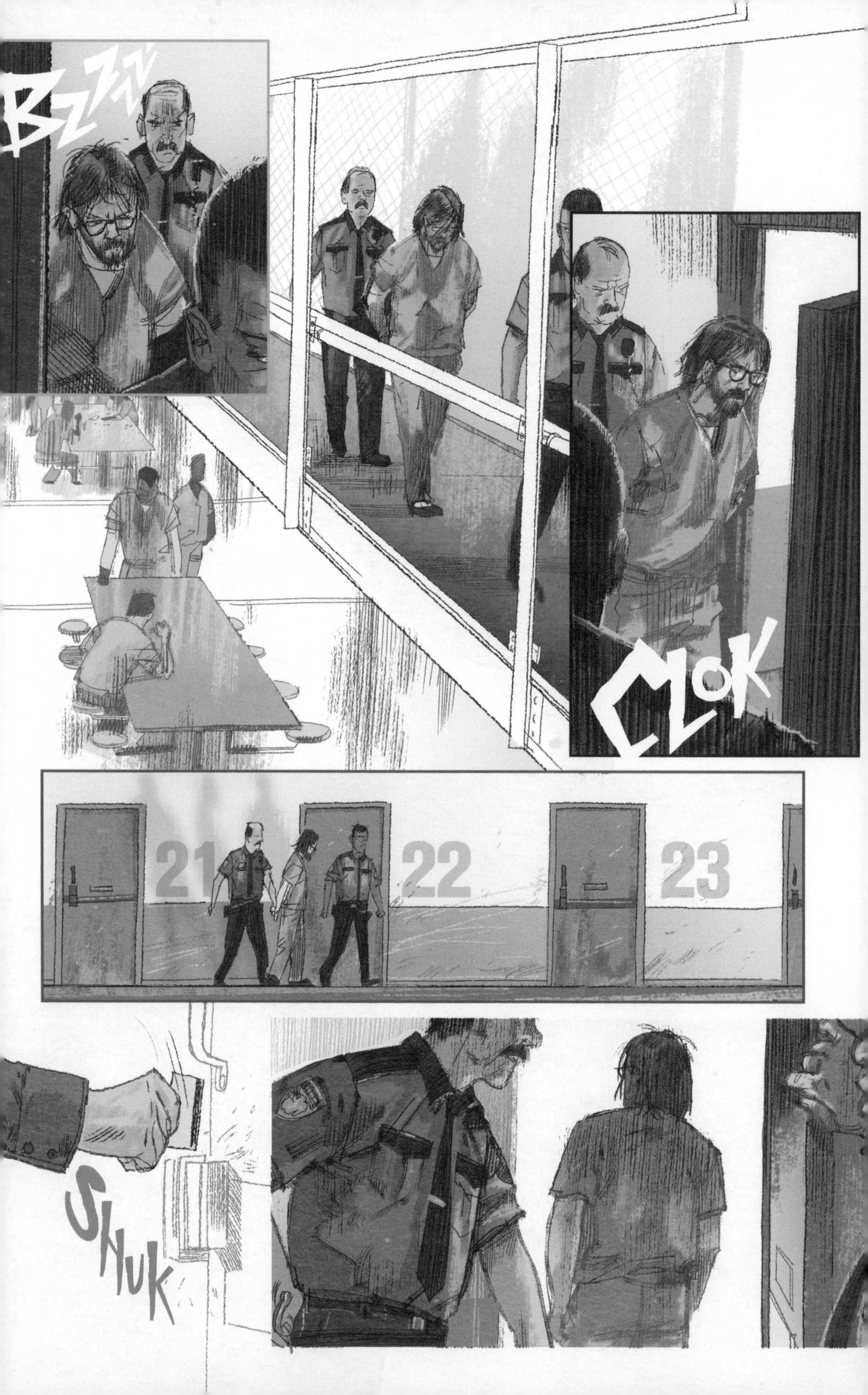
BZZZZ
CLOK
21
22
23
SHUK

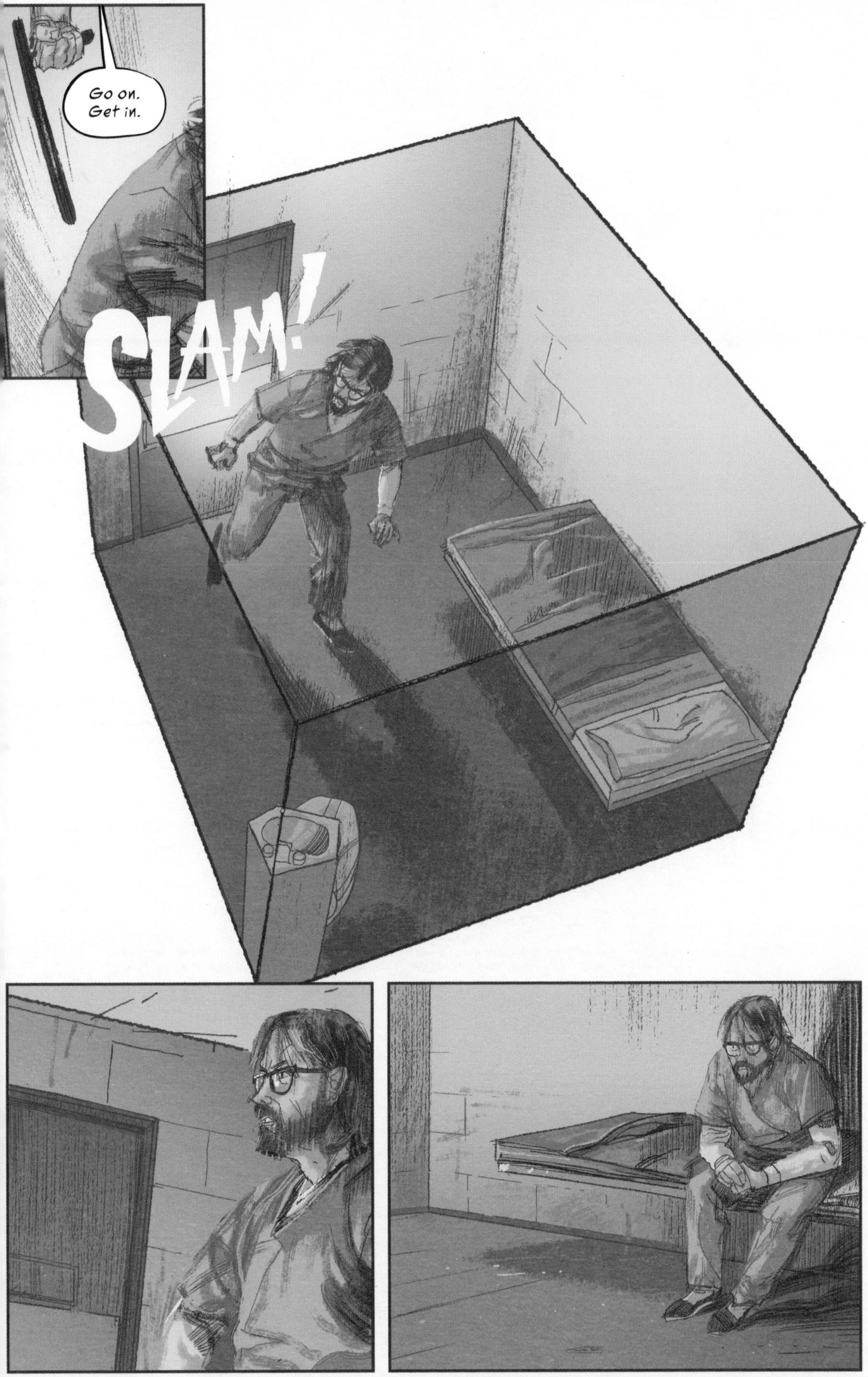
Go on.
Get in.
SLAM!

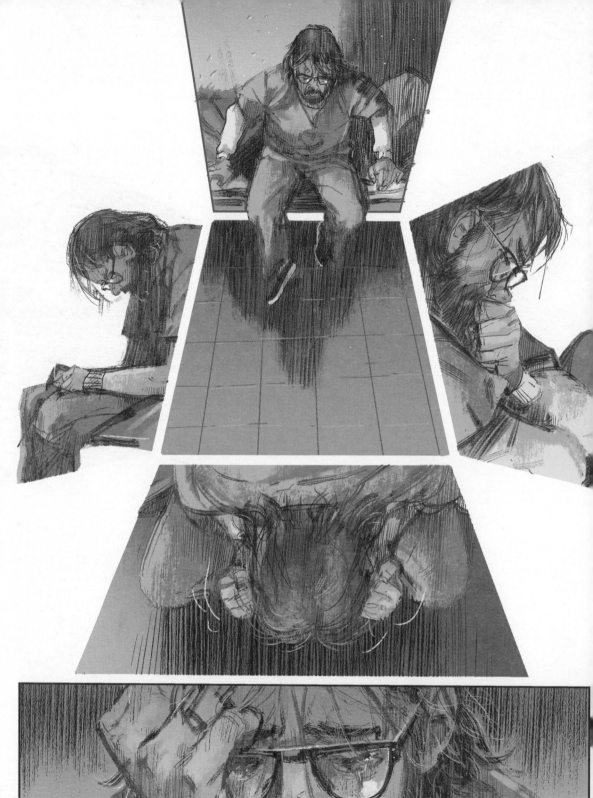

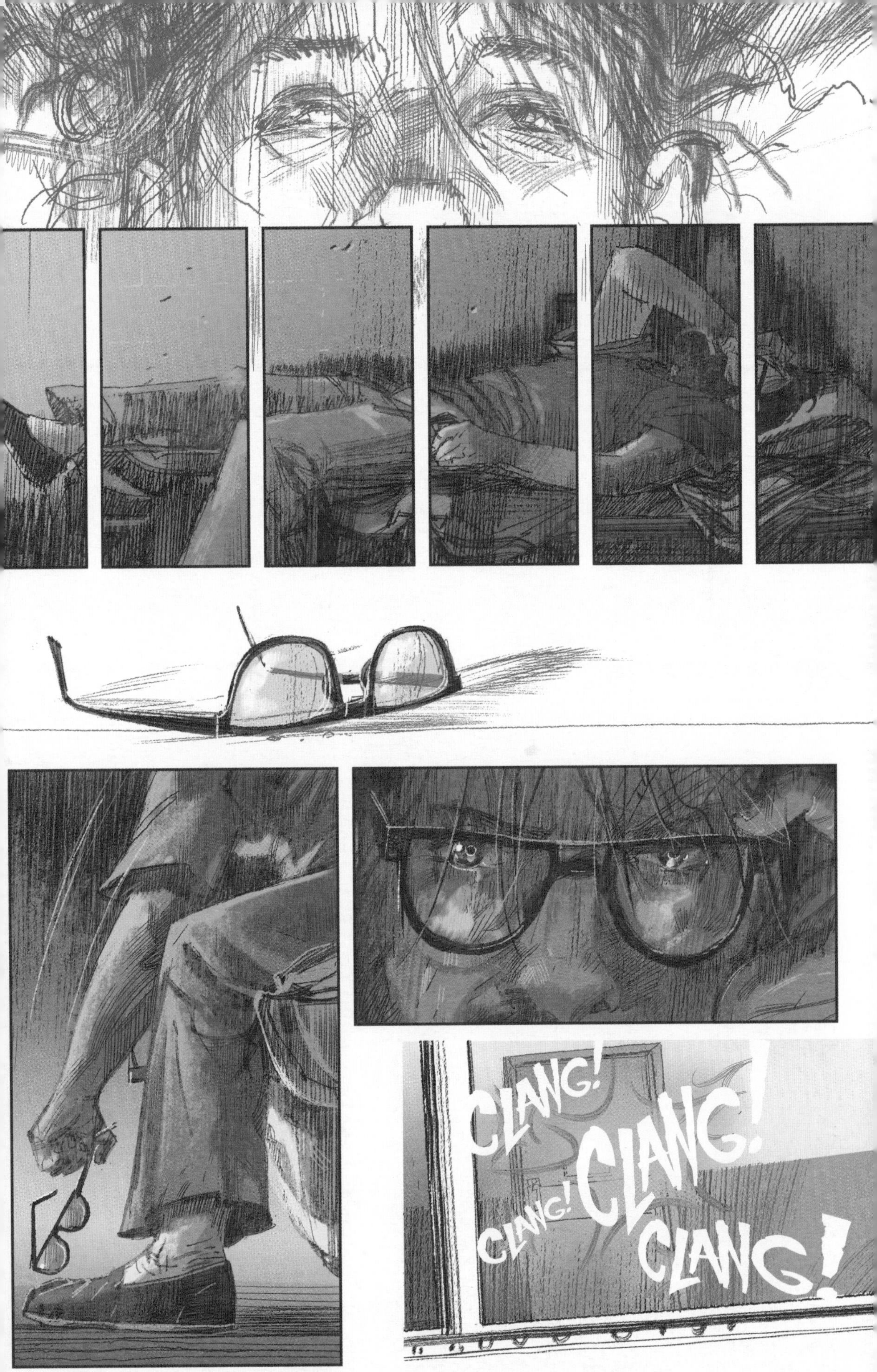
CLANG!
CLANG!
CLANG!
CLANG!

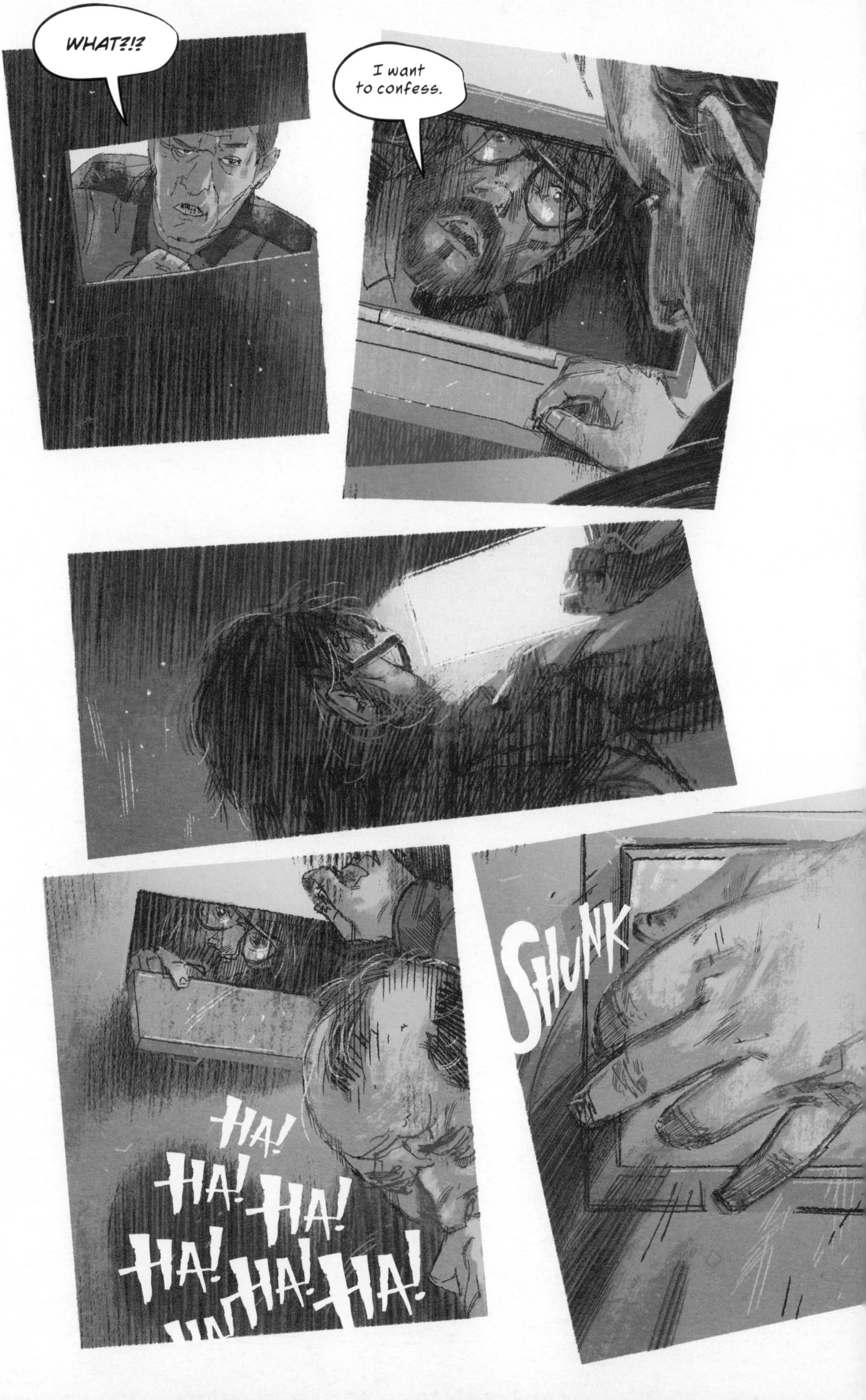
WHAT?!?
I want to confess.
SHUNK
HA! HA! HA! HA! HA! HA!

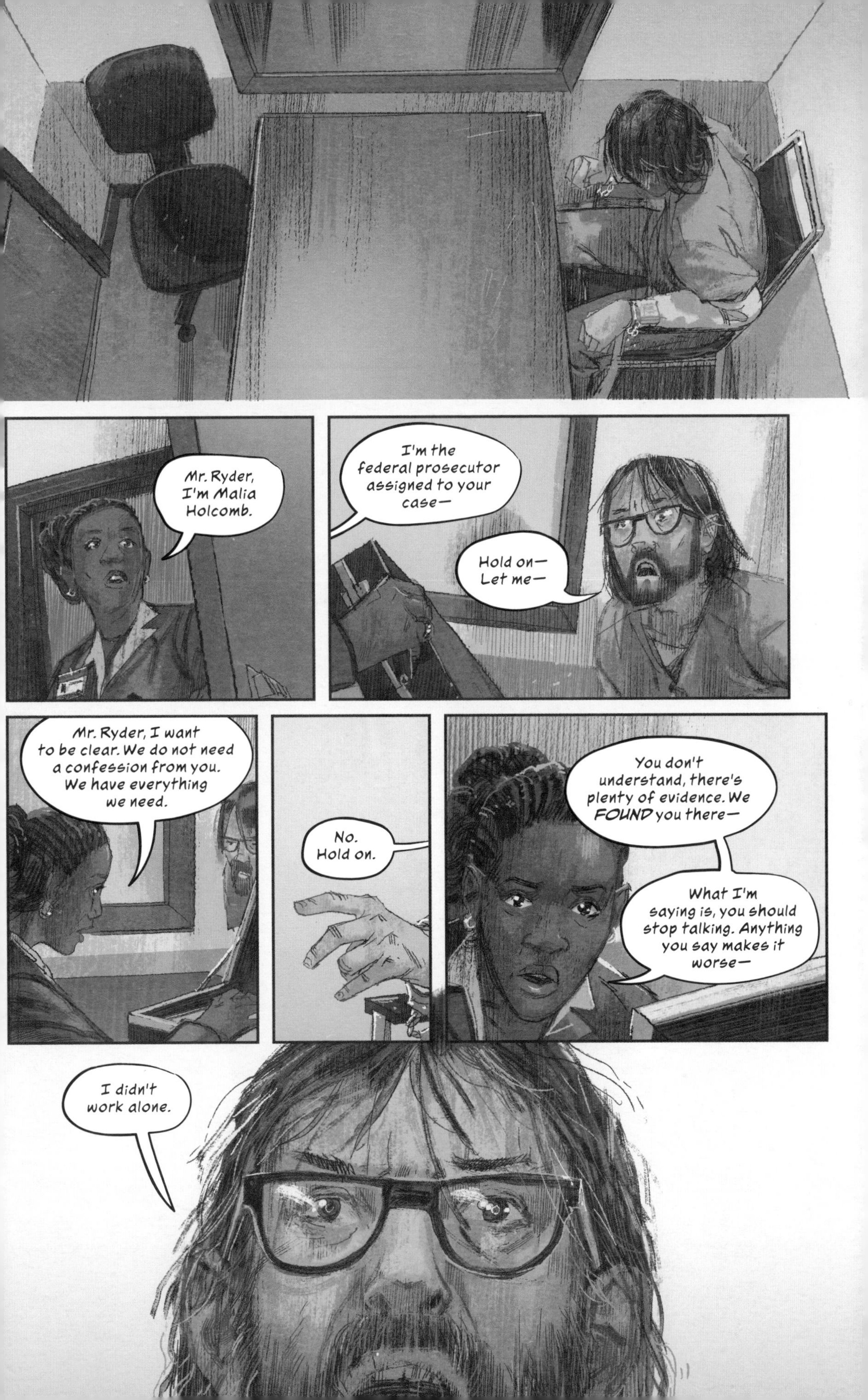
Mr. Ryder, I'm Malia Holcomb.
I'm the federal prosecutor assigned to your case—
Hold on— Let me—
Mr. Ryder, I want to be clear. We do not need a confession from you. We have everything we need.
No. Hold on.
You don't understand, there's plenty of evidence. We FOUND you there—
What I'm saying is, you should stop talking. Anything you say makes it worse—
I didn't work alone.

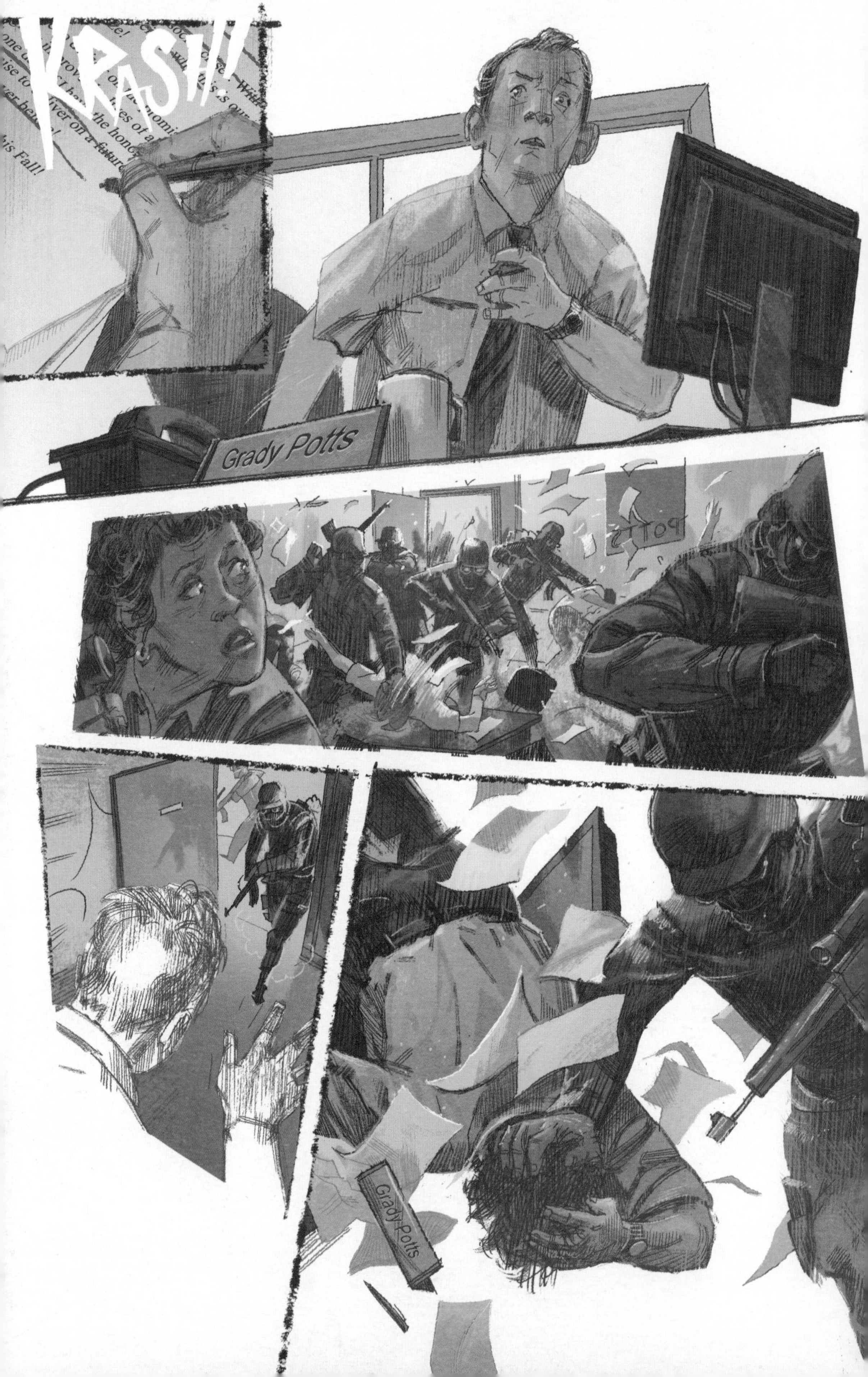
KRASH!!
Grady Potts
Grady Potts

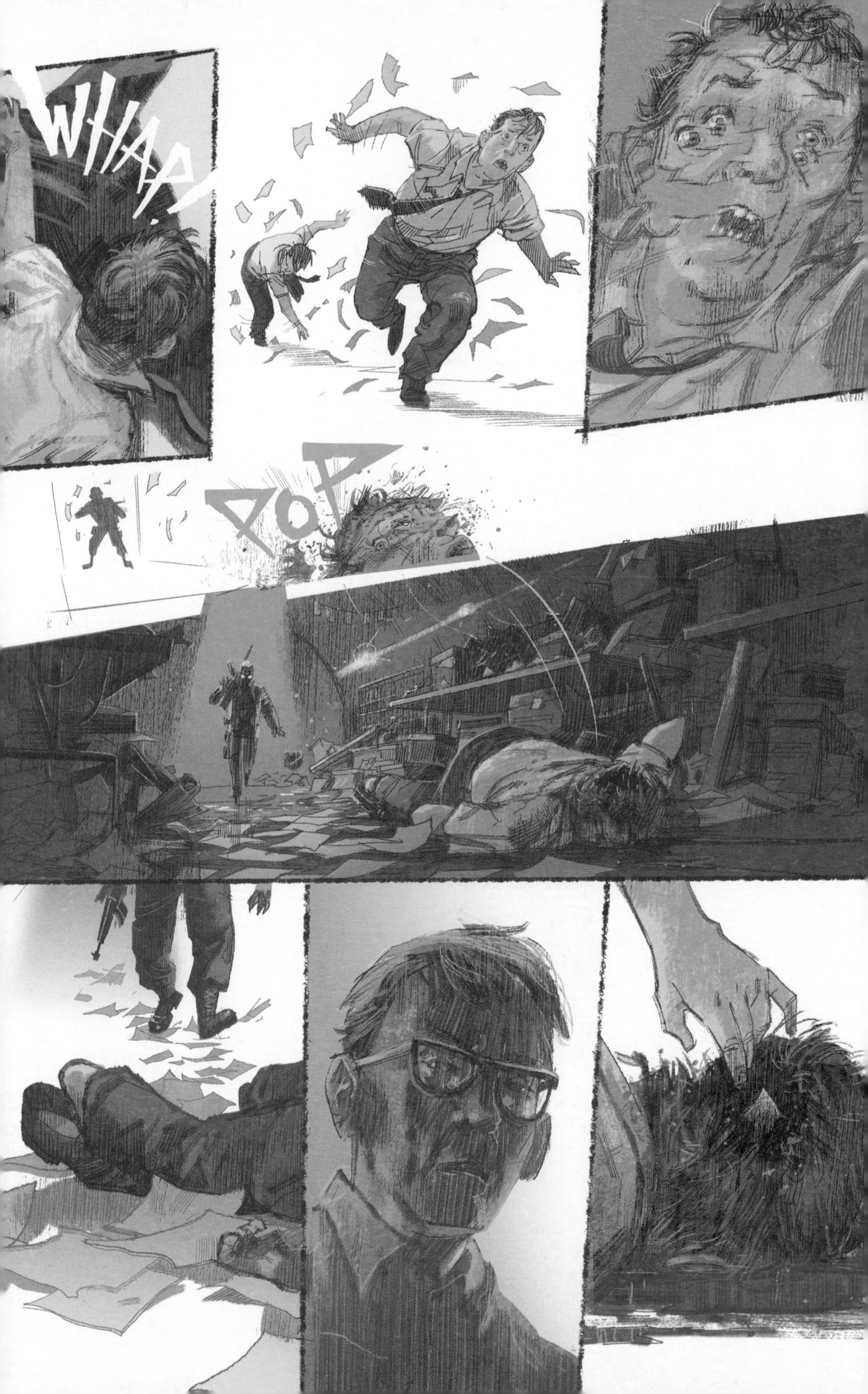
WHAP!
POP

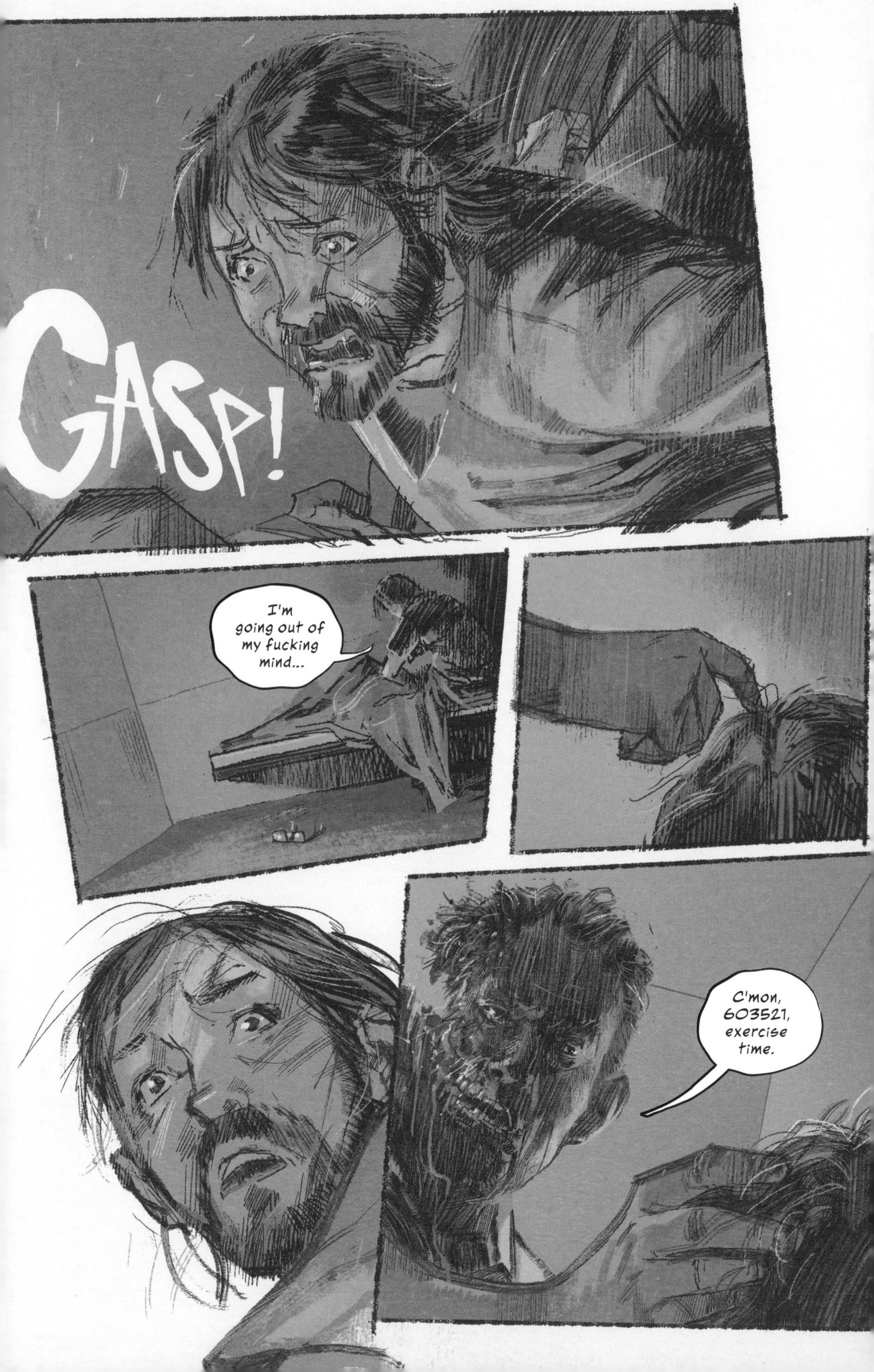
GASP!
I'm going out of my fucking mind...
C'mon, 603521, exercise time.

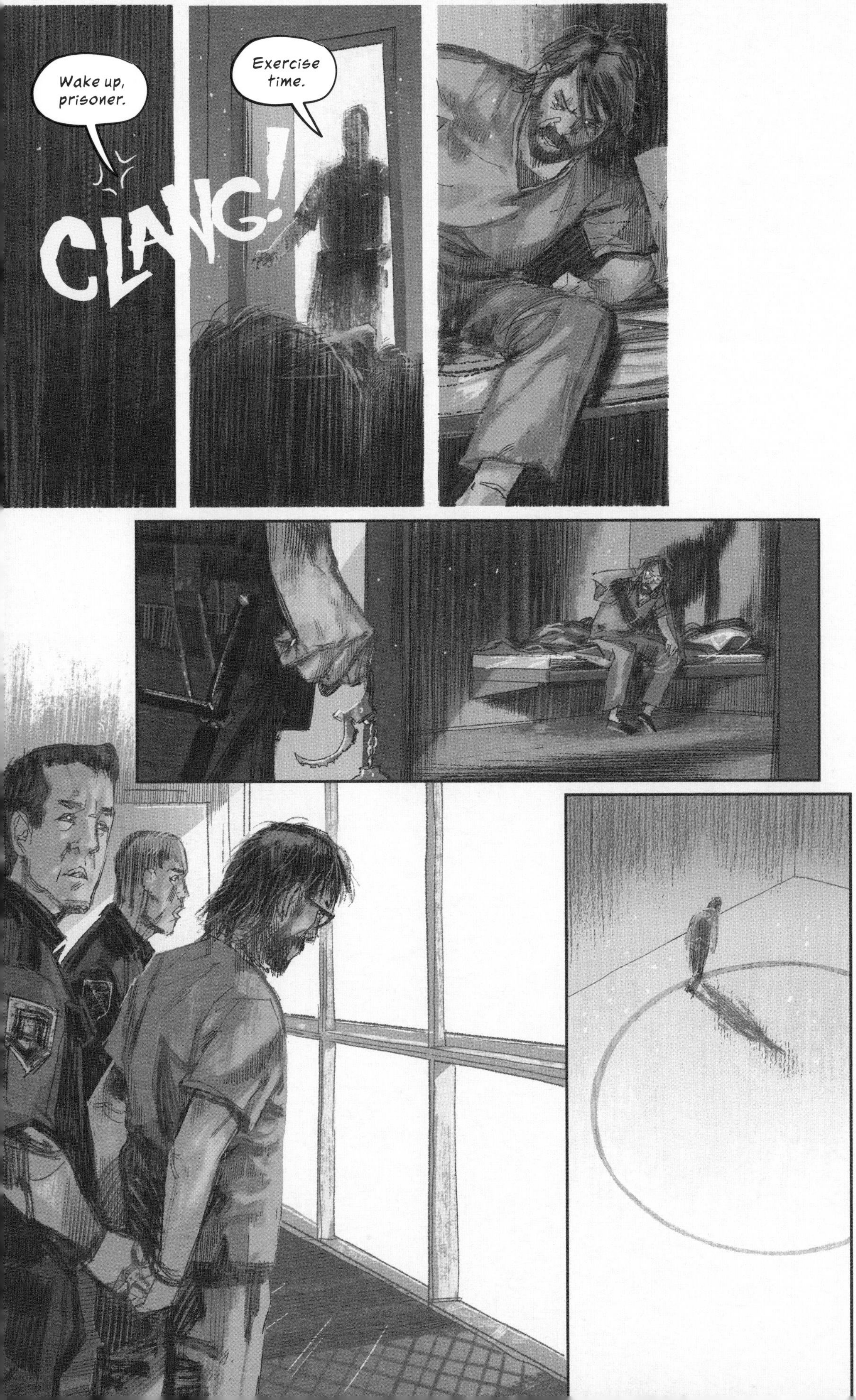
Wake up, prisoner.
CLANG!
Exercise time.

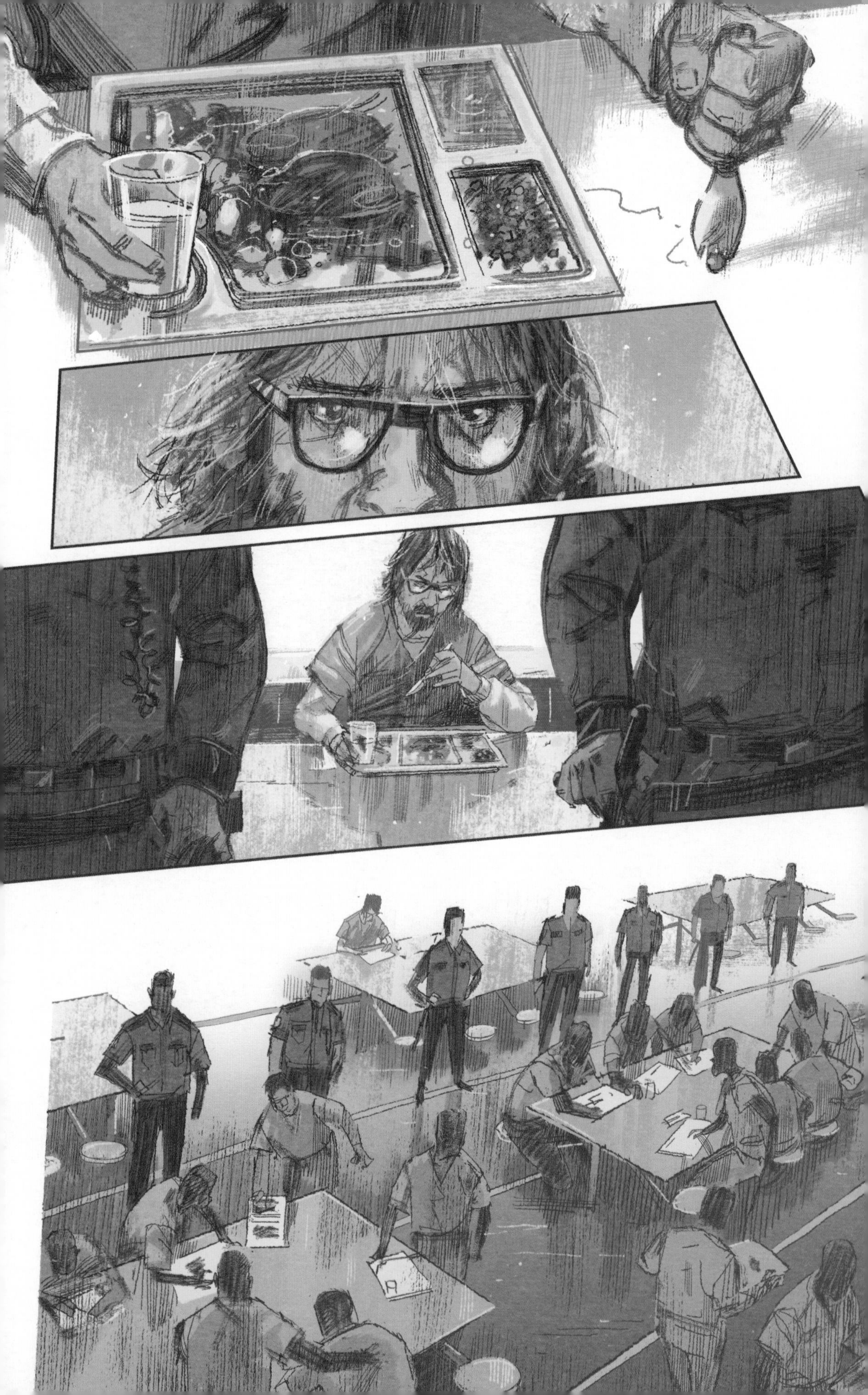

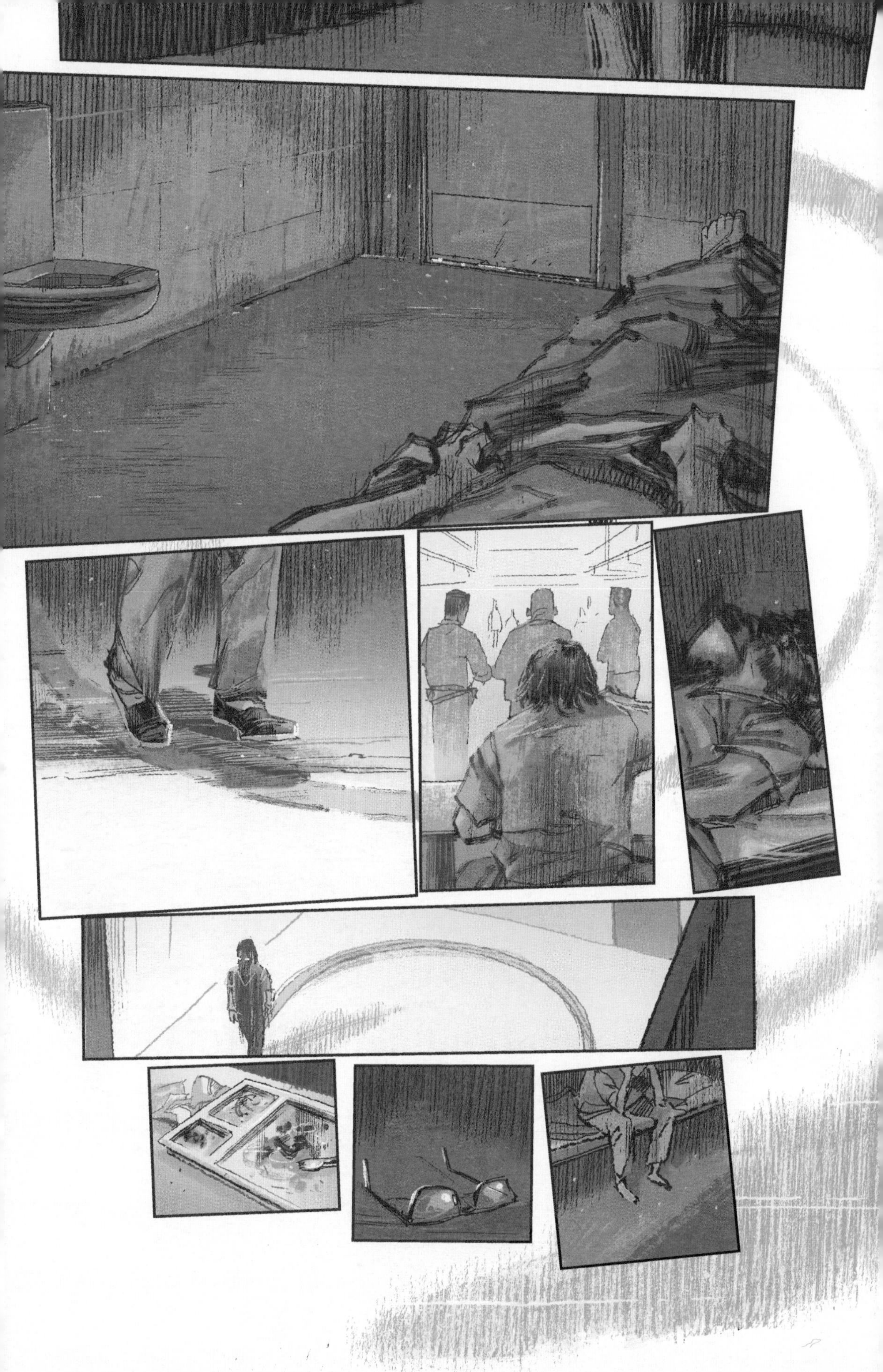

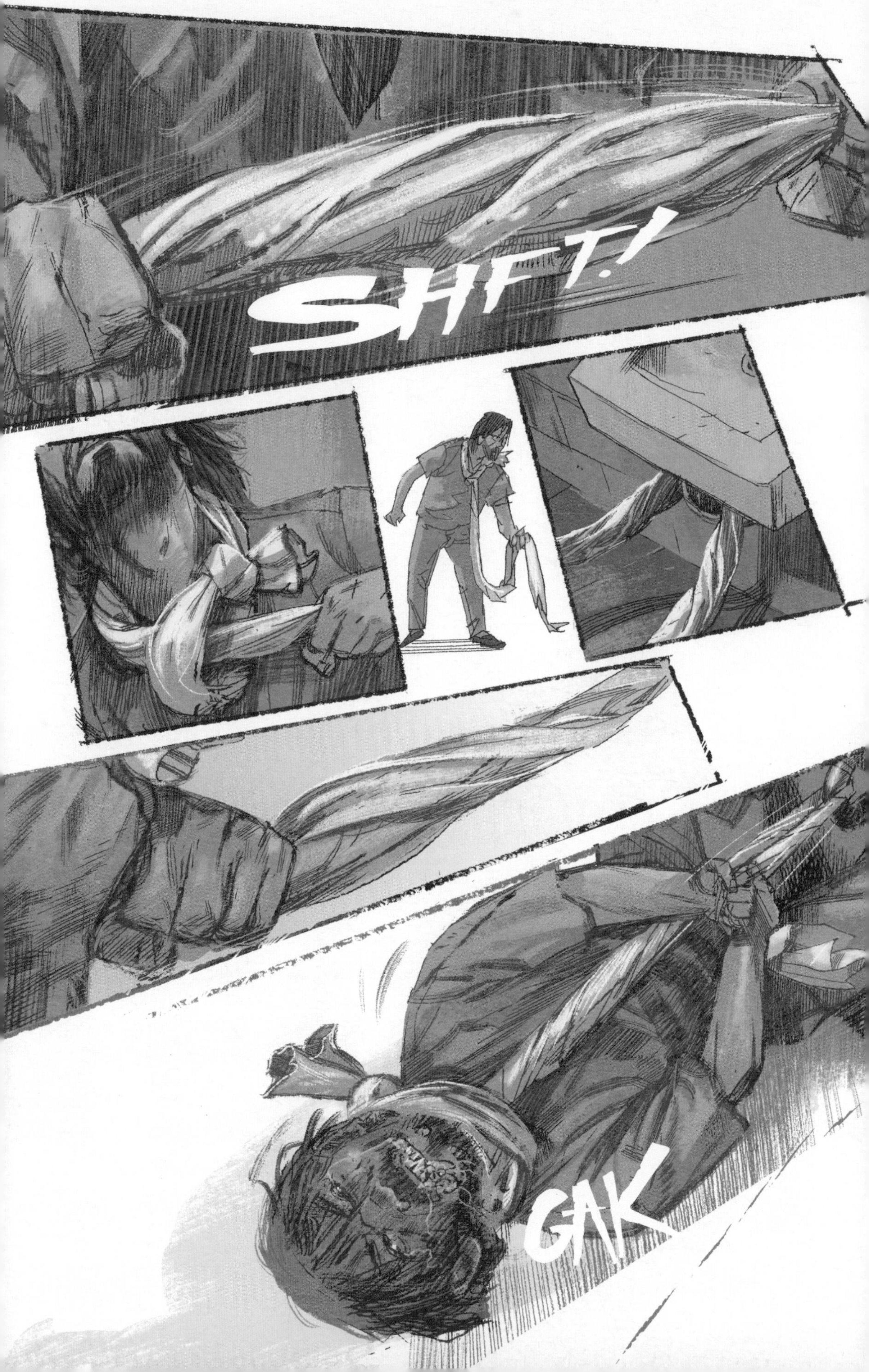
SHFT!
GAK

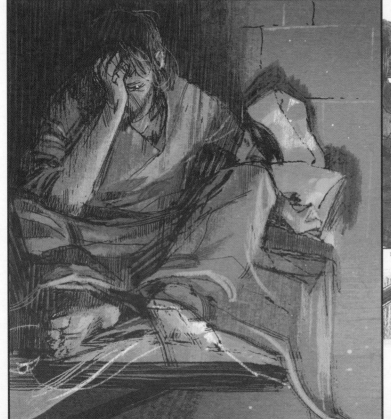

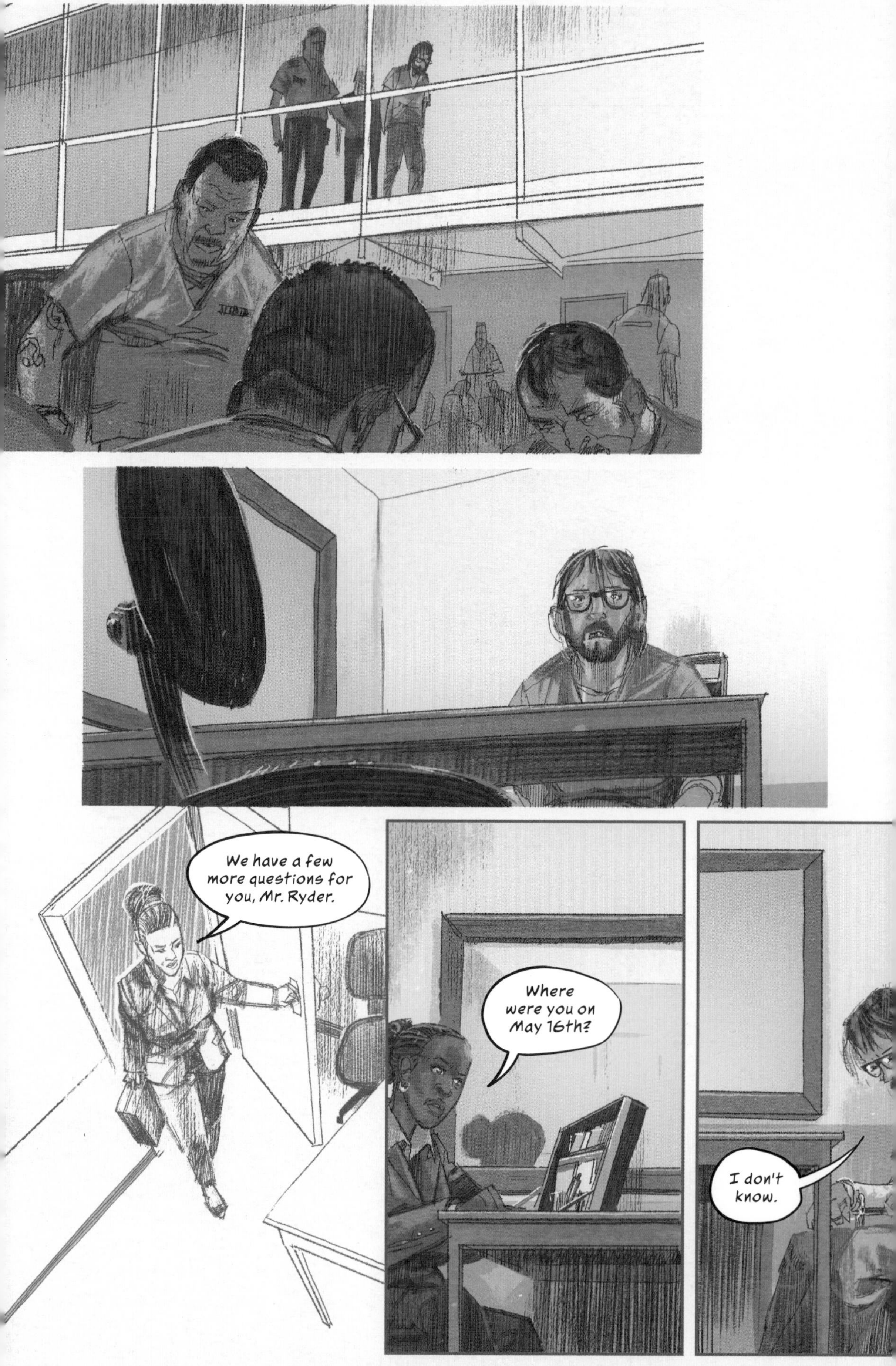
We have a few more questions for you, Mr. Ryder.
Where were you on May 16th?
I don't know.

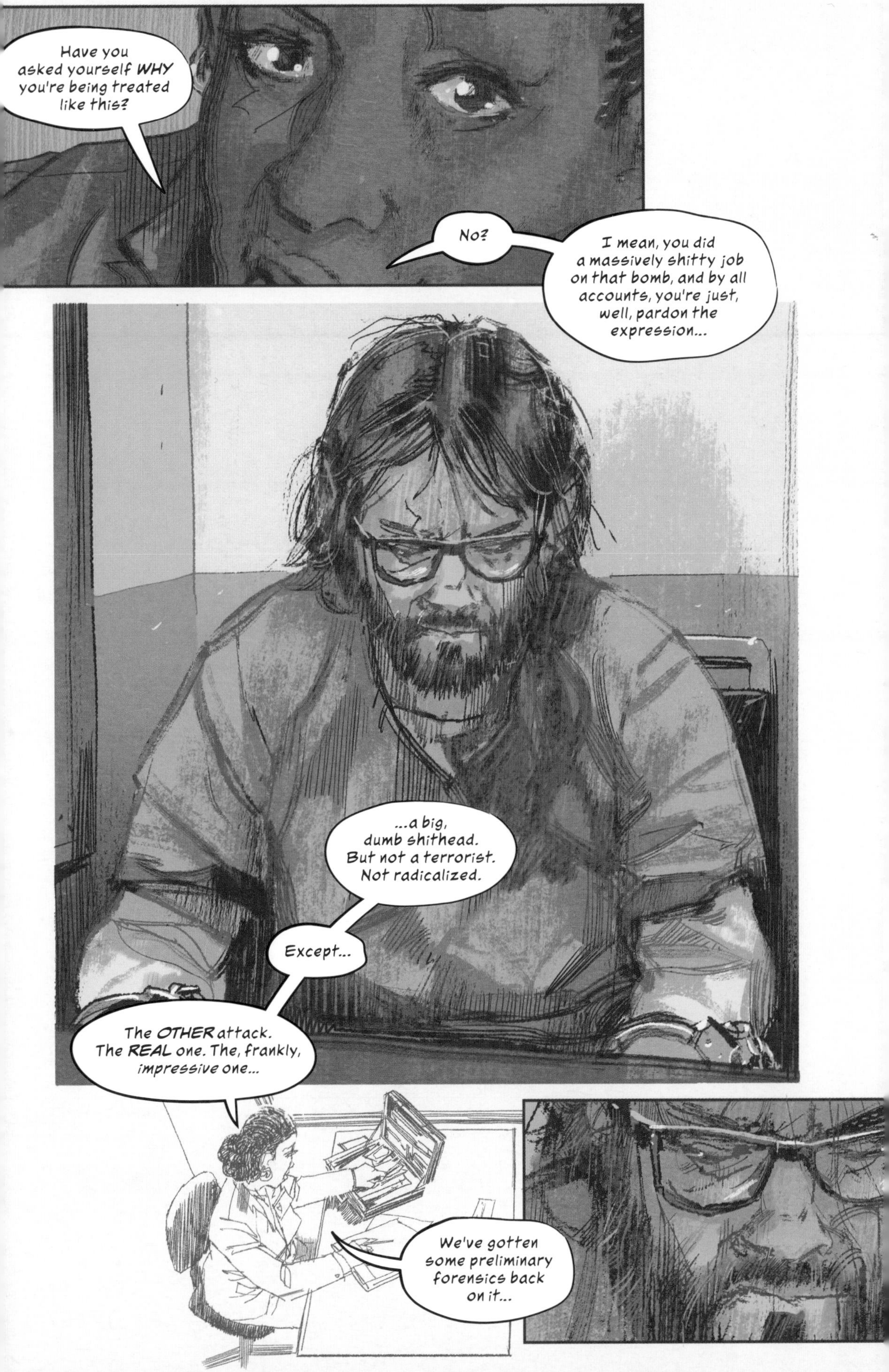

Have you asked yourself **WHY** you're being treated like this?
No?
I mean, you did a massively shitty job on that bomb, and by all accounts, you're just, well, pardon the expression...
...a big, dumb shithead. But not a terrorist. Not radicalized.
Except...
The **OTHER** attack. The **REAL** one. The, frankly, *impressive* one...
We've gotten some preliminary forensics back on it...

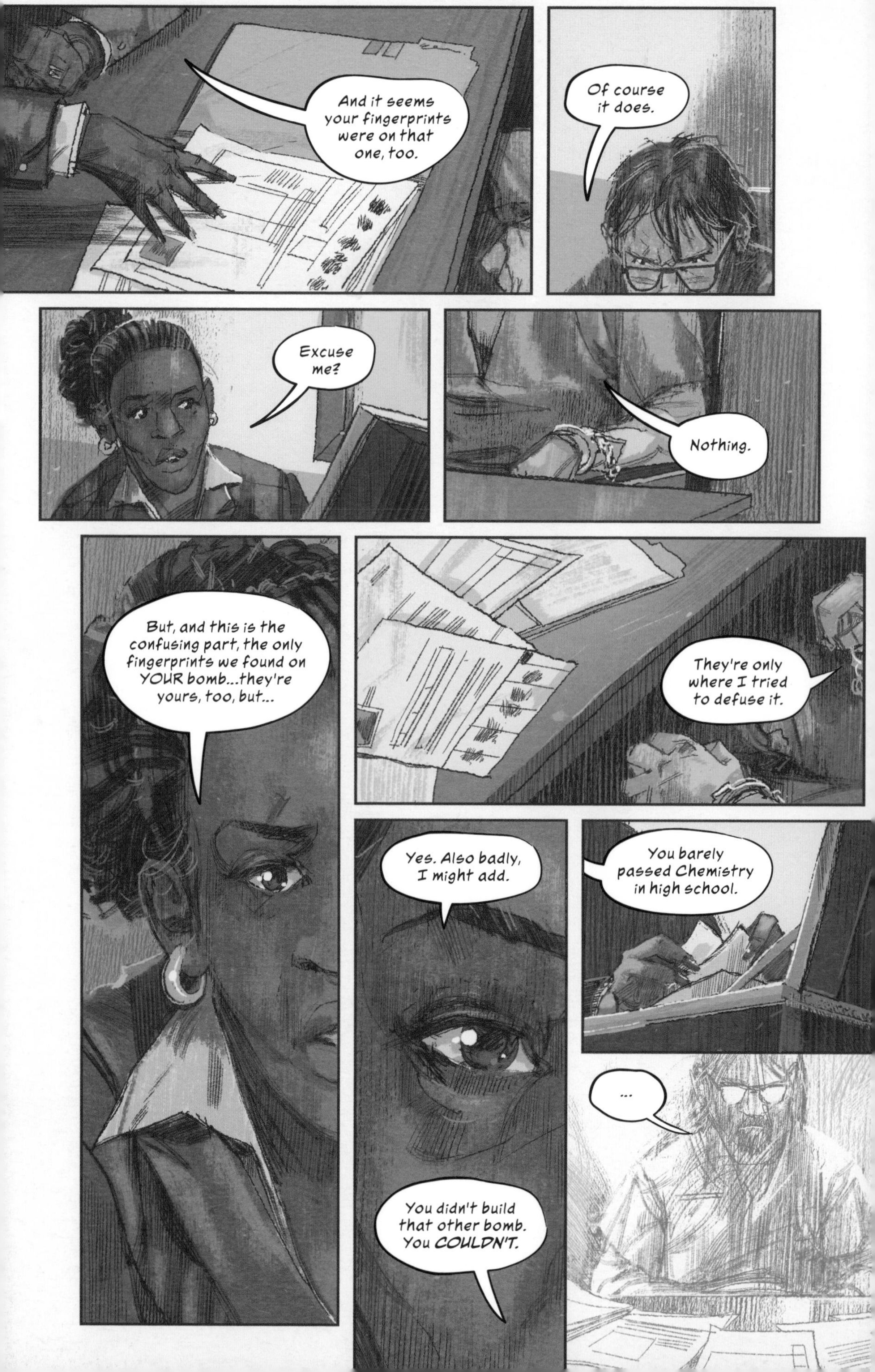
And it seems your fingerprints were on that one, too.
Of course it does.
Excuse me?
Nothing.
But, and this is the confusing part, the only fingerprints we found on YOUR bomb...they're yours, too, but...
They're only where I tried to defuse it.
Yes. Also badly, I might add.
You barely passed Chemistry in high school.
...
You didn't build that other bomb. You COULDN'T.

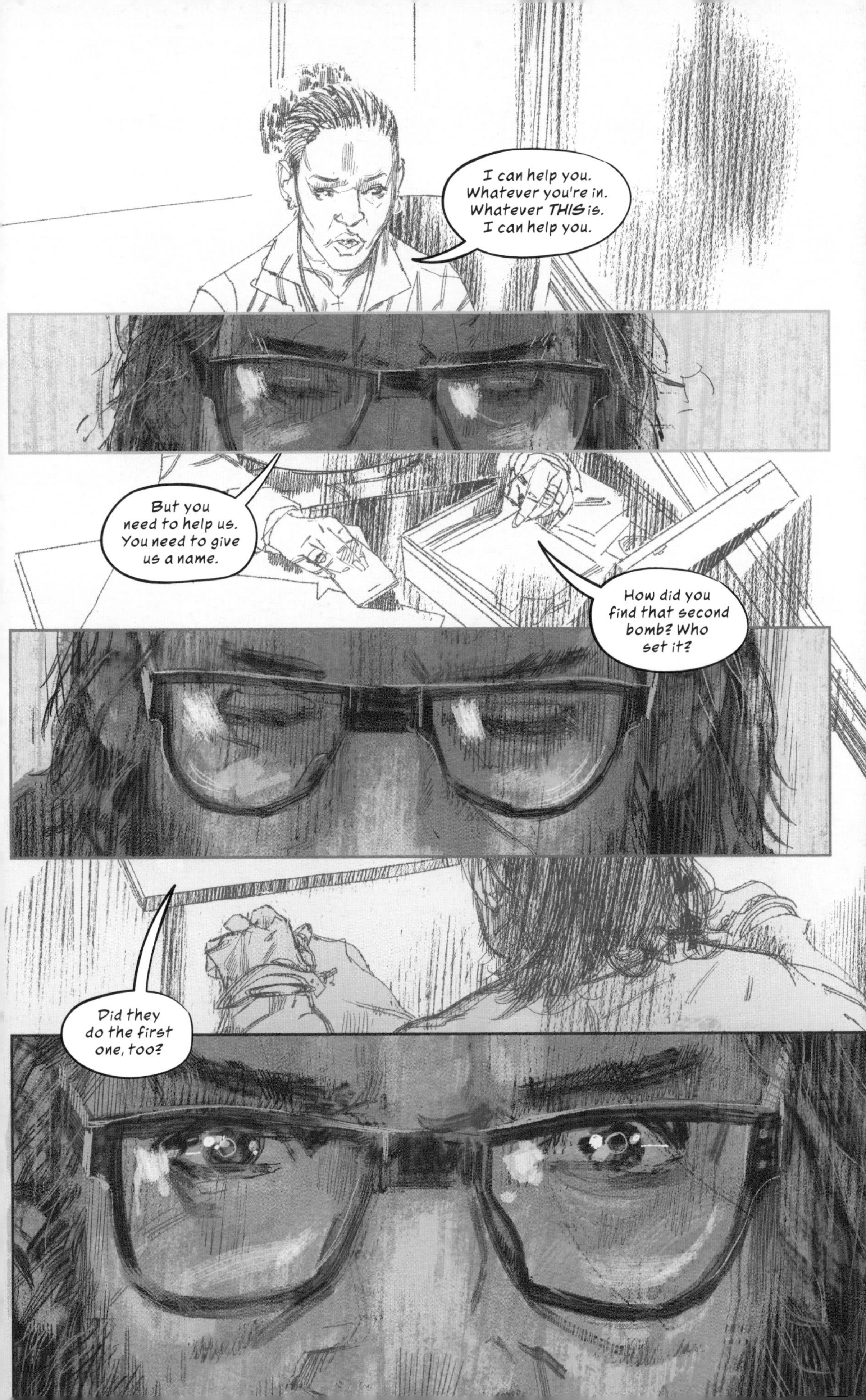
I can help you. Whatever you're in. Whatever THIS is. I can help you.
But you need to help us. You need to give us a name.
How did you find that second bomb? Who set it?
Did they do the first one, too?

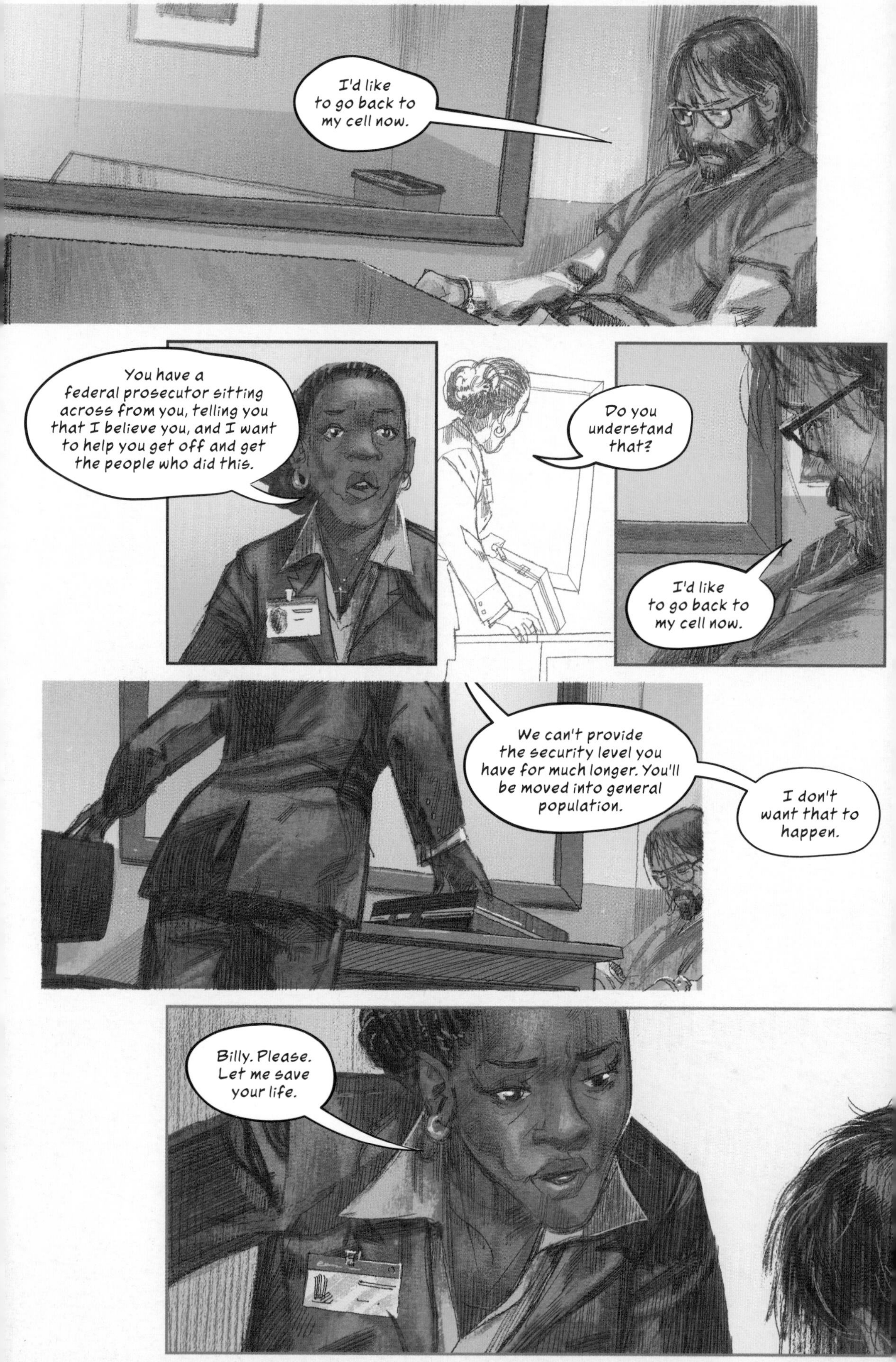
I'd like to go back to my cell now.
You have a federal prosecutor sitting across from you, telling you that I believe you, and I want to help you get off and get the people who did this.
Do you understand that?
I'd like to go back to my cell now.
We can't provide the security level you have for much longer. You'll be moved into general population.
I don't want that to happen.
Billy. Please. Let me save your life.

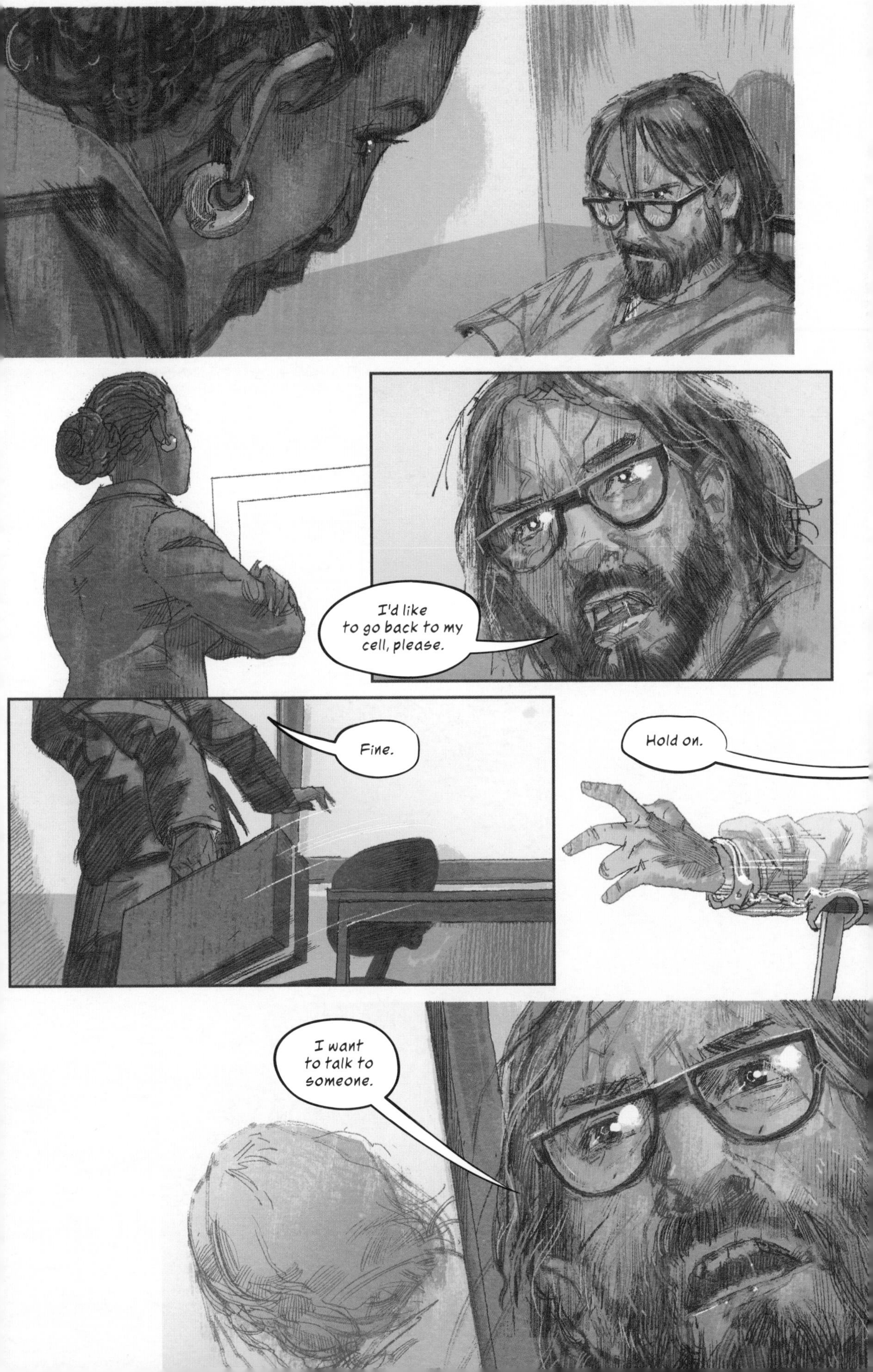
I'd like to go back to my cell, please.
Fine.
Hold on.
I want to talk to someone.

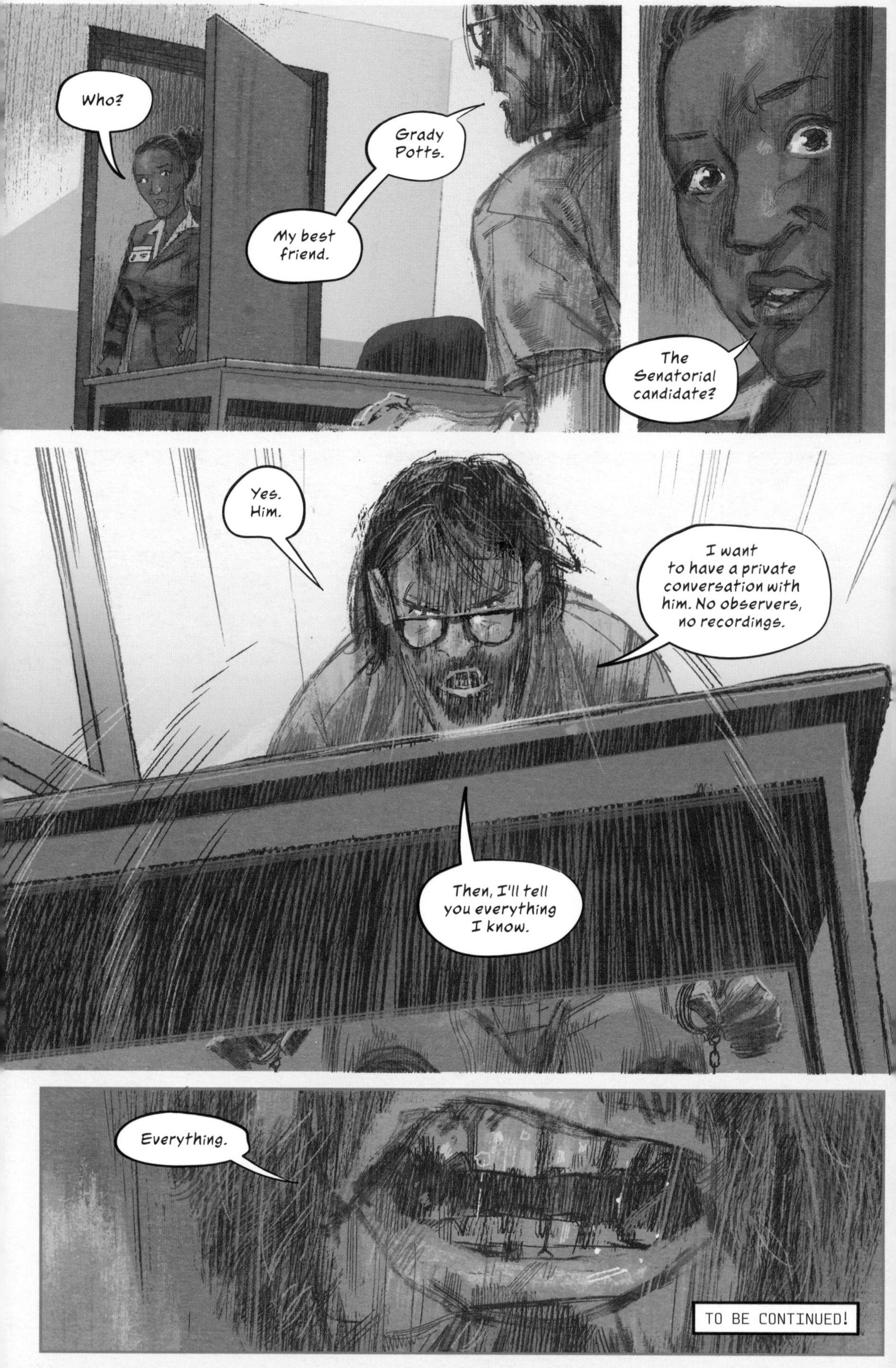
Who?
Grady Potts.
My best friend.
The Senatorial candidate?
Yes. Him.
I want to have a private conversation with him. No observers, no recordings.
Then, I'll tell you everything I know.
Everything.
TO BE CONTINUED!

CHAPTER
12

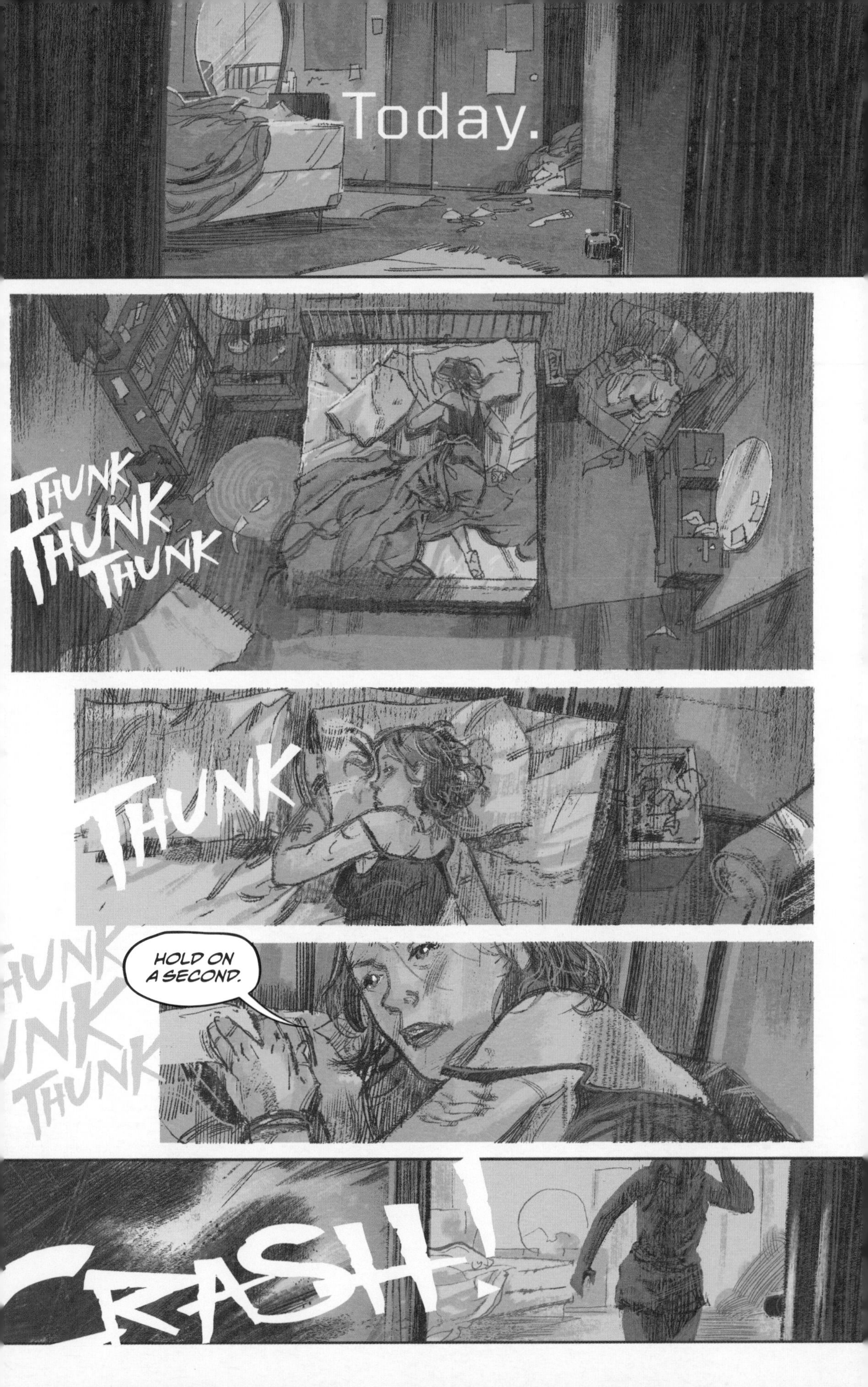
Today.
THUNK THUNK THUNK
THUNK
THUNK THUNK THUNK
HOLD ON A SECOND.
CRASH!

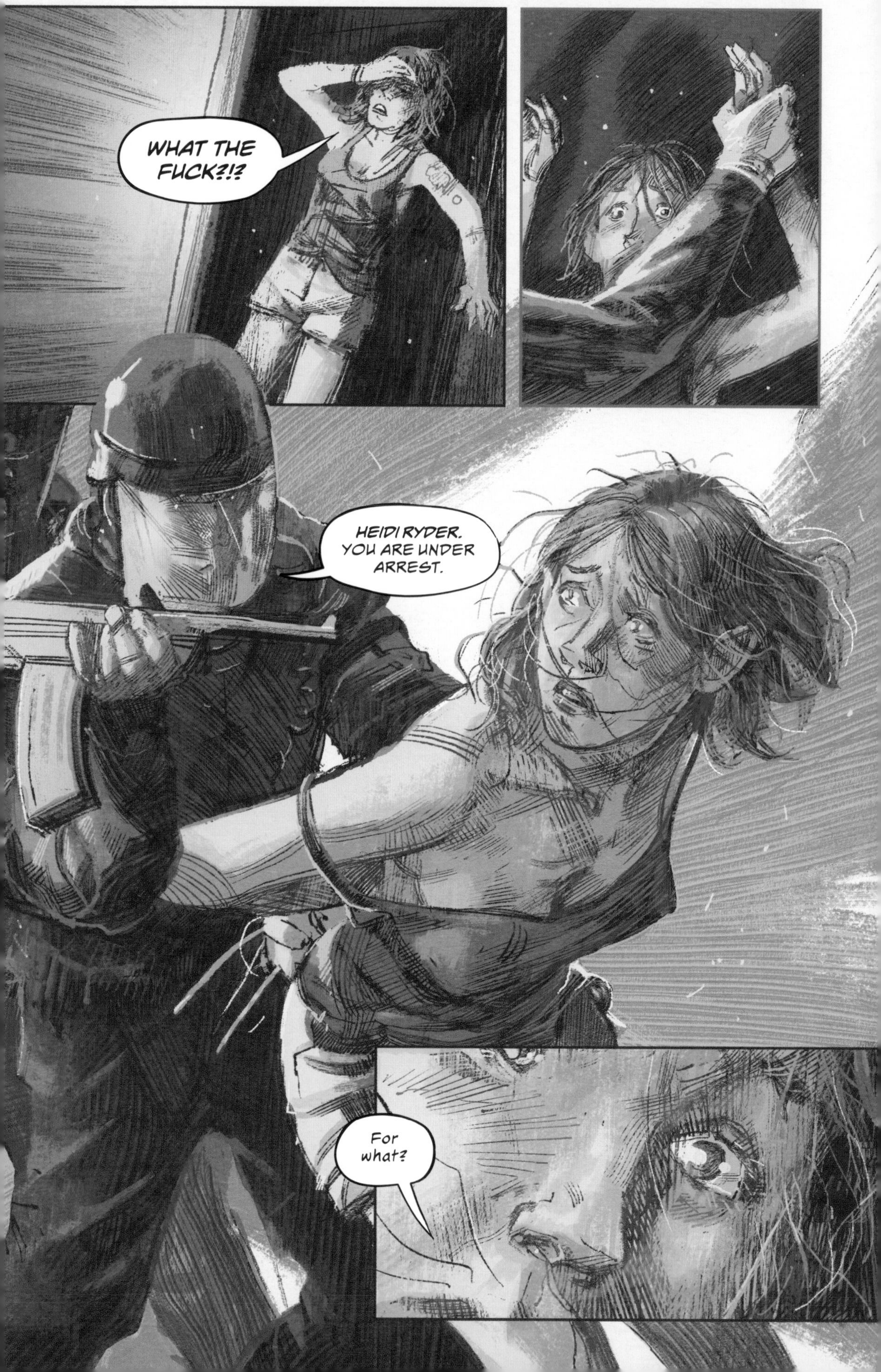
WHAT THE FUCK?!?
HEIDI RYDER. YOU ARE UNDER ARREST.
For what?

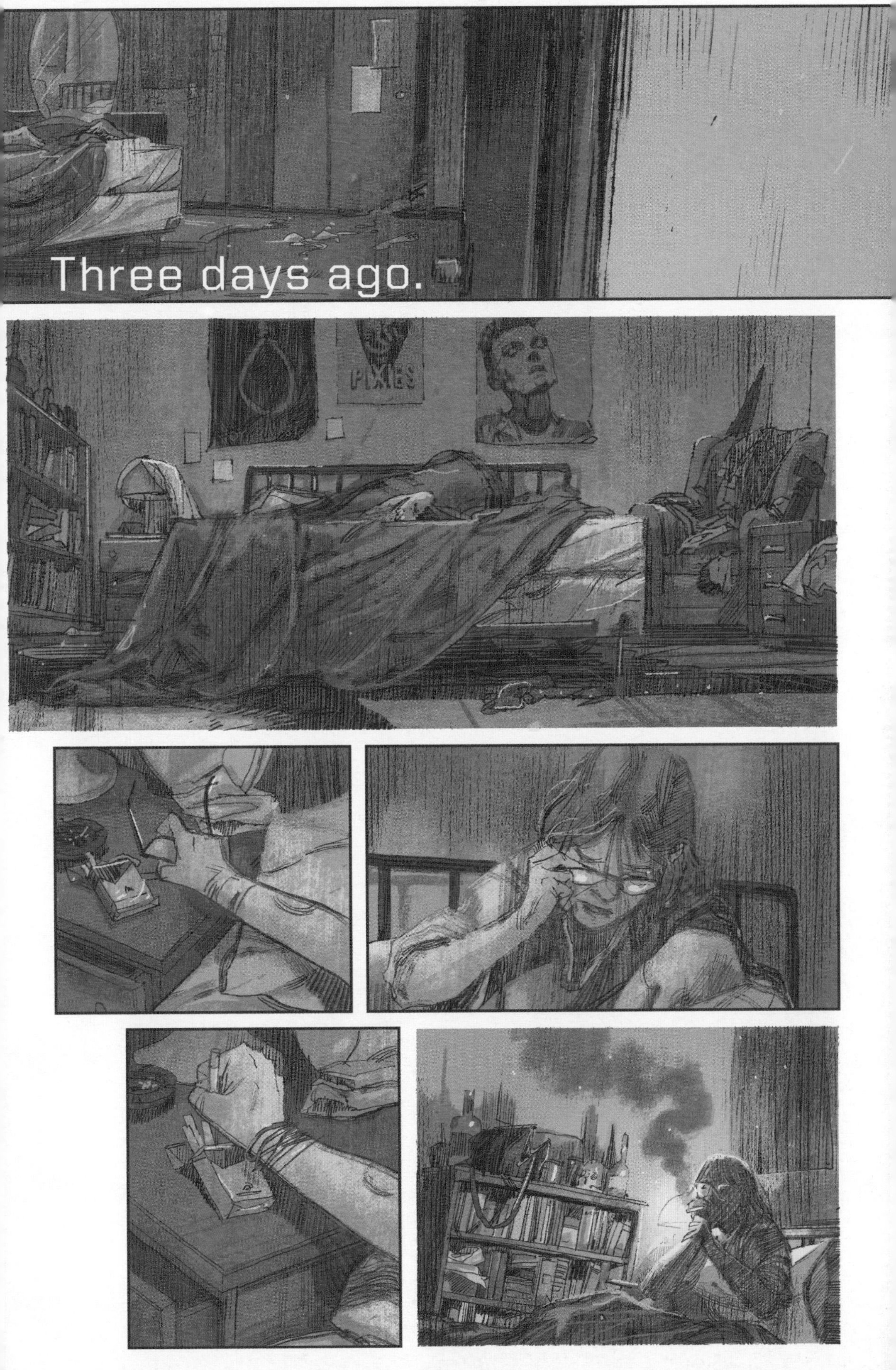
Three days ago.
PIXIES

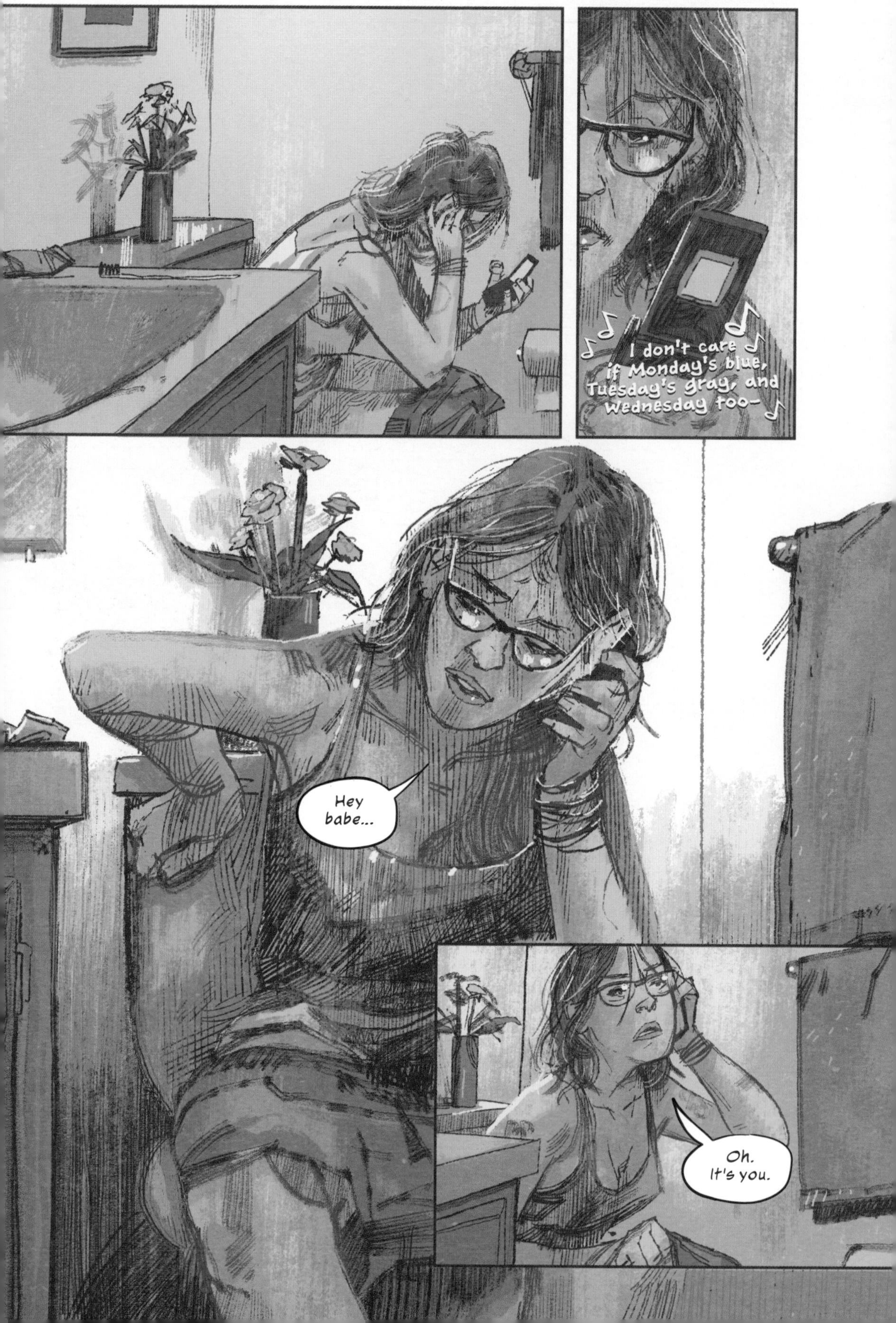
I don't care if Monday's blue, Tuesday's gray, and Wednesday too–
Hey babe...
Oh. It's you.

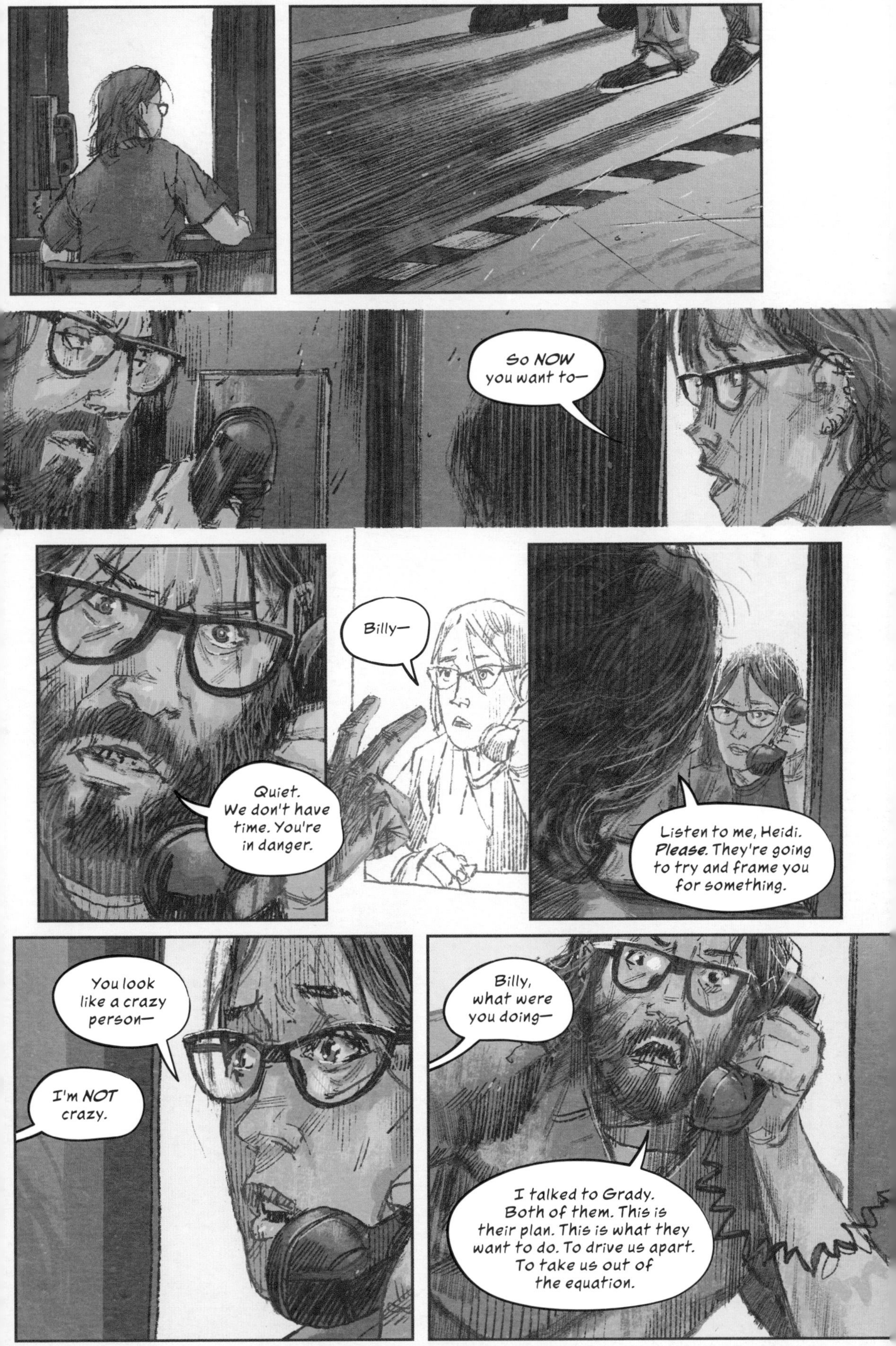
So NOW you want to—
Billy—
Quiet. We don't have time. You're in danger.
Listen to me, Heidi. Please. They're going to try and frame you for something.
You look like a crazy person—
I'm NOT crazy.
Billy, what were you doing—
I talked to Grady. Both of them. This is their plan. This is what they want to do. To drive us apart. To take us out of the equation.

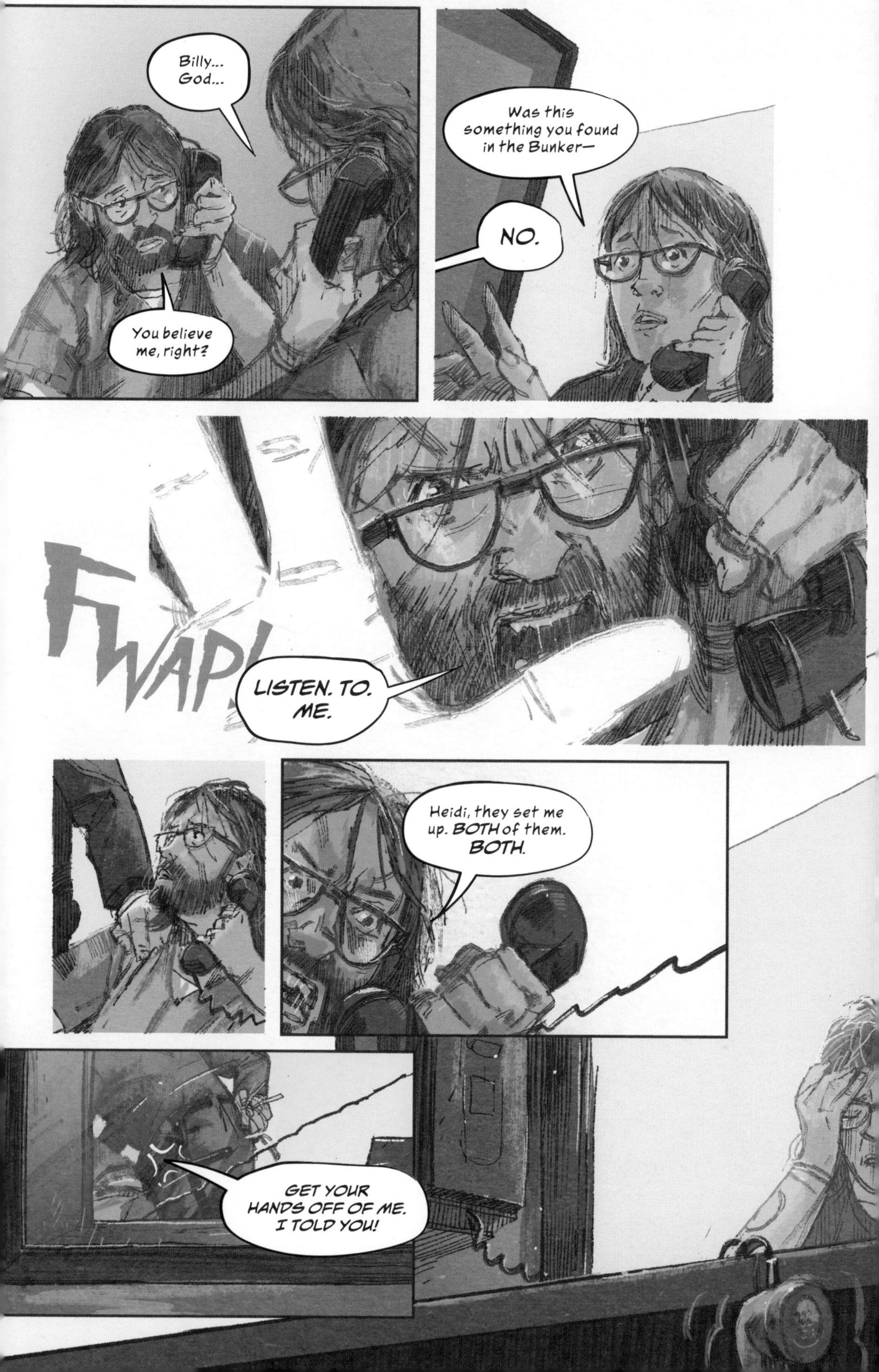
Billy... God...
You believe me, right?
Was this something you found in the Bunker—
NO.
FWAP!
LISTEN. TO. ME.
Heidi, they set me up. BOTH of them. BOTH.
GET YOUR HANDS OFF OF ME. I TOLD YOU!

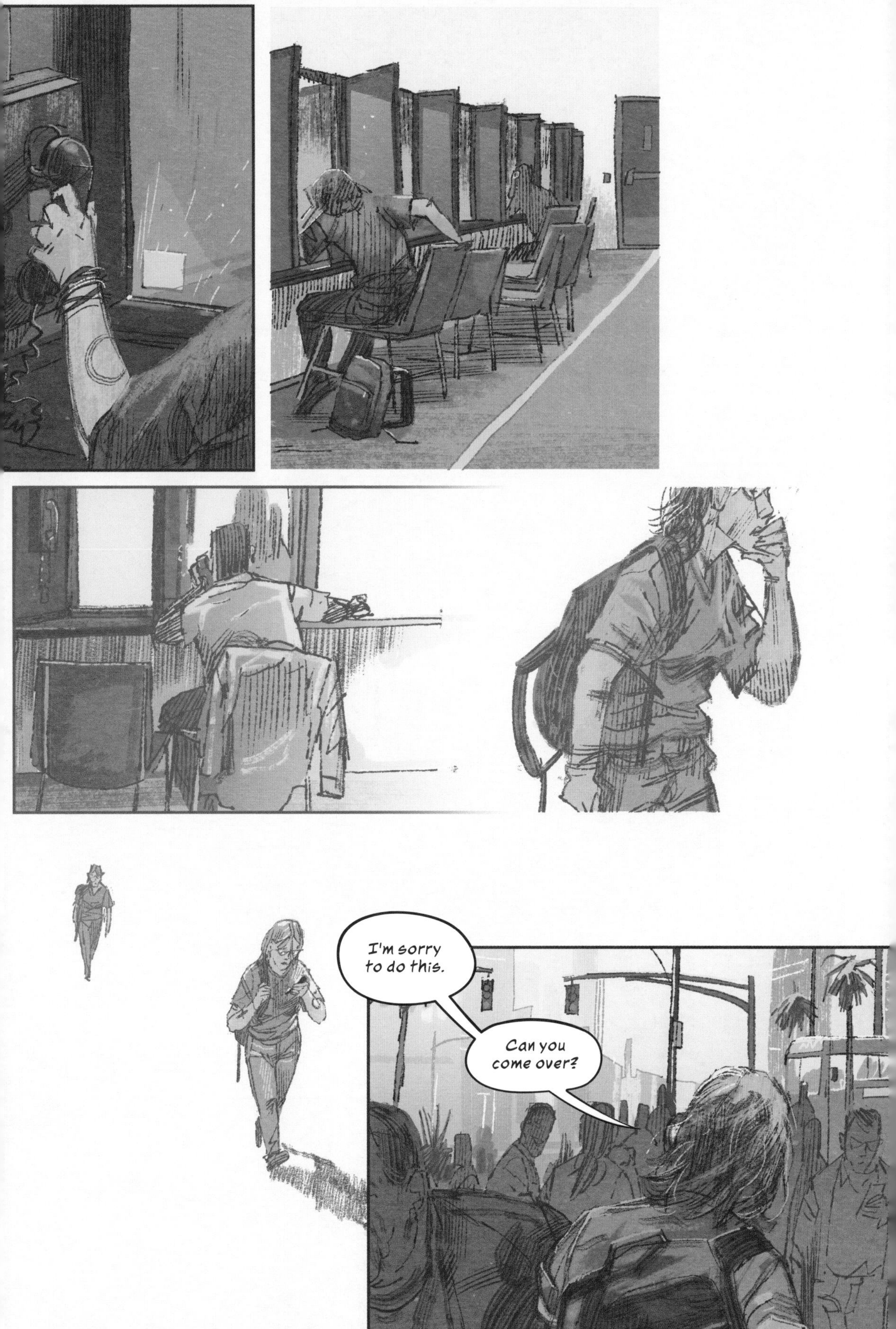
I'm sorry to do this.
Can you come over?

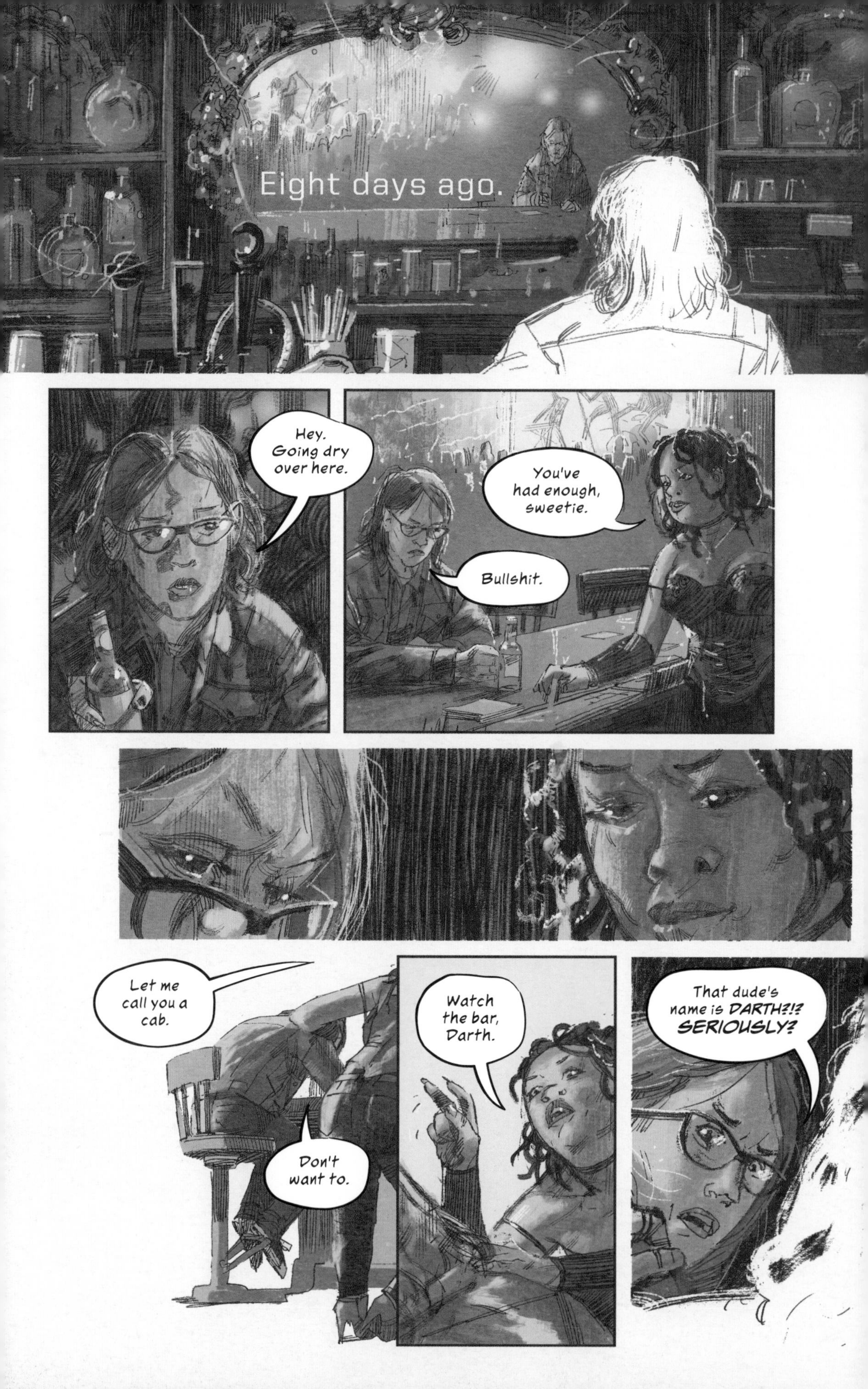
Eight days ago.
Hey. Going dry over here.
You've had enough, sweetie.
Bullshit.
Let me call you a cab.
Don't want to.
Watch the bar, Darth.
That dude's name is DARTH?!? SERIOUSLY?

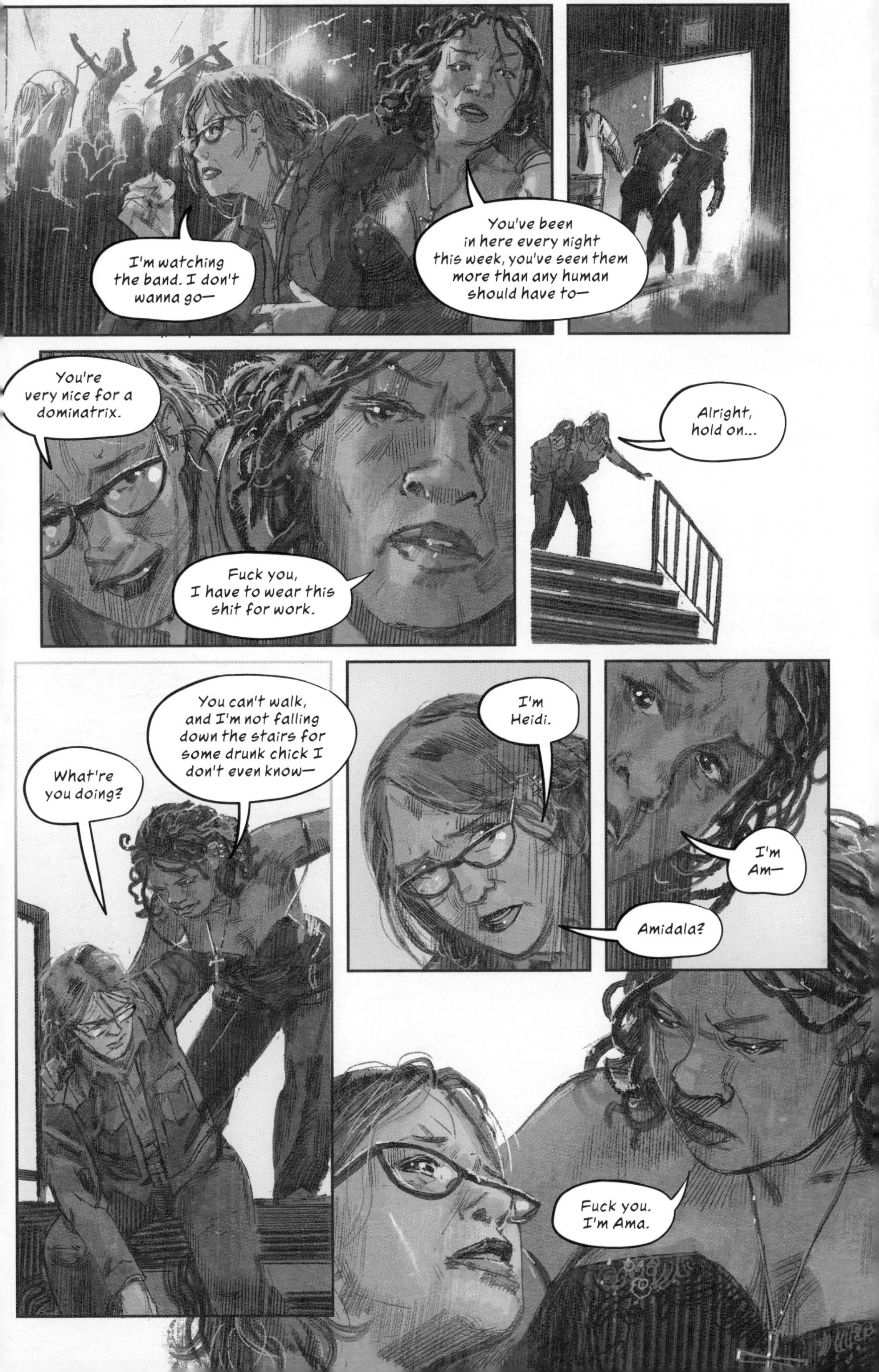
I'm watching the band. I don't wanna go—
You've been in here every night this week, you've seen them more than any human should have to—
You're very nice for a dominatrix.
Fuck you, I have to wear this shit for work.
Alright, hold on...
What're you doing?
You can't walk, and I'm not falling down the stairs for some drunk chick I don't even know—
I'm Heidi.
I'm Am—
Amidala?
Fuck you. I'm Ama.

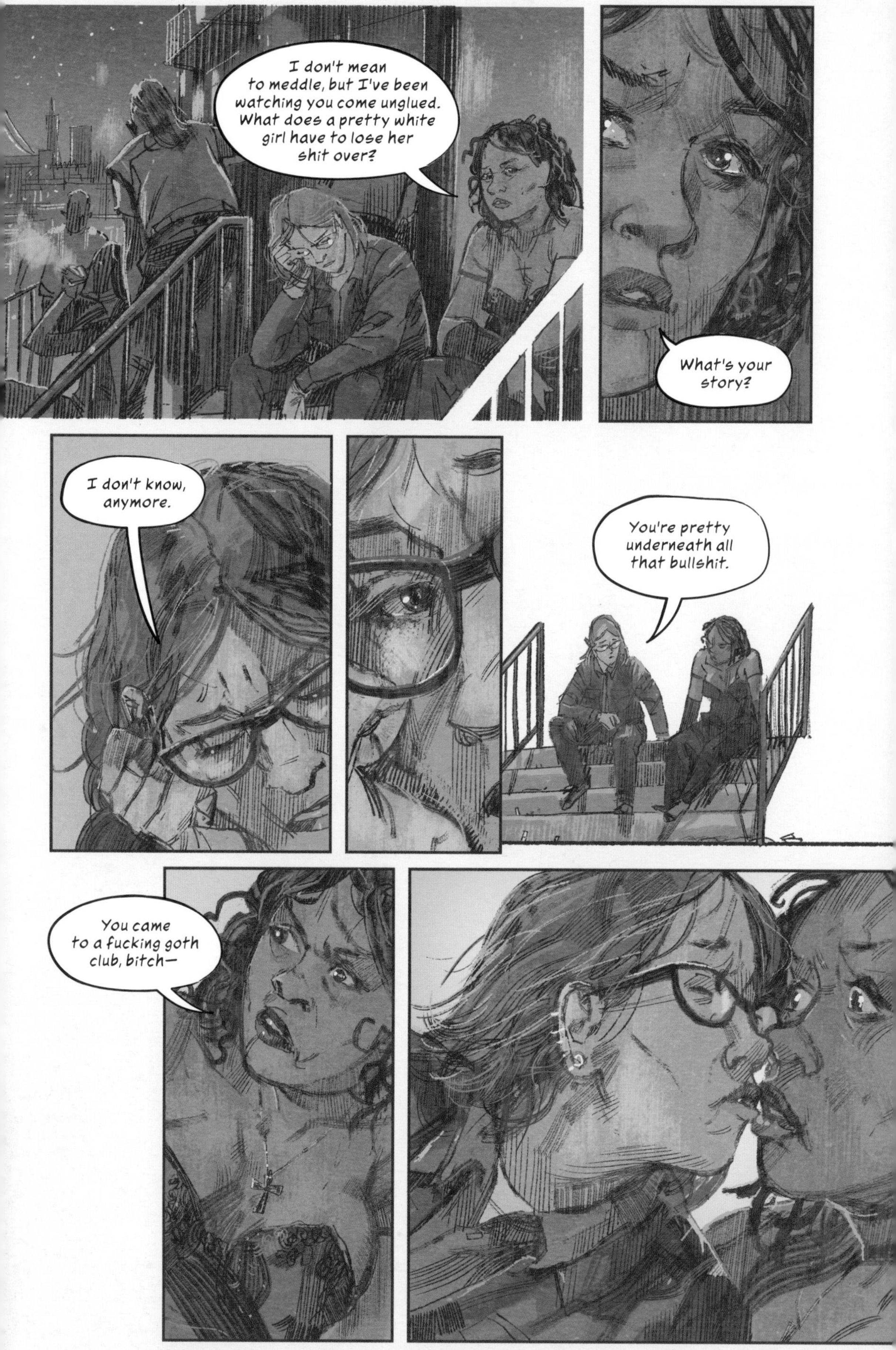
I don't mean to meddle, but I've been watching you come unglued. What does a pretty white girl have to lose her shit over?
What's your story?
I don't know, anymore.
You're pretty underneath all that bullshit.
You came to a fucking goth club, bitch—

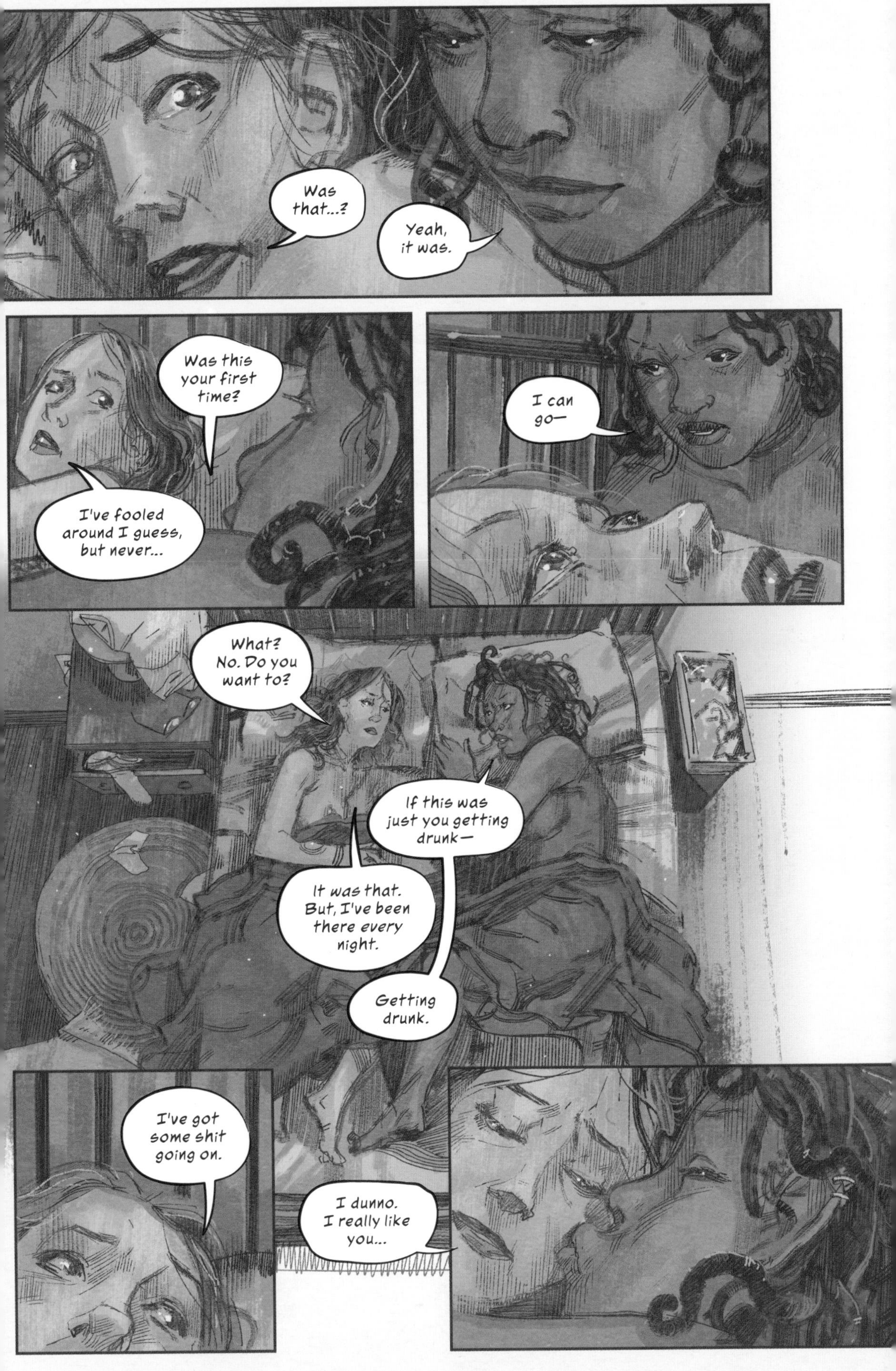
Was that...?
Yeah, it was.
Was this your first time?
I've fooled around I guess, but never...
I can go—
What? No. Do you want to?
If this was just you getting drunk—
It was that. But, I've been there every night.
Getting drunk.
I've got some shit going on.
I dunno. I really like you...

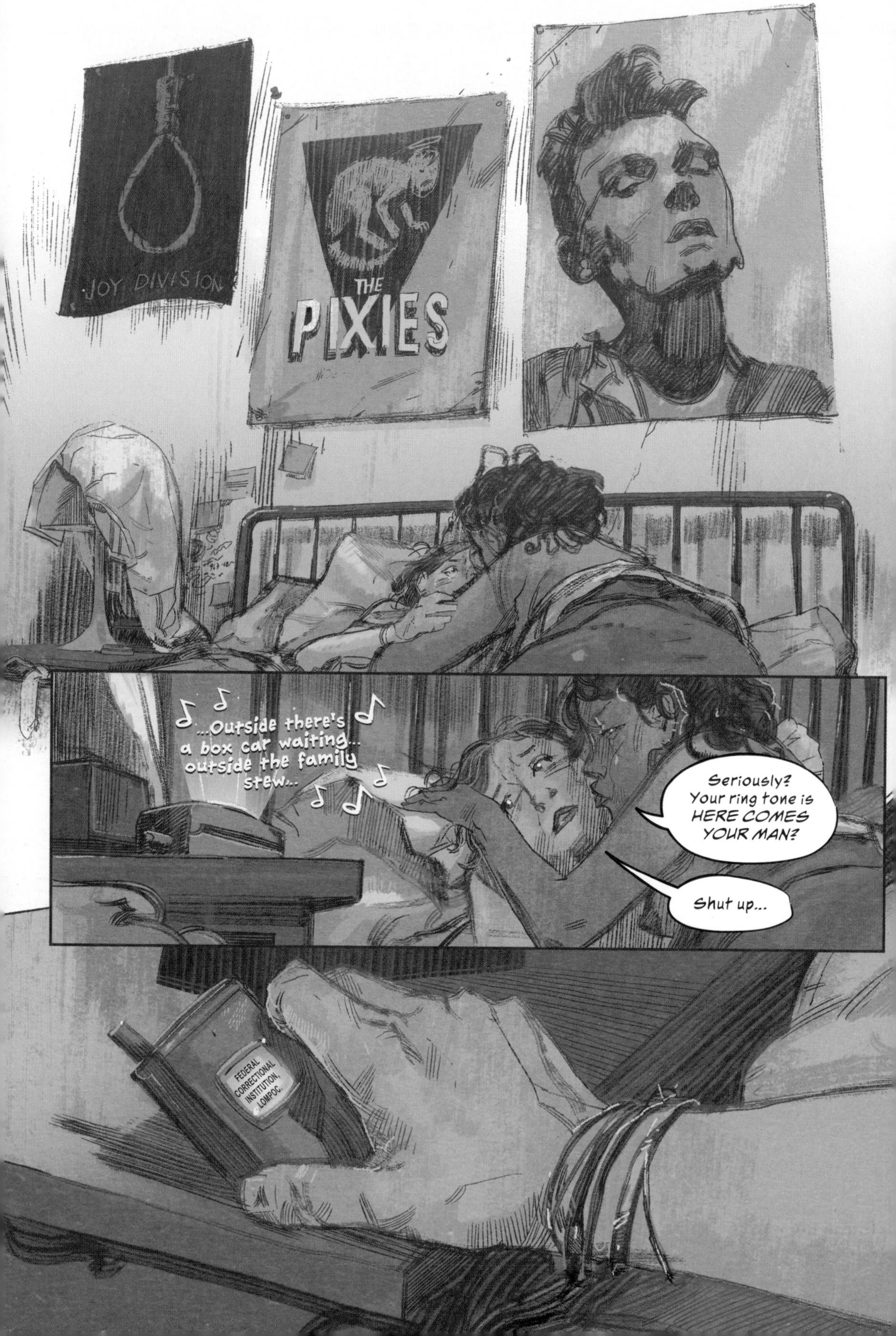
JOY DIVISION
THE PIXIES
...Outside there's a box car waiting... outside the family stew...
Seriously? Your ring tone is HERE COMES YOUR MAN?
Shut up...
FEDERAL CORRECTIONAL INSTITUTION, LOMPOC.

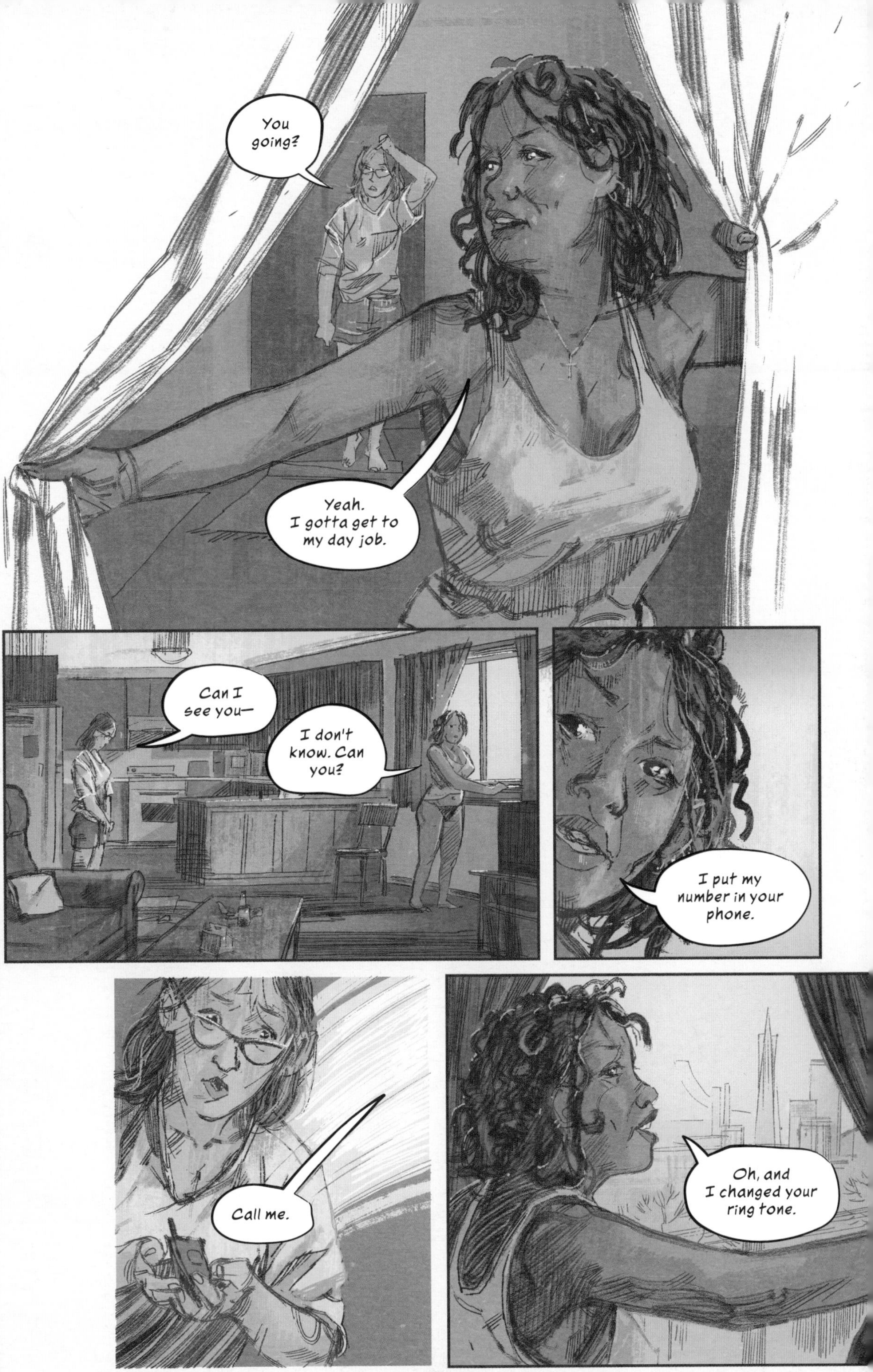
You going?
Yeah. I gotta get to my day job.
Can I see you—
I don't know. Can you?
I put my number in your phone.
Call me.
Oh, and I changed your ring tone.

Nine days ago.

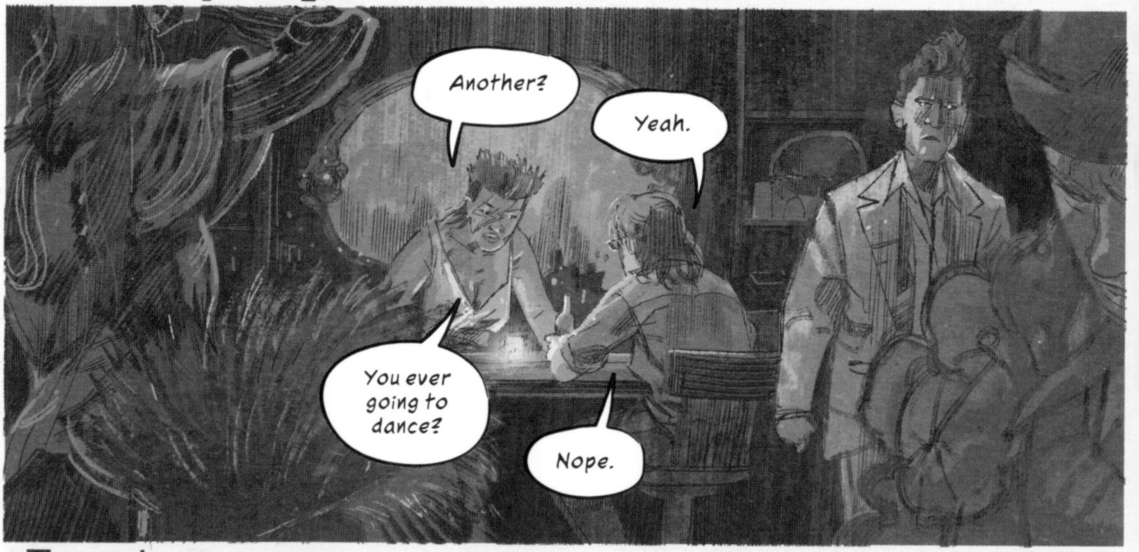
Another?
Yeah.
You ever going to dance?
Nope.

Ten days ago.

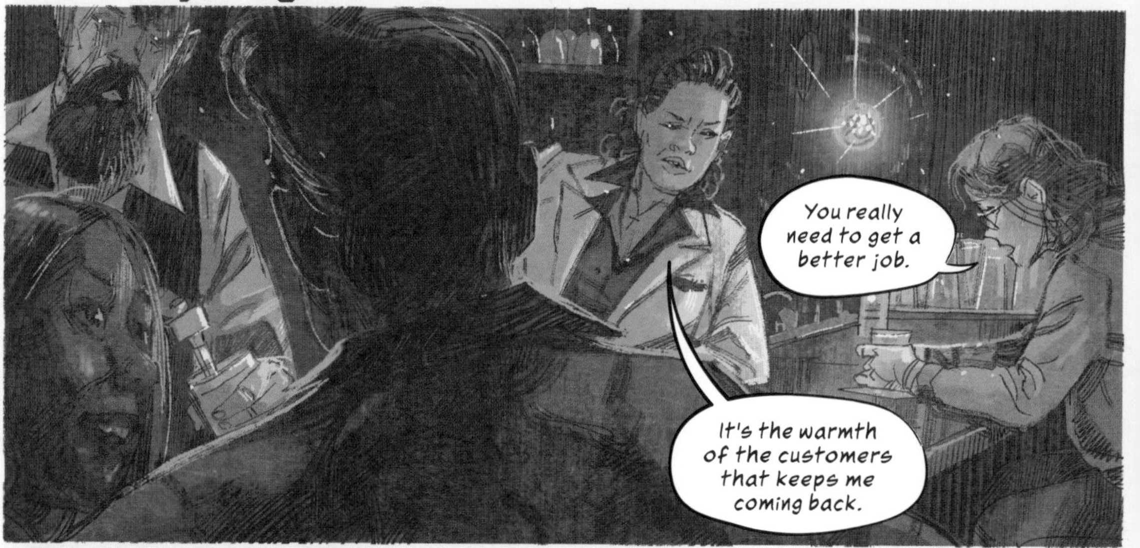
You really need to get a better job.
It's the warmth of the customers that keeps me coming back.

Eleven days ago.

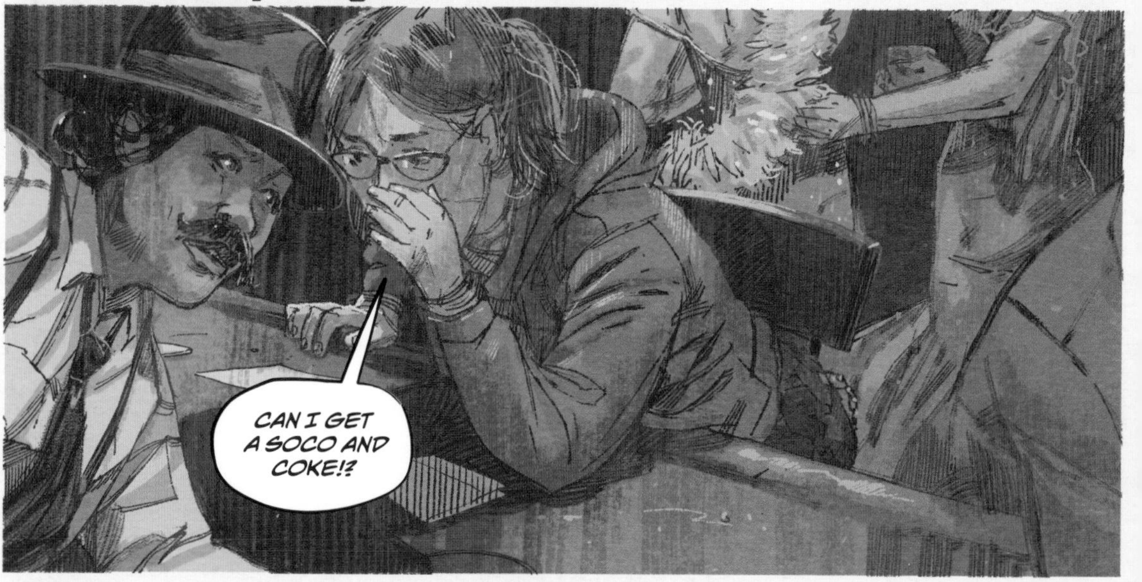
CAN I GET A SOCO AND COKE!?

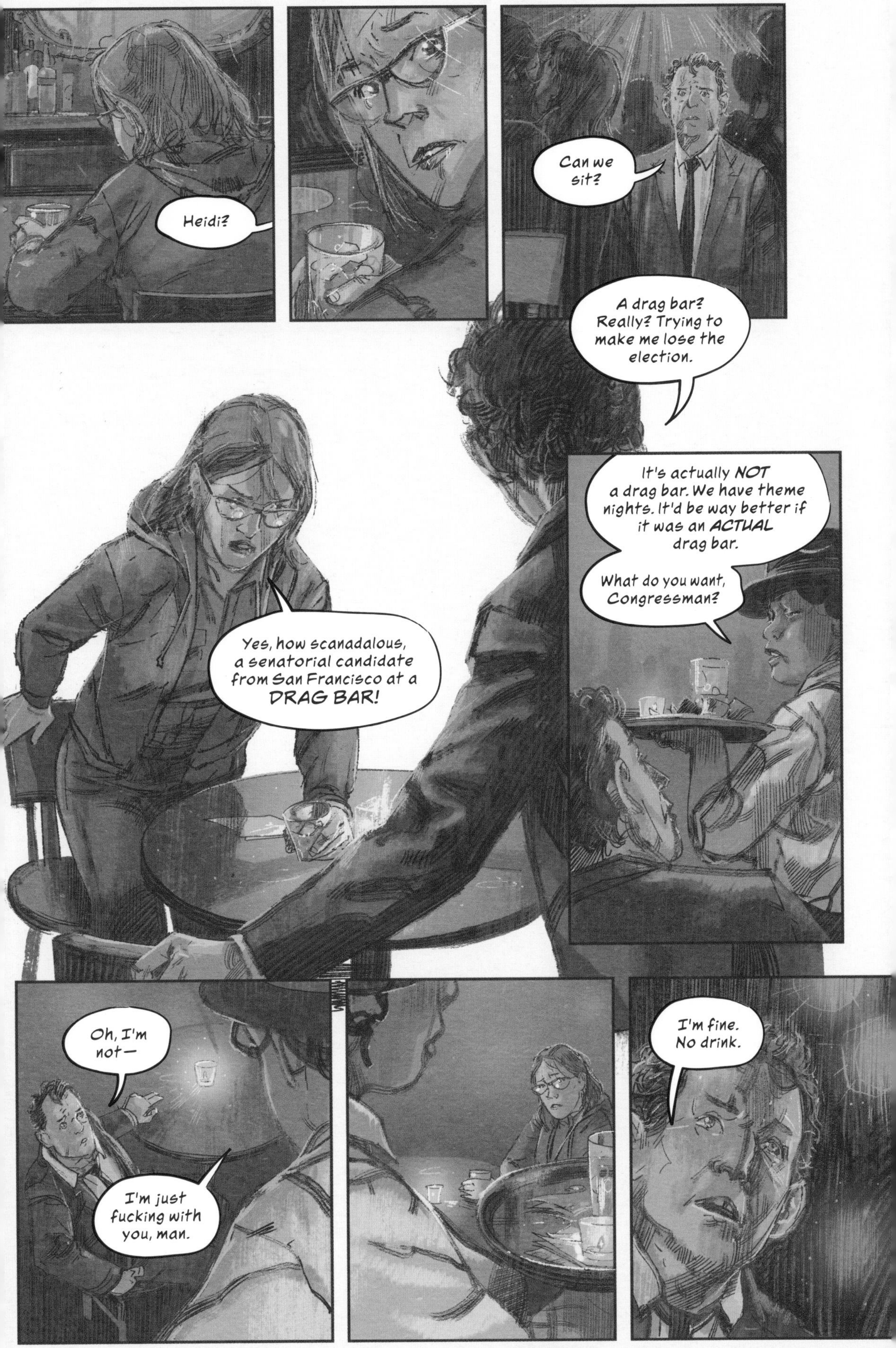

Heidi?
Can we sit?
A drag bar? Really? Trying to make me lose the election.
Yes, how scanadalous, a senatorial candidate from San Francisco at a DRAG BAR!
It's actually NOT a drag bar. We have theme nights. It'd be way better if it was an ACTUAL drag bar.
What do you want, Congressman?
Oh, I'm not—
I'm just fucking with you, man.
I'm fine. No drink.

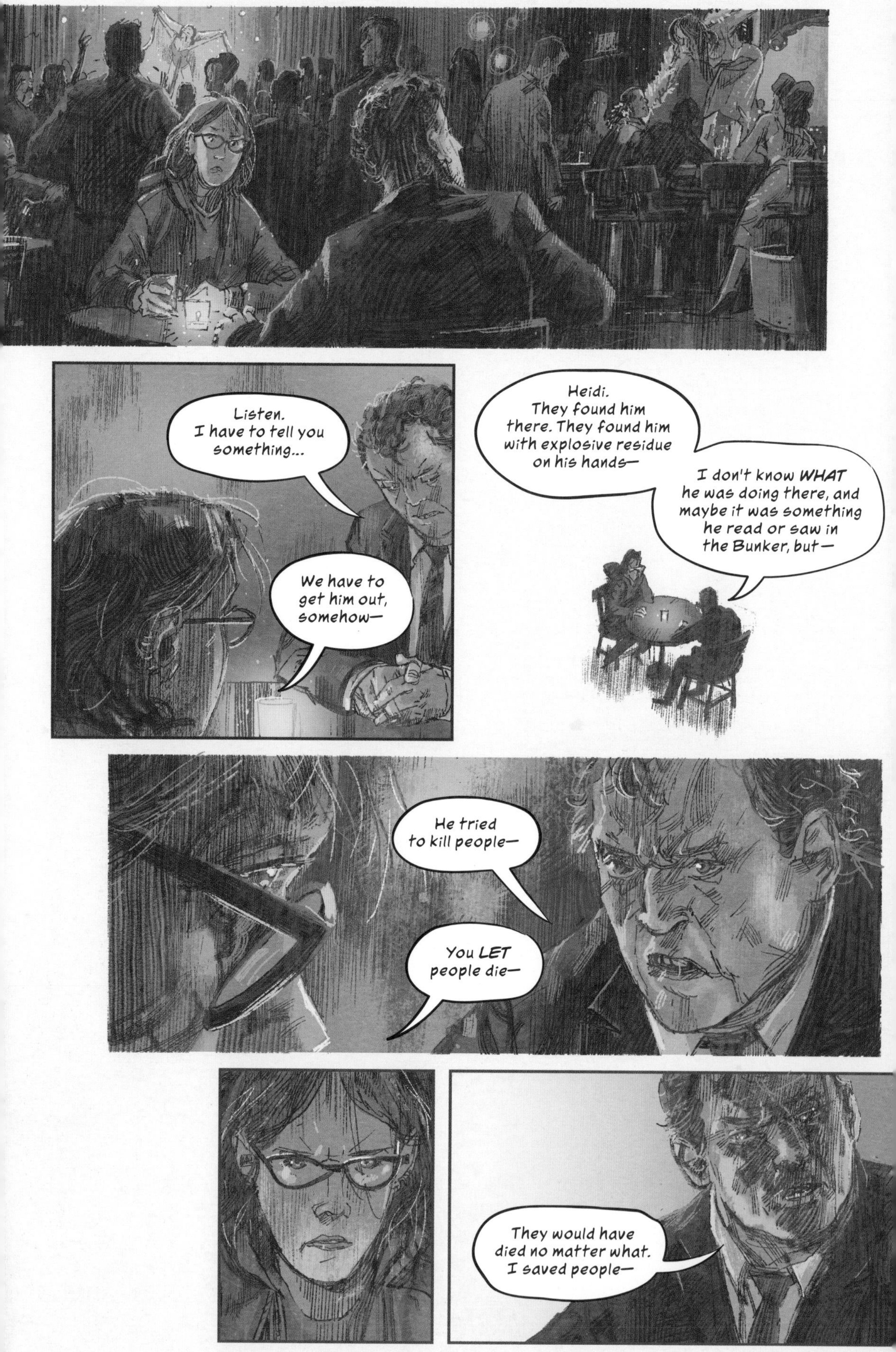
Listen.
I have to tell you
something...
We have to
get him out,
somehow—
Heidi.
They found him
there. They found him
with explosive residue
on his hands—
I don't know **WHAT**
he was doing there, and
maybe it was something
he read or saw in
the Bunker, but—
He tried
to kill people—
You **LET**
people die—
They would have
died no matter what.
I saved people—

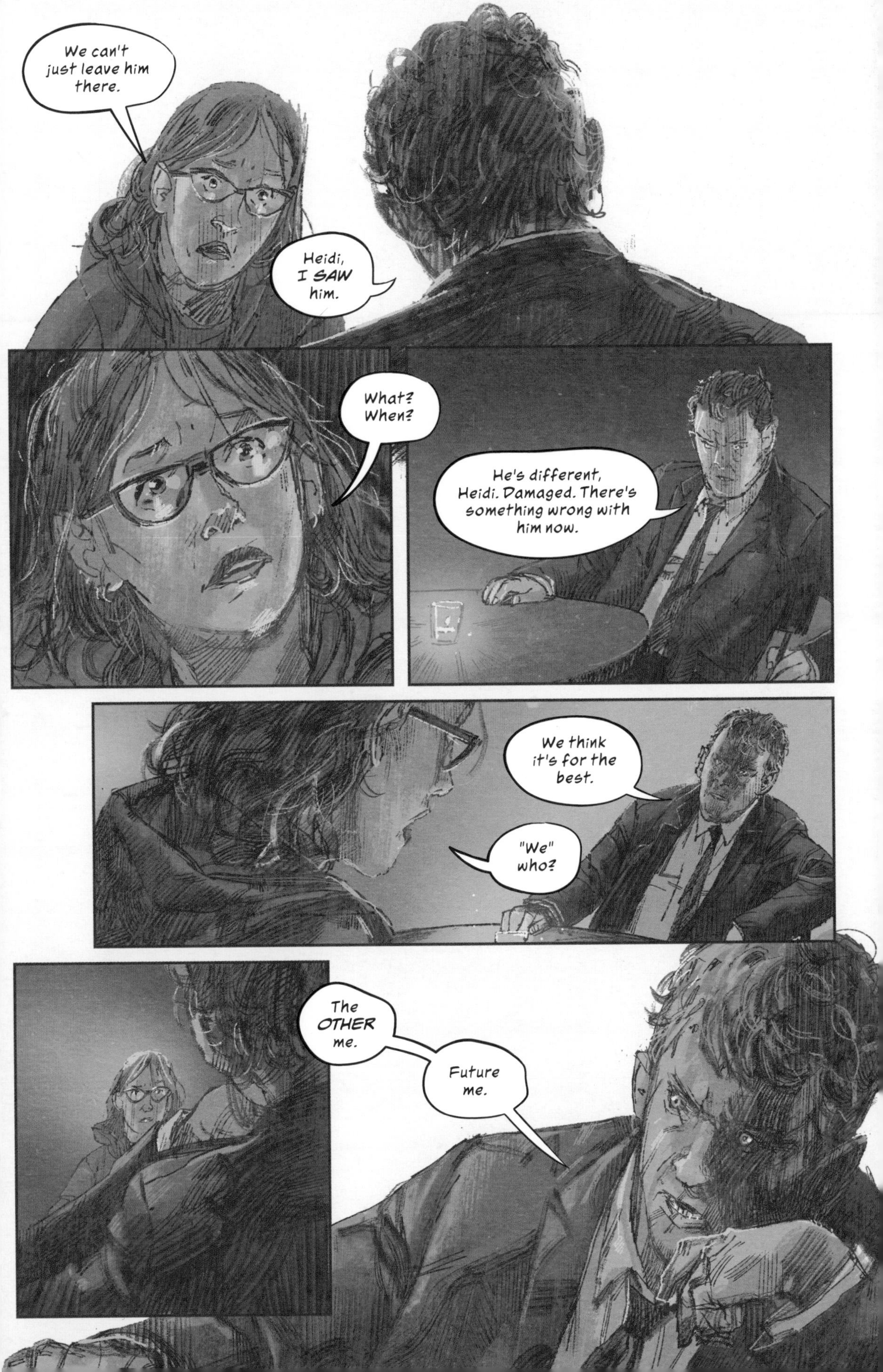
We can't just leave him there.
Heidi, I SAW him.
What? When?
He's different, Heidi. Damaged. There's something wrong with him now.
We think it's for the best.
"We" who?
The OTHER me.
Future me.

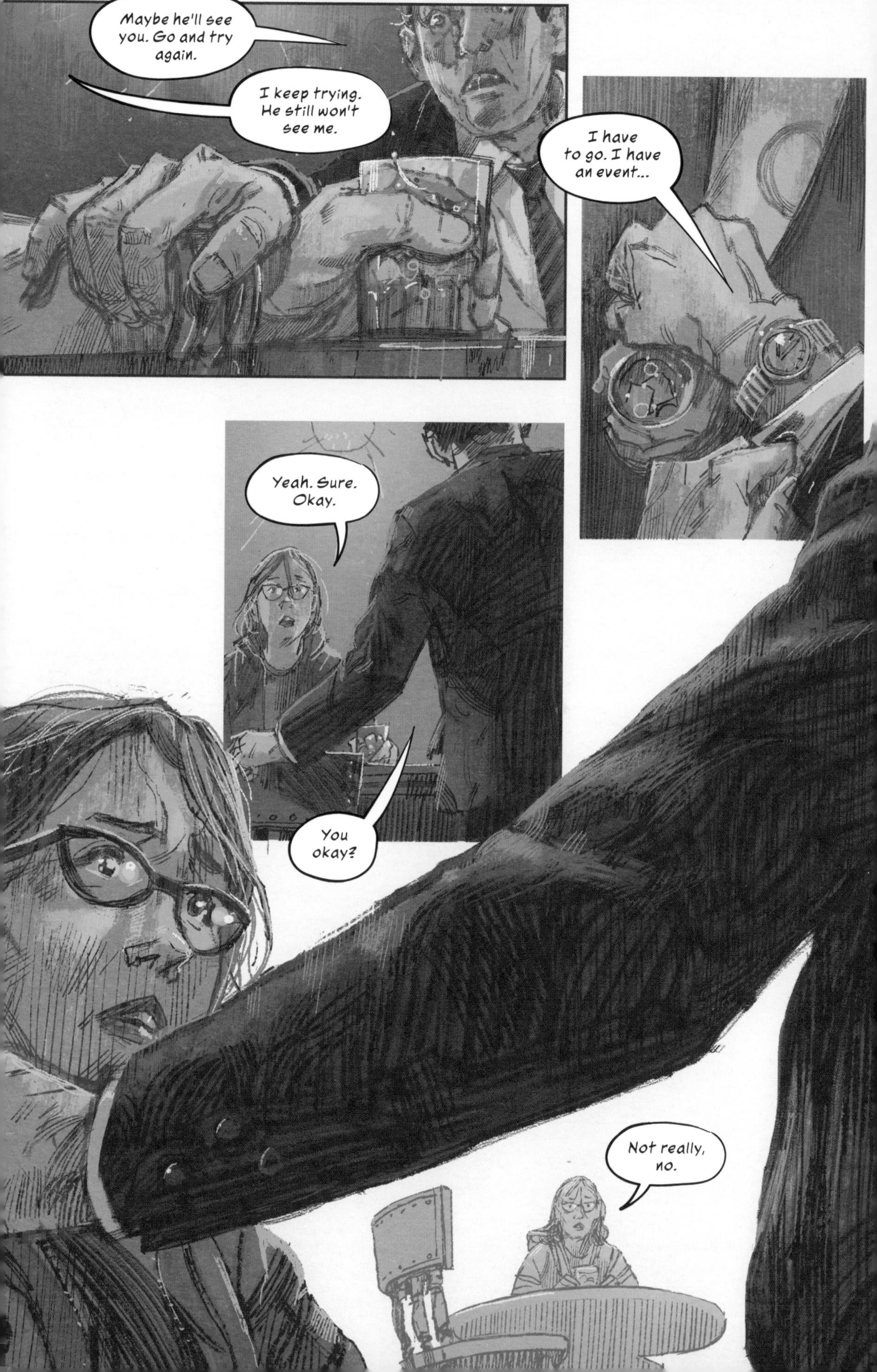
Maybe he'll see you. Go and try again.
I keep trying. He still won't see me.
I have to go. I have an event...
Yeah. Sure. Okay.
You okay?
Not really, no.

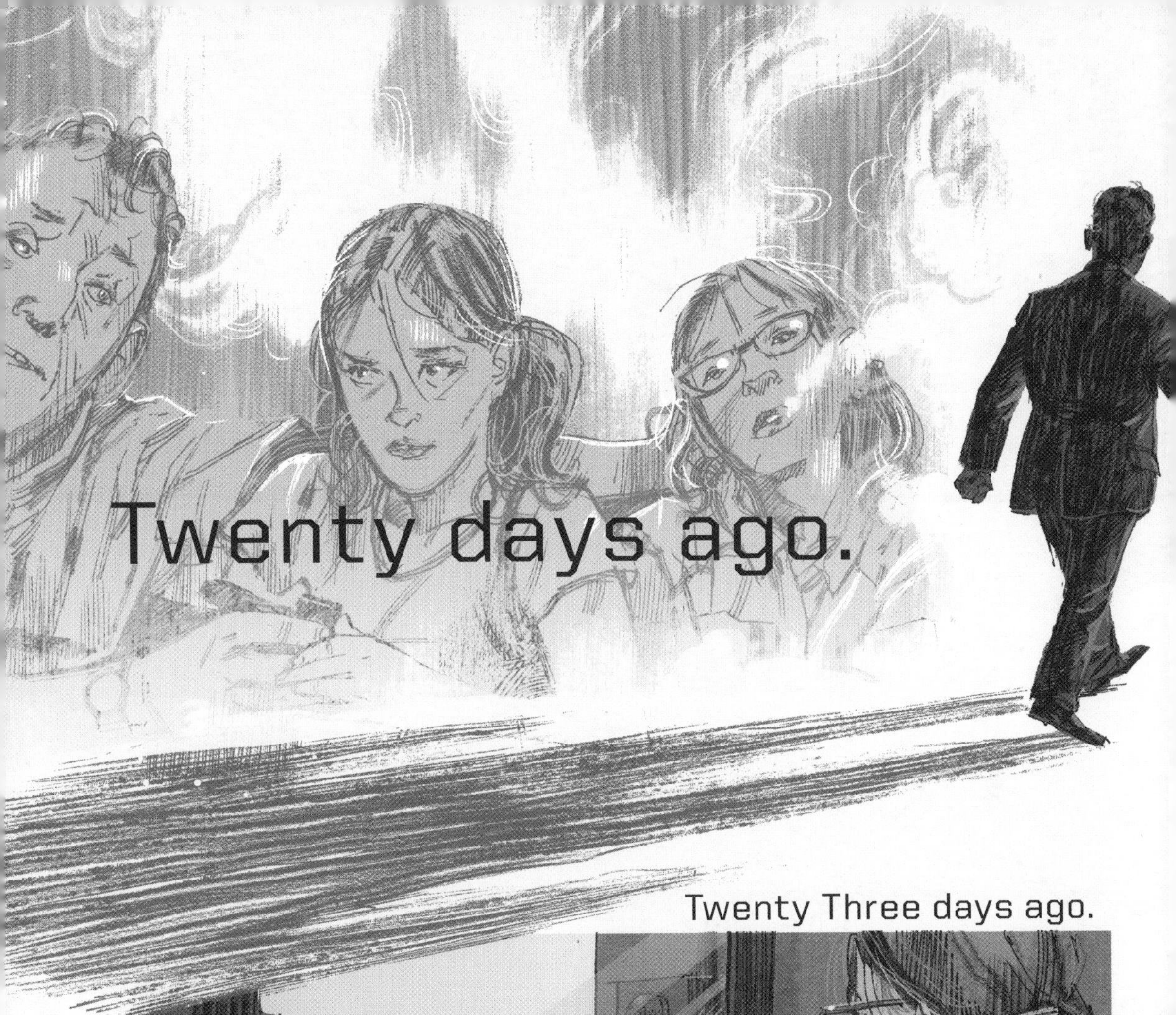
Twenty days ago.

Twenty Three days ago.

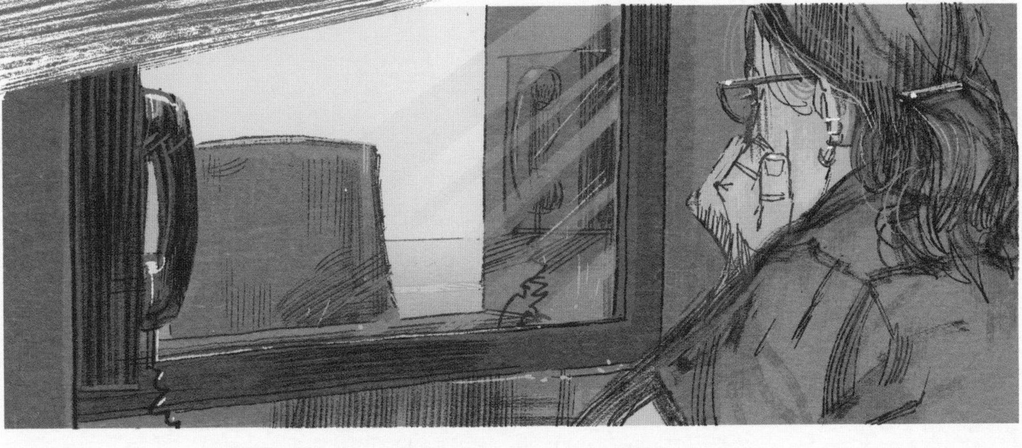

Thirty days ago.

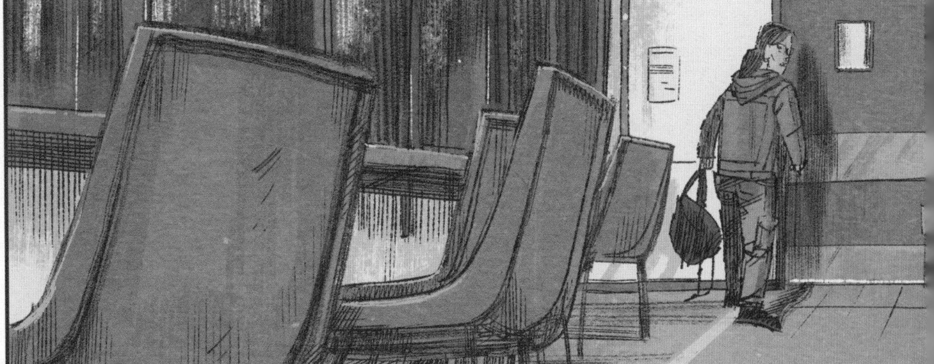

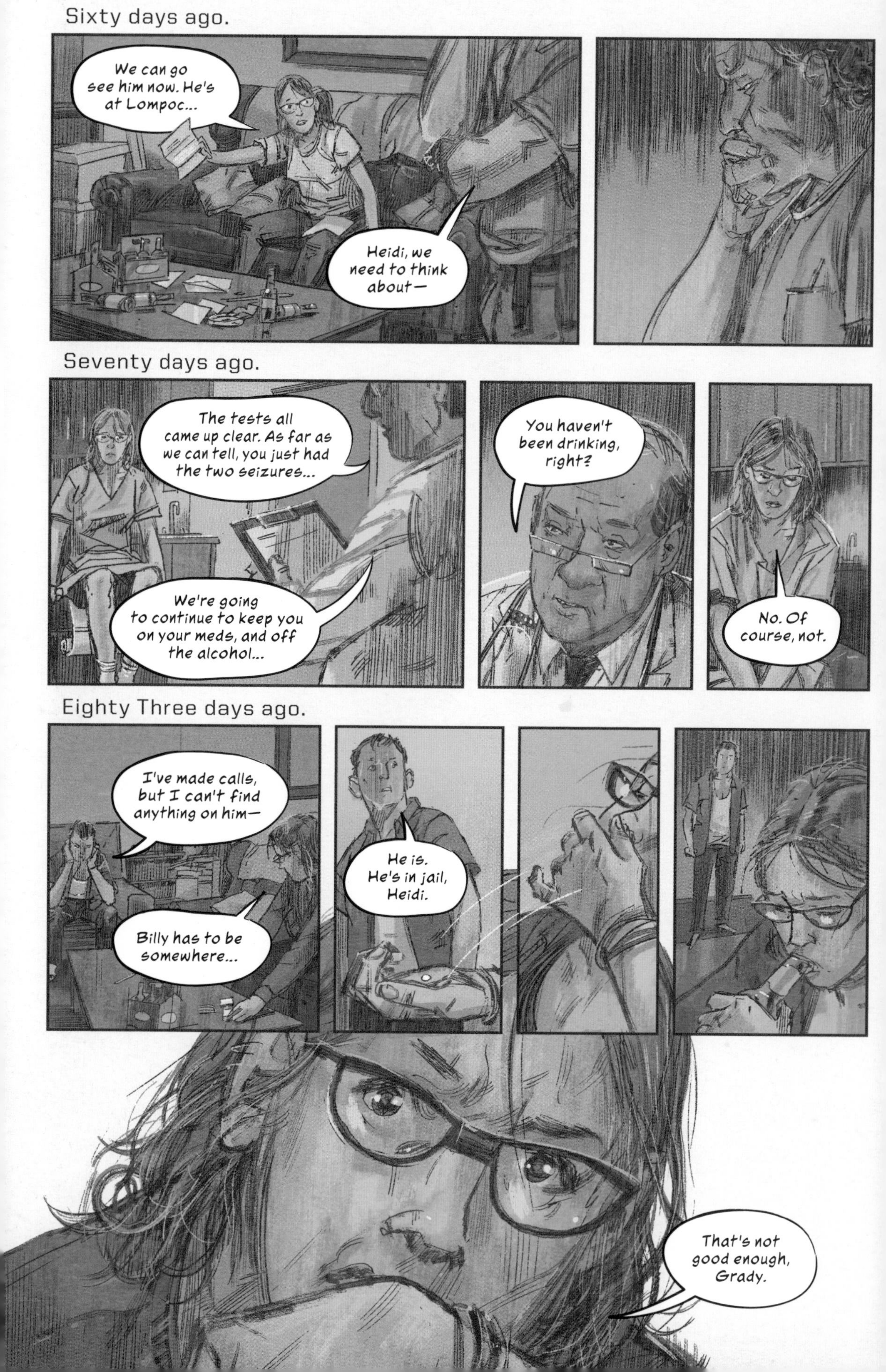
Sixty days ago.
We can go see him now. He's at Lompoc...
Heidi, we need to think about—
Seventy days ago.
The tests all came up clear. As far as we can tell, you just had the two seizures...
We're going to continue to keep you on your meds, and off the alcohol...
You haven't been drinking, right?
No. Of course, not.
Eighty Three days ago.
I've made calls, but I can't find anything on him—
Billy has to be somewhere...
He is. He's in jail, Heidi.
That's not good enough, Grady.

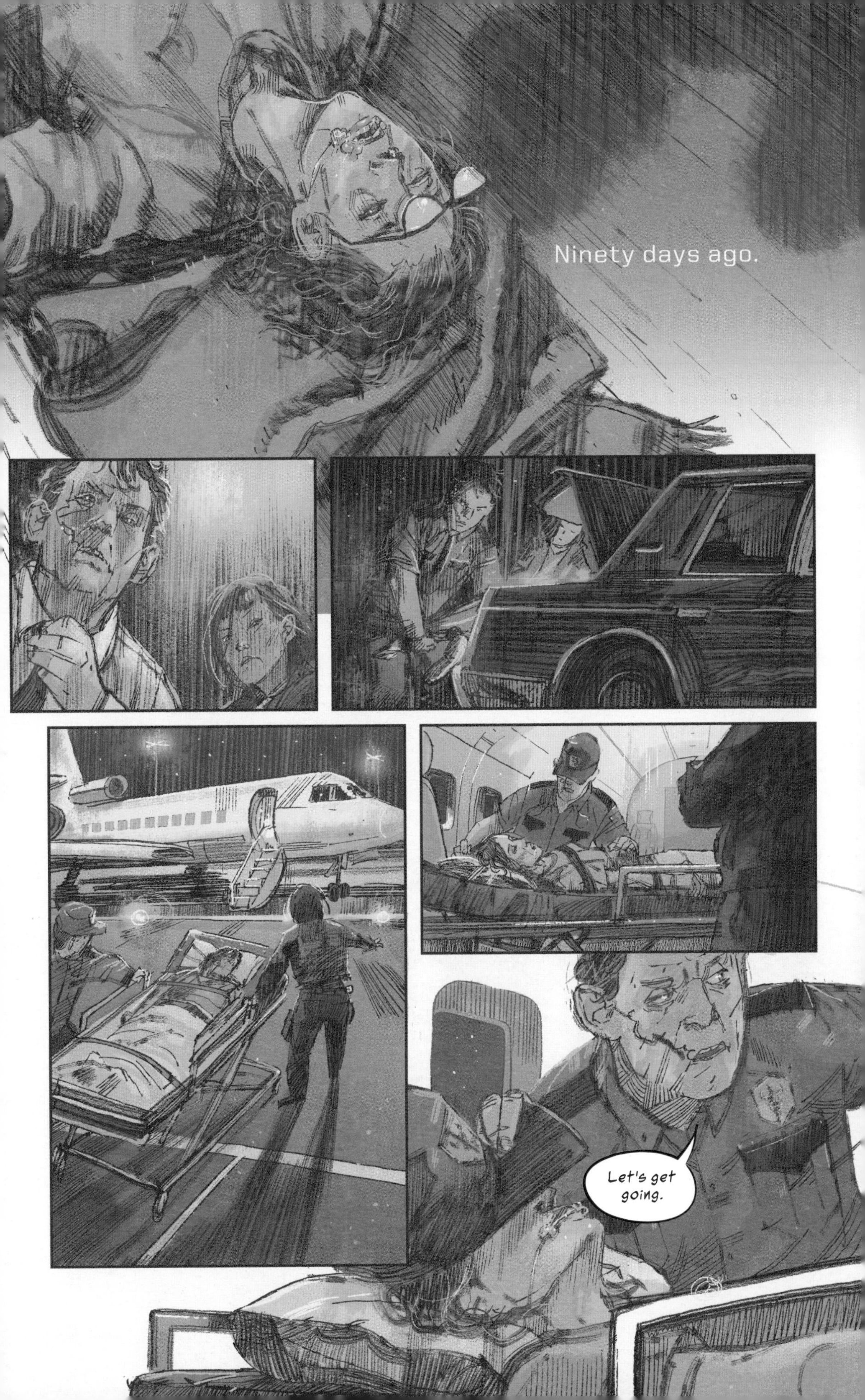
Ninety days ago.
Let's get going.

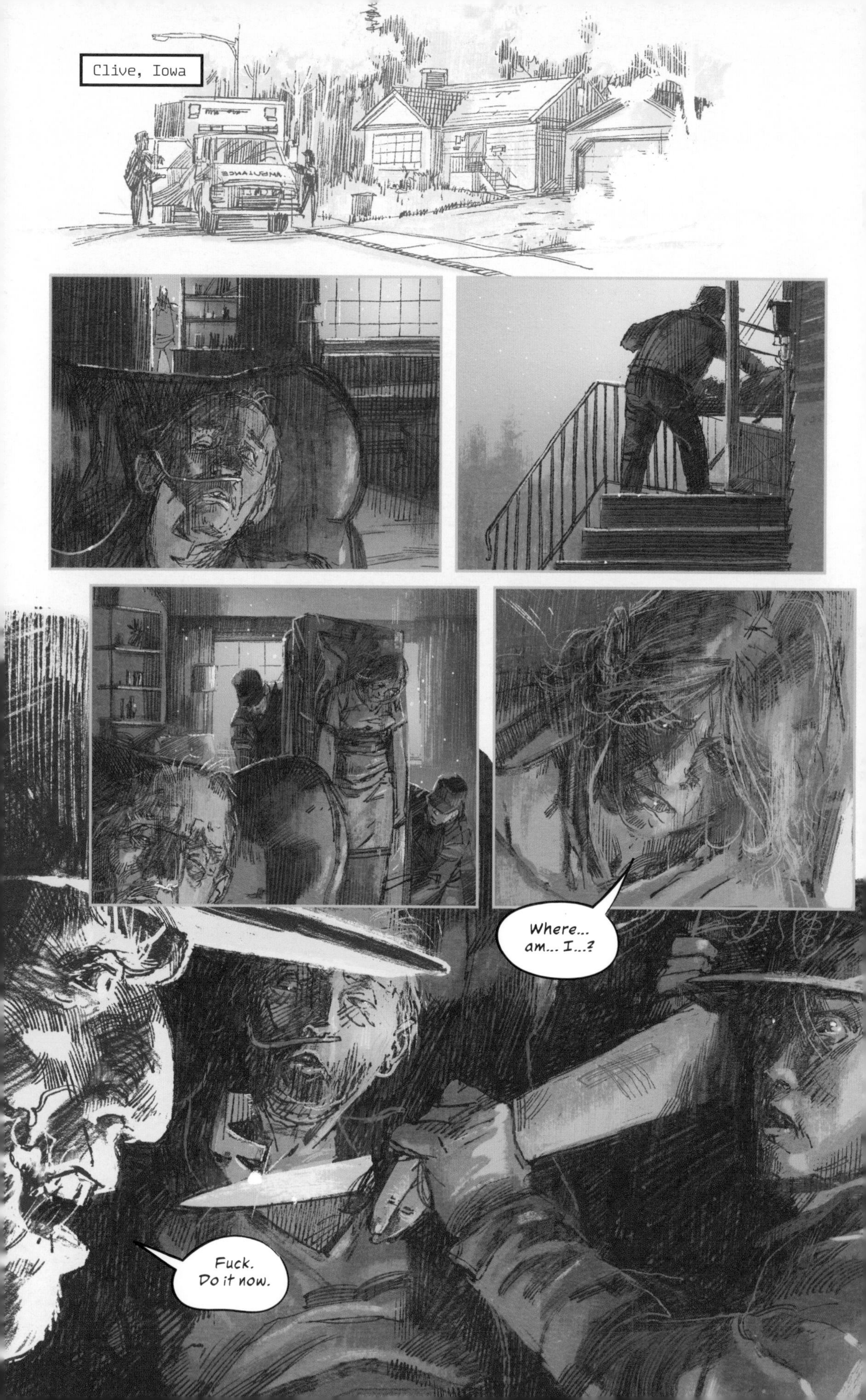
Clive, Iowa
Where... am... I...?
Fuck. Do it now.

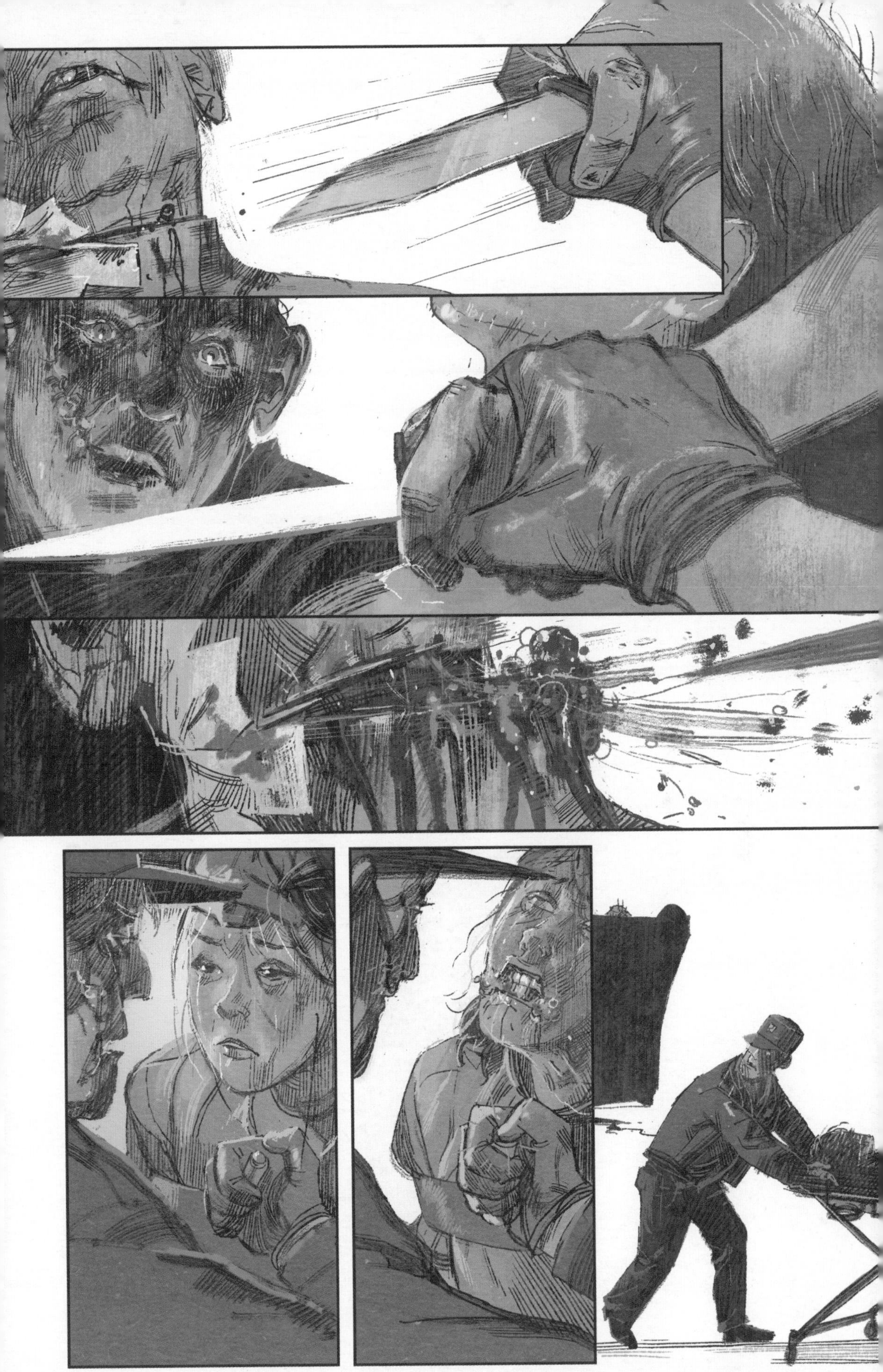

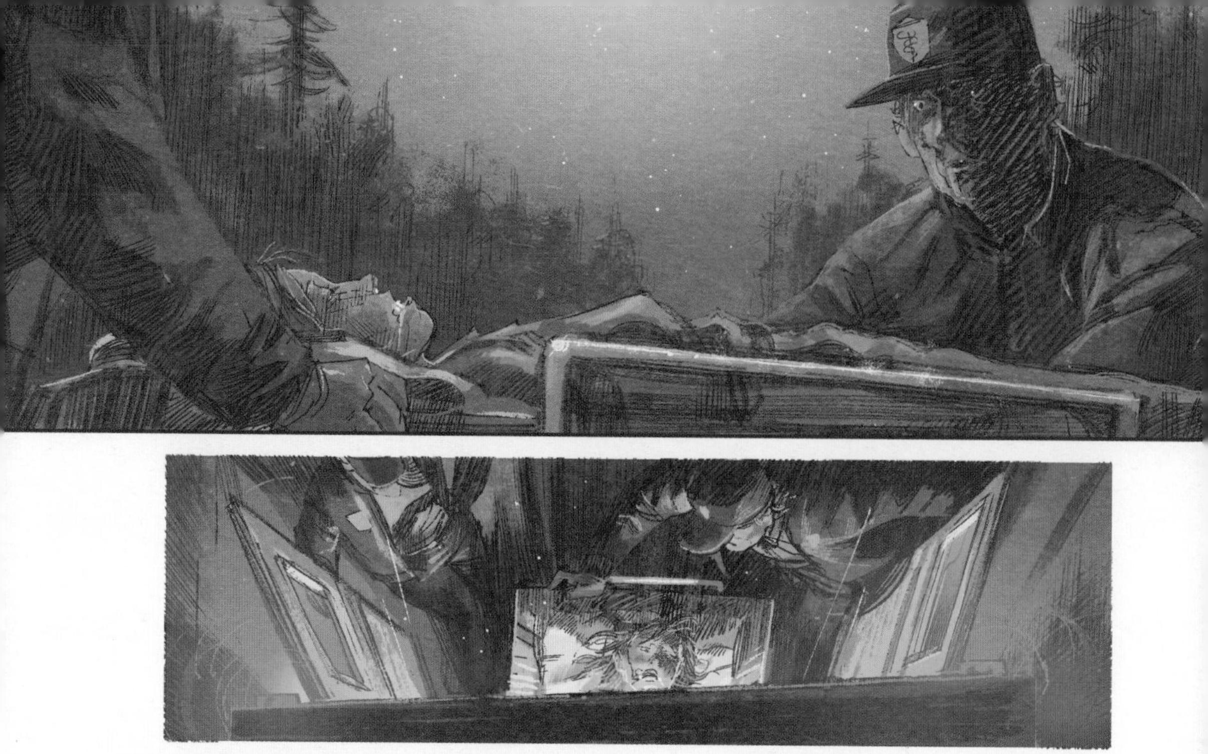

Eighty Nine days ago.

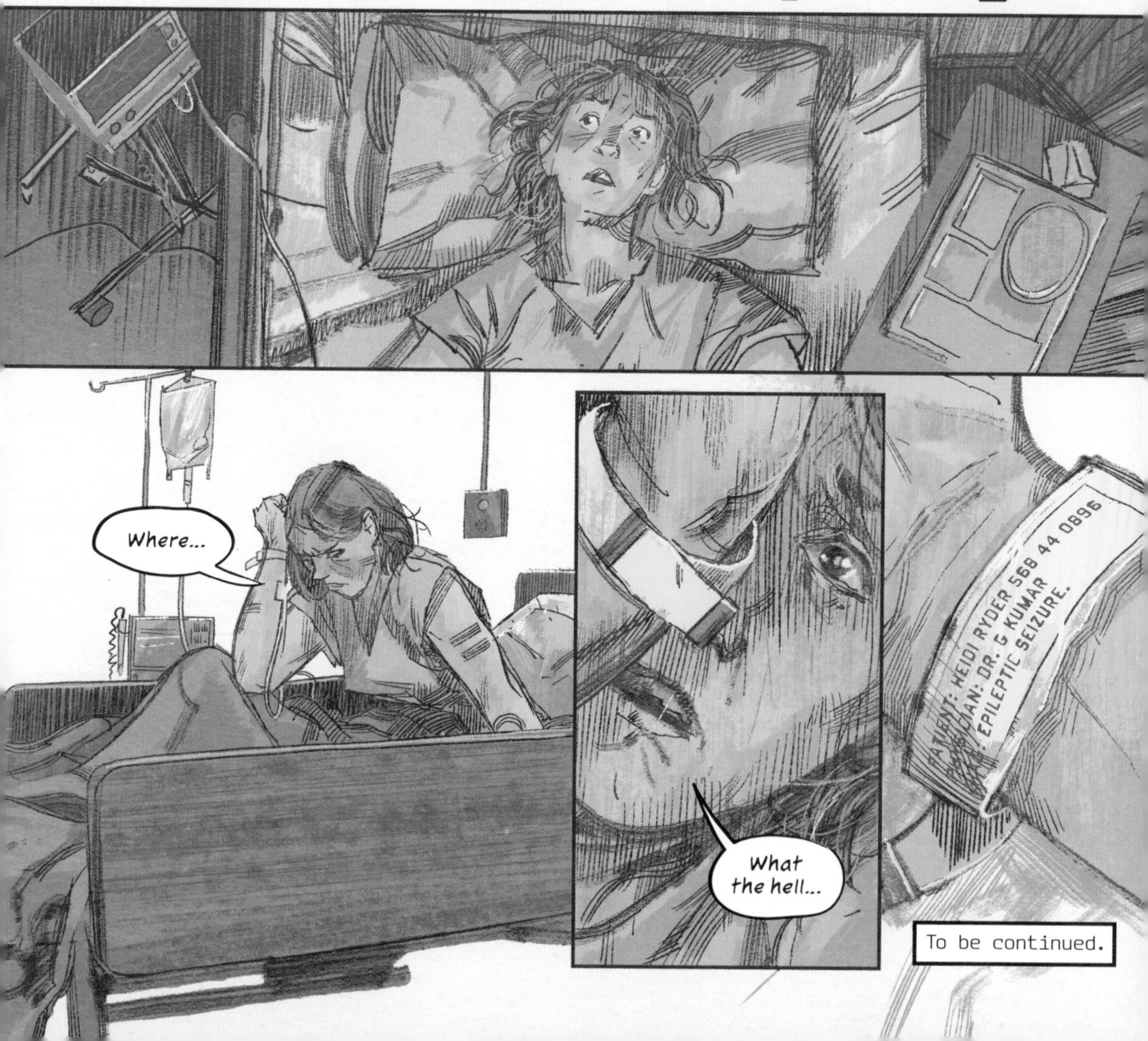
Where...
What the hell...
HEIDI RYDER 568 44 0896
DR. G KUMAR
EPILEPTIC SEIZURE.
To be continued.

CHAPTER
13

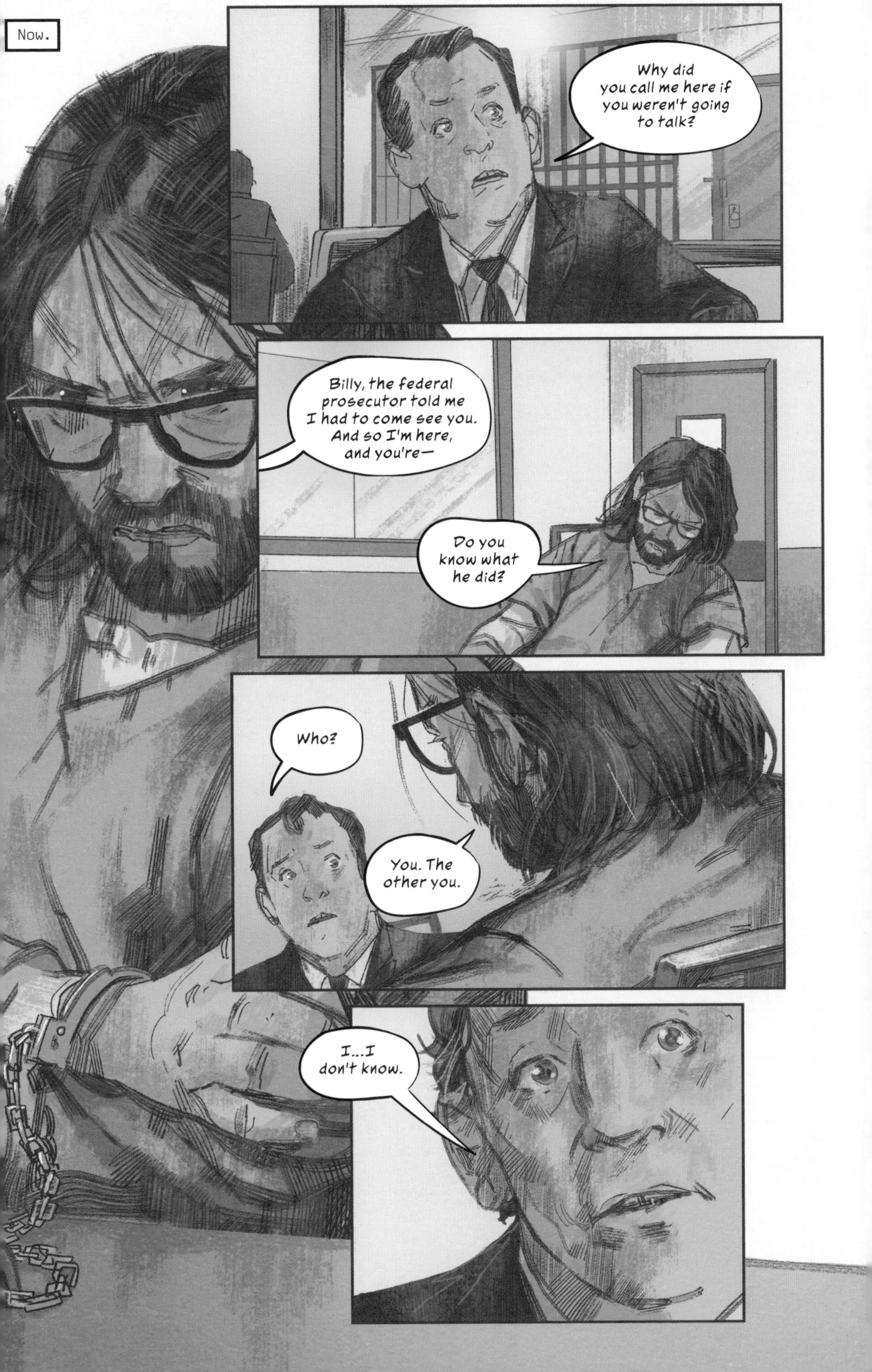
Now.
Why did you call me here if you weren't going to talk?
Billy, the federal prosecutor told me I had to come see you. And so I'm here, and you're—
Do you know what he did?
Who?
You. The other you.
I...I don't know.

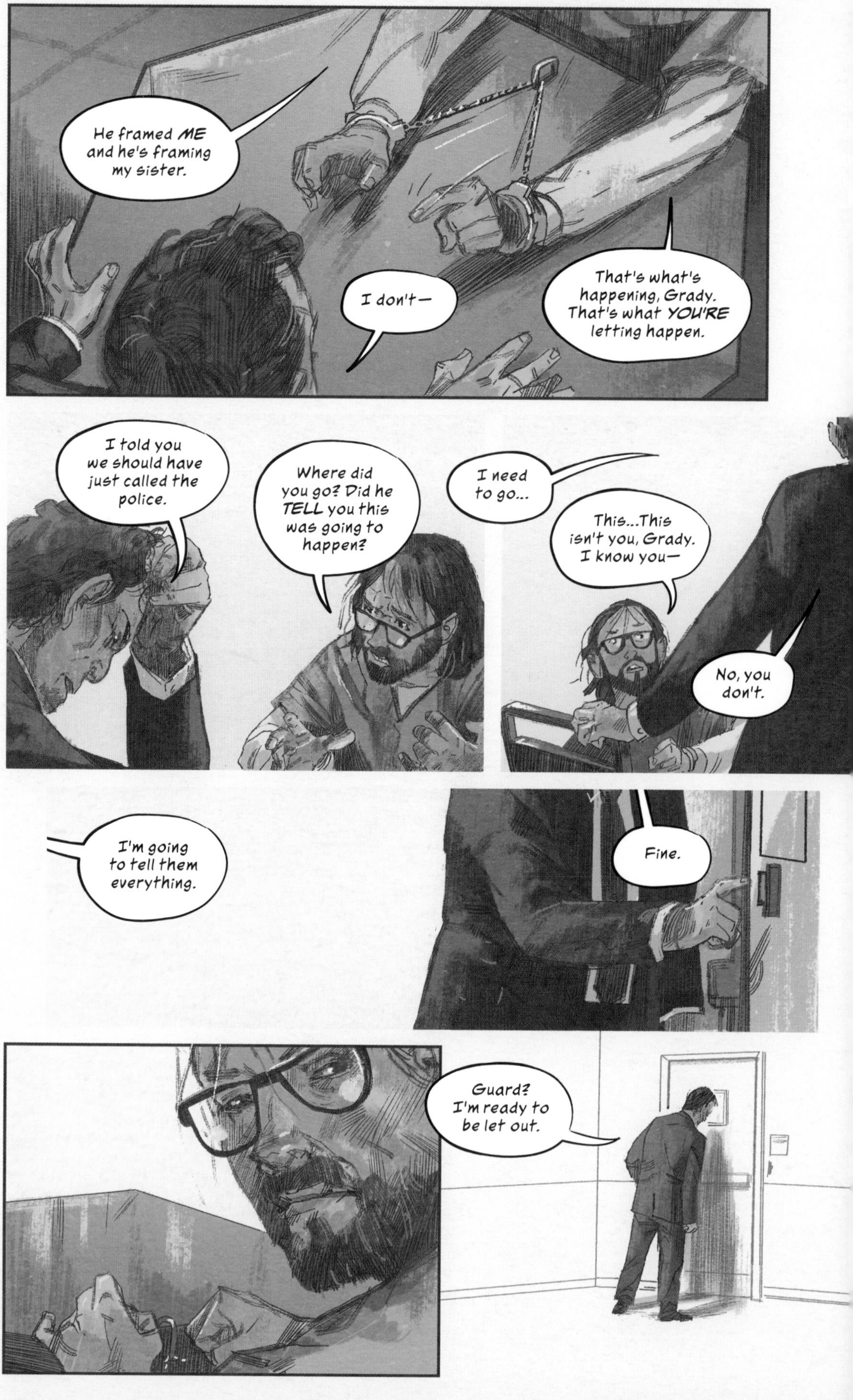
He framed ME and he's framing my sister.
I don't—
That's what's happening, Grady. That's what YOU'RE letting happen.
I told you we should have just called the police.
Where did you go? Did he TELL you this was going to happen?
I need to go...
This...This isn't you, Grady. I know you—
No, you don't.
I'm going to tell them everything.
Fine.
Guard? I'm ready to be let out.

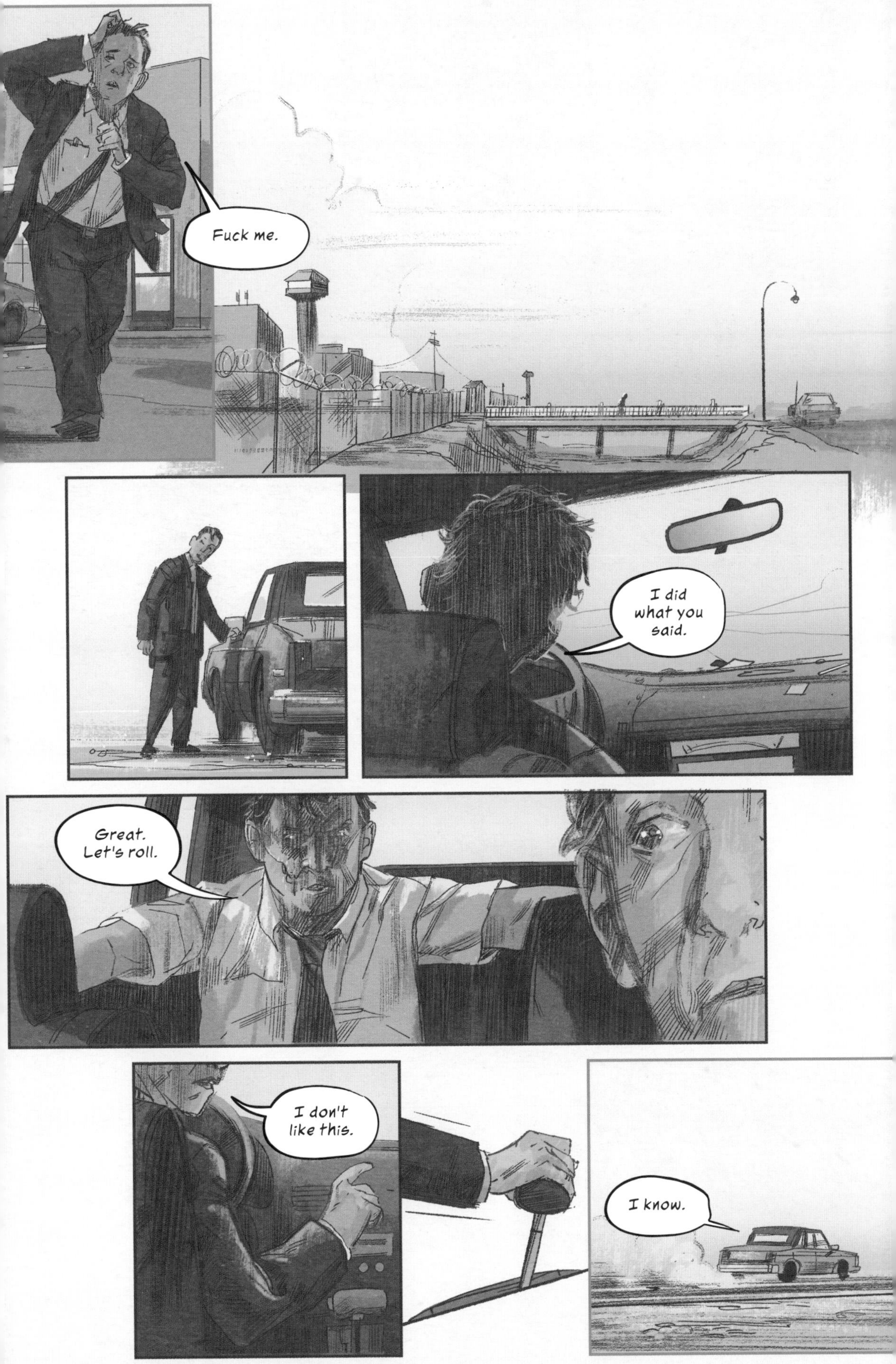
Fuck me.
I did what you said.
Great. Let's roll.
I don't like this.
I know.

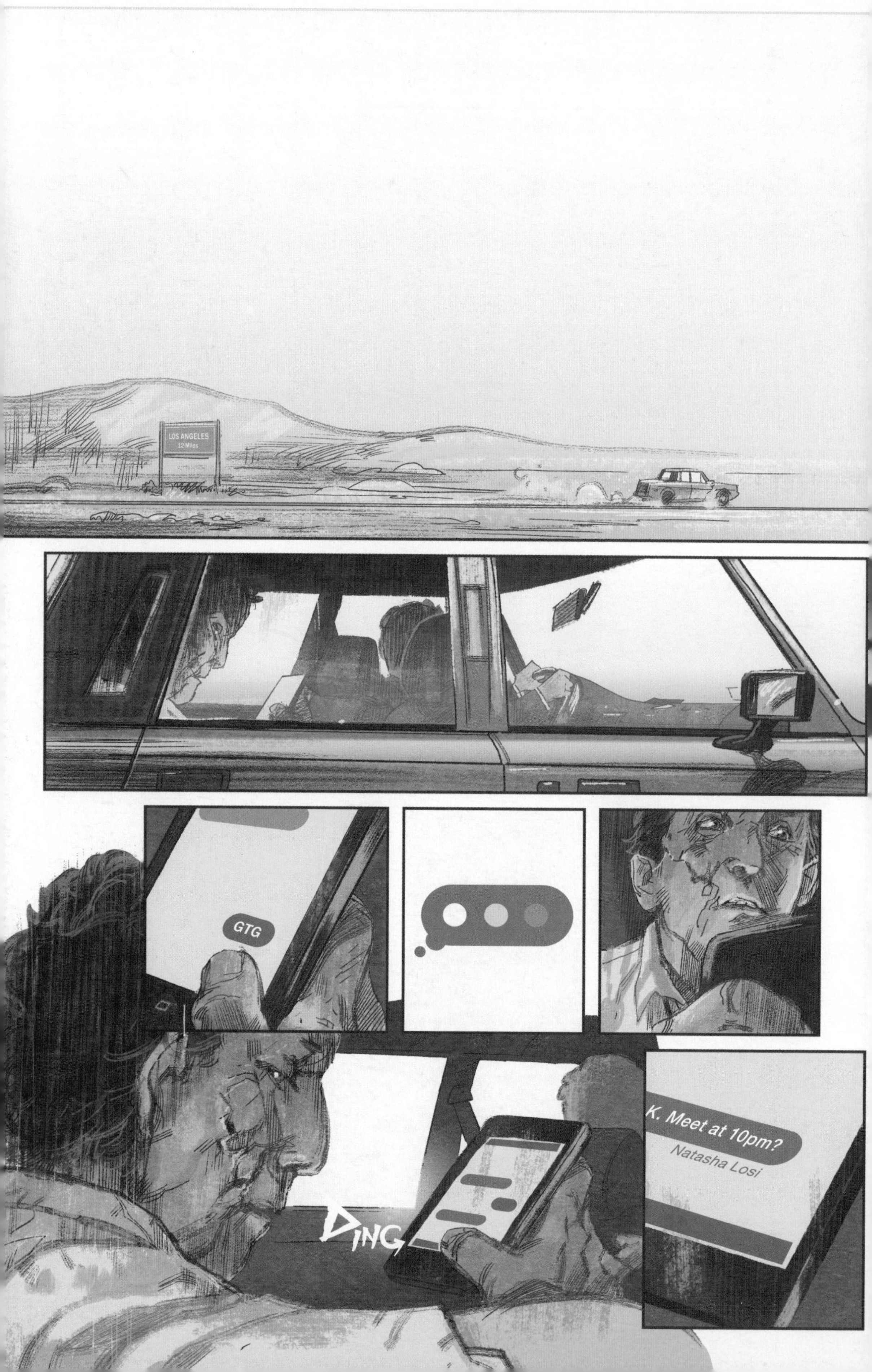
LOS ANGELES
12 Miles
GTG
DING
K. Meet at 10pm?
Natasha Losi

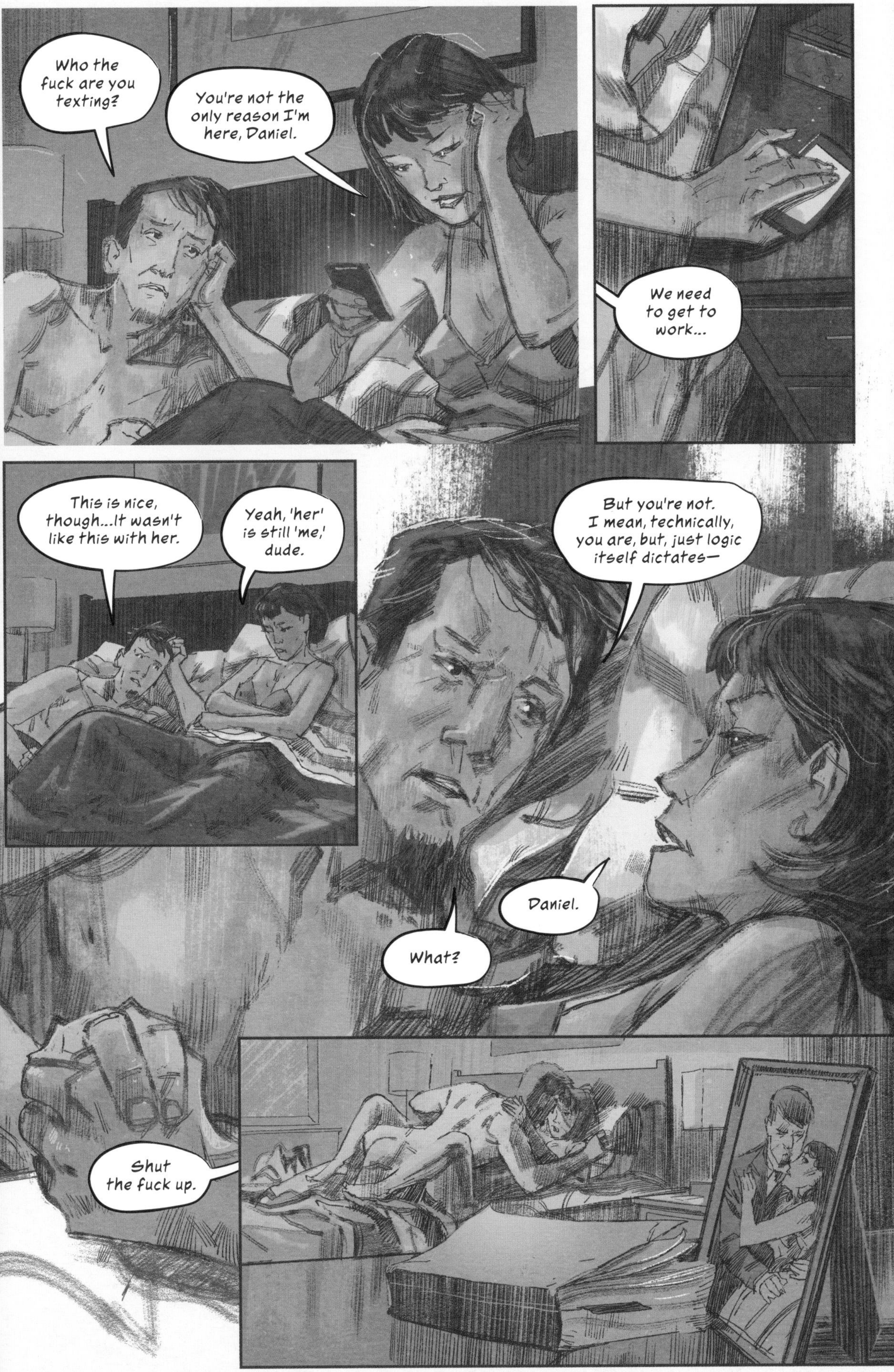

Who the fuck are you texting?
You're not the only reason I'm here, Daniel.
We need to get to work...
This is nice, though...It wasn't like this with her.
Yeah, 'her' is still 'me,' dude.
But you're not. I mean, technically, you are, but, just logic itself dictates—
Daniel.
What?
Shut the fuck up.

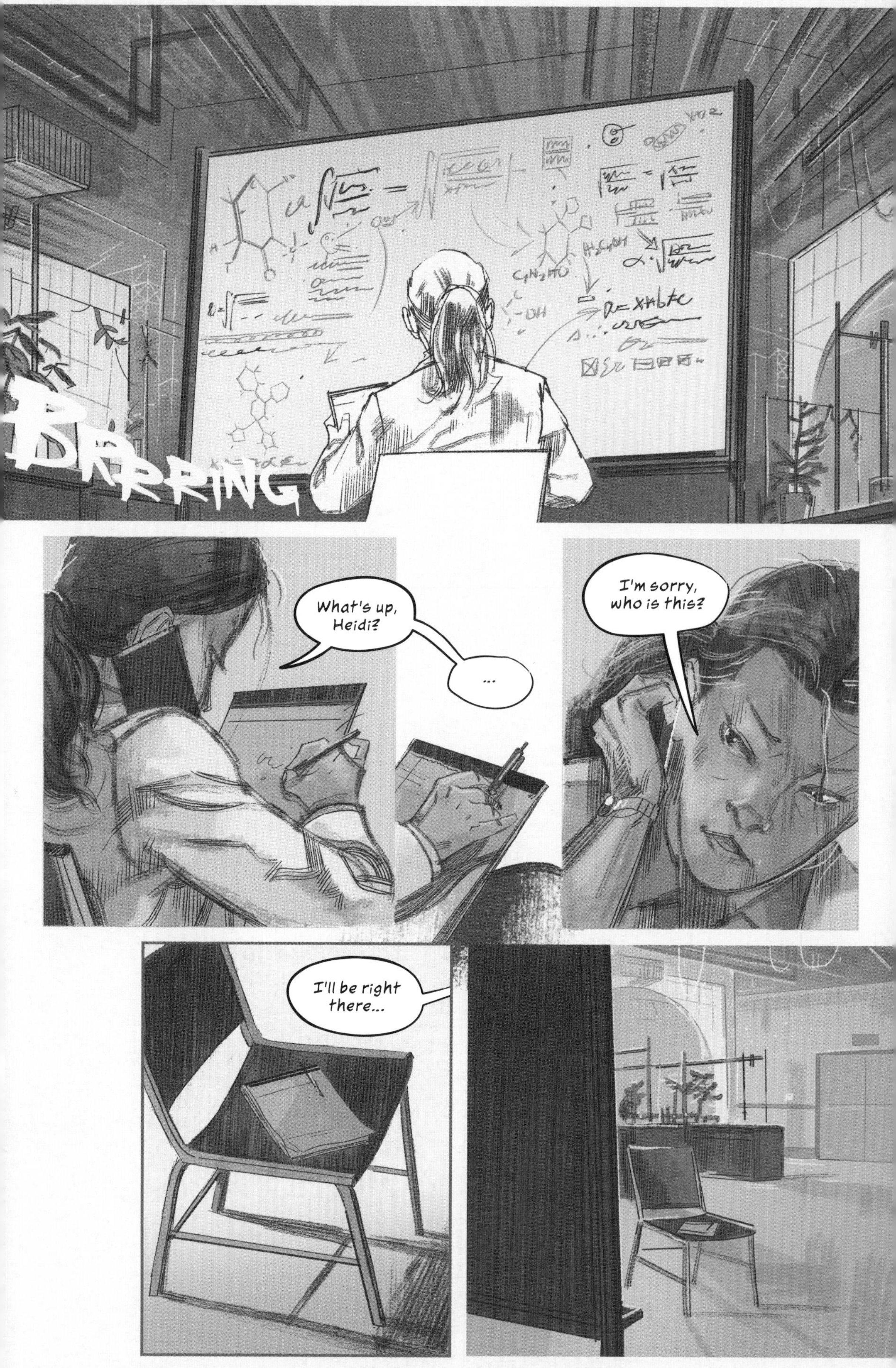
BRRRING
What's up, Heidi?
...
I'm sorry, who is this?
I'll be right there...

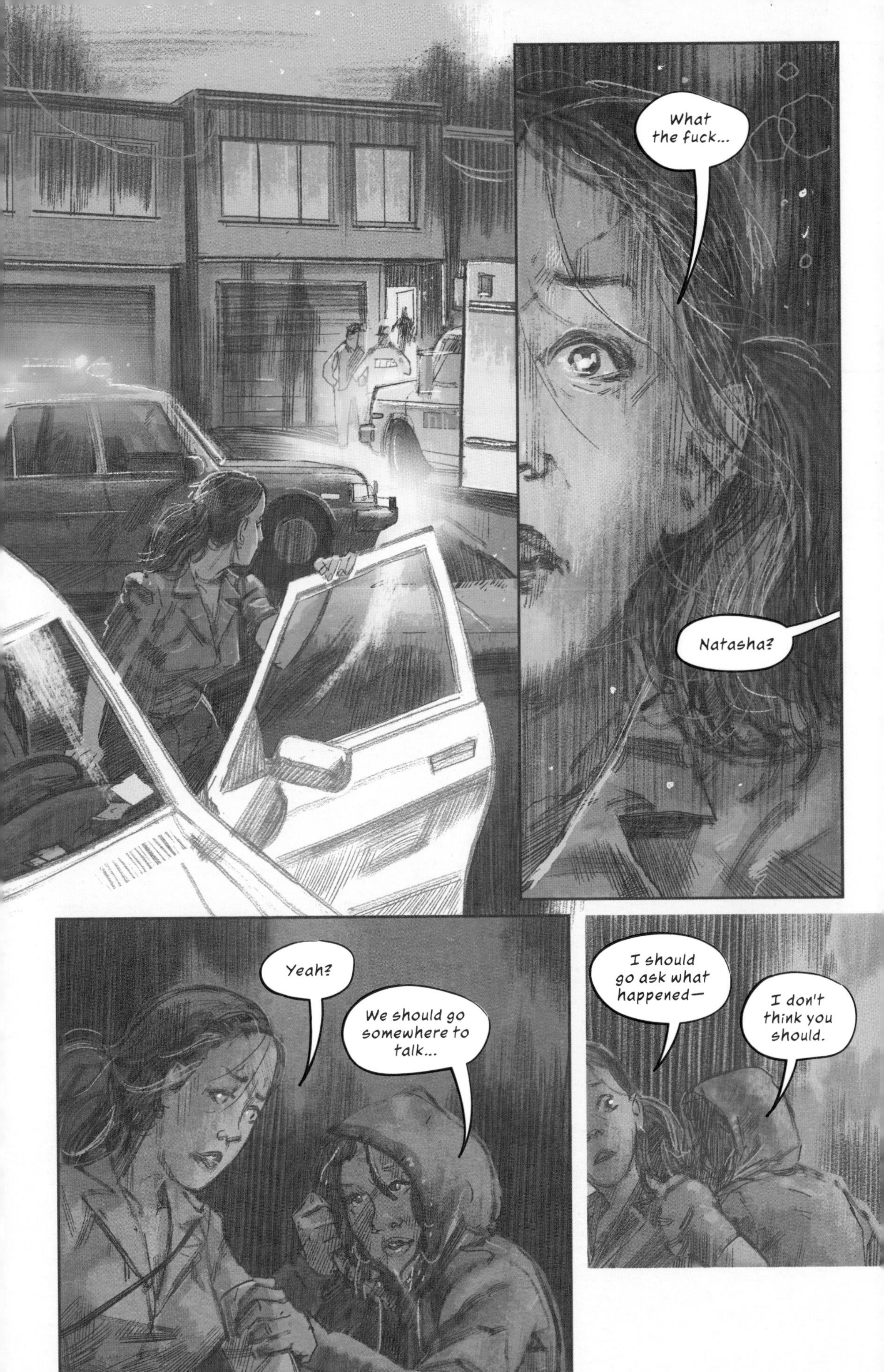
What the fuck...
Natasha?
Yeah?
We should go somewhere to talk...
I should go ask what happened—
I don't think you should.

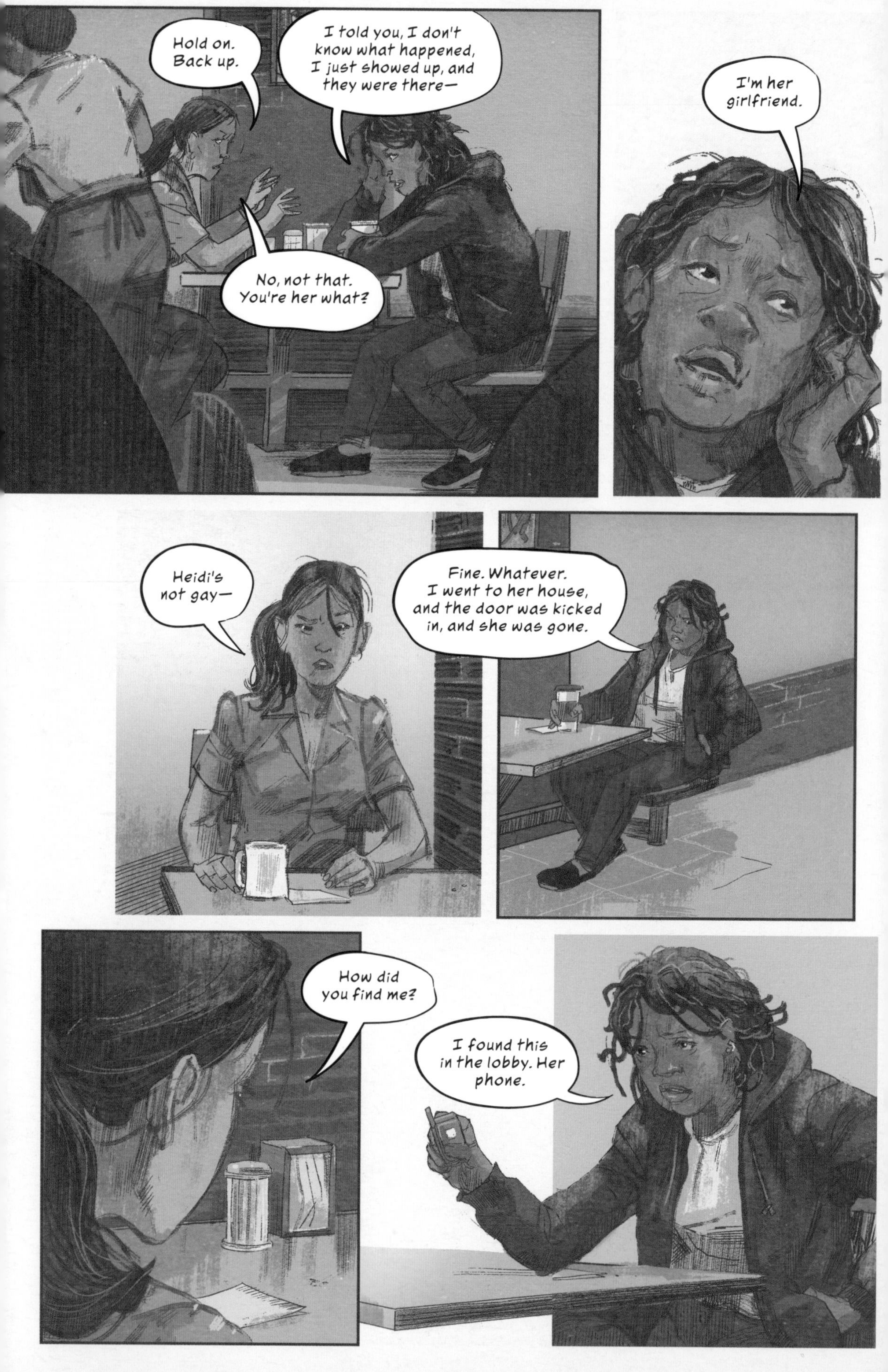
Hold on. Back up.
I told you, I don't know what happened, I just showed up, and they were there—
No, not that. You're her what?
I'm her girlfriend.
Heidi's not gay—
Fine. Whatever. I went to her house, and the door was kicked in, and she was gone.
How did you find me?
I found this in the lobby. Her phone.

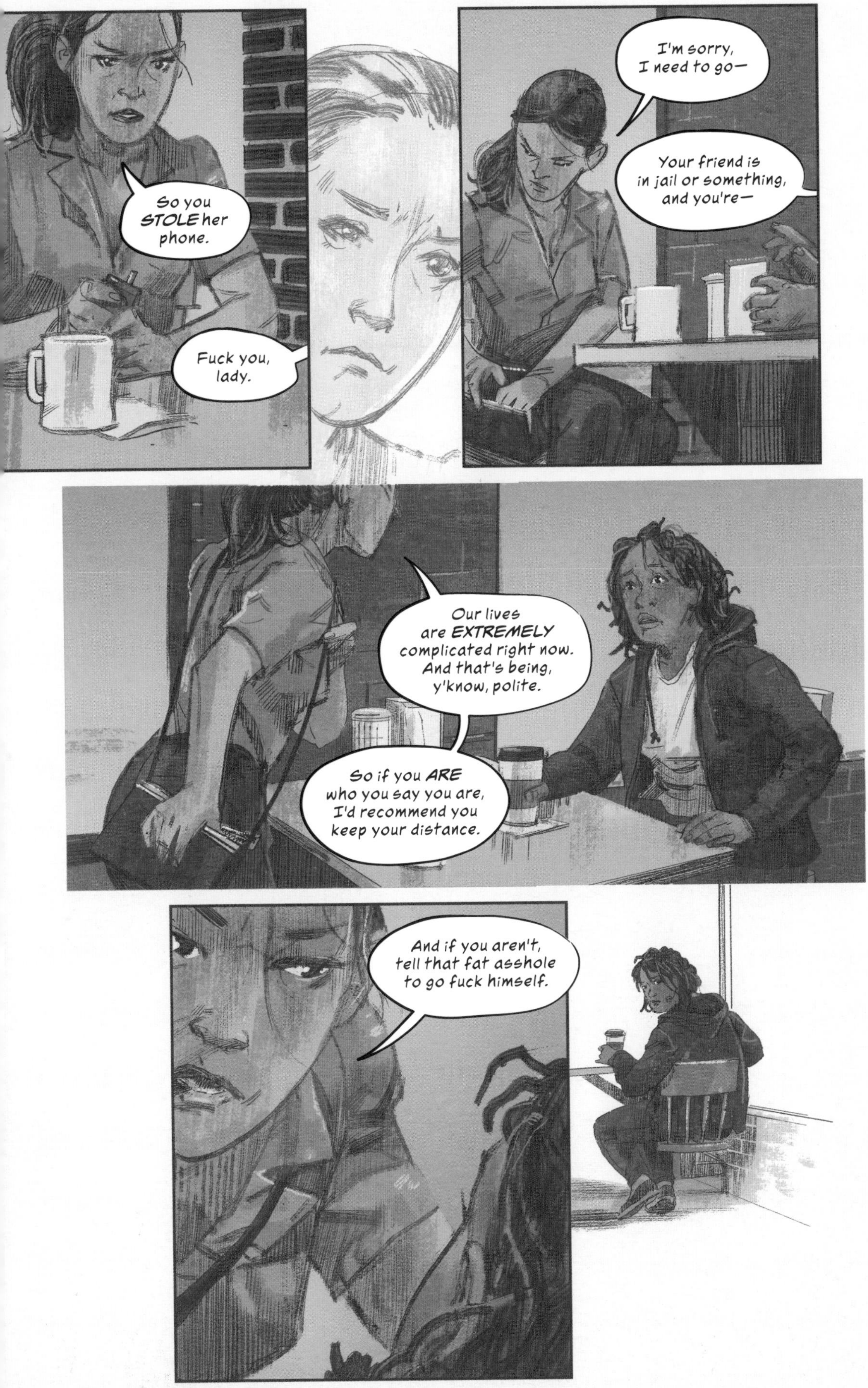
So you STOLE her phone.
Fuck you, lady.
I'm sorry, I need to go—
Your friend is in jail or something, and you're—
Our lives are EXTREMELY complicated right now. And that's being, y'know, polite.
So if you ARE who you say you are, I'd recommend you keep your distance.
And if you aren't, tell that fat asshole to go fuck himself.

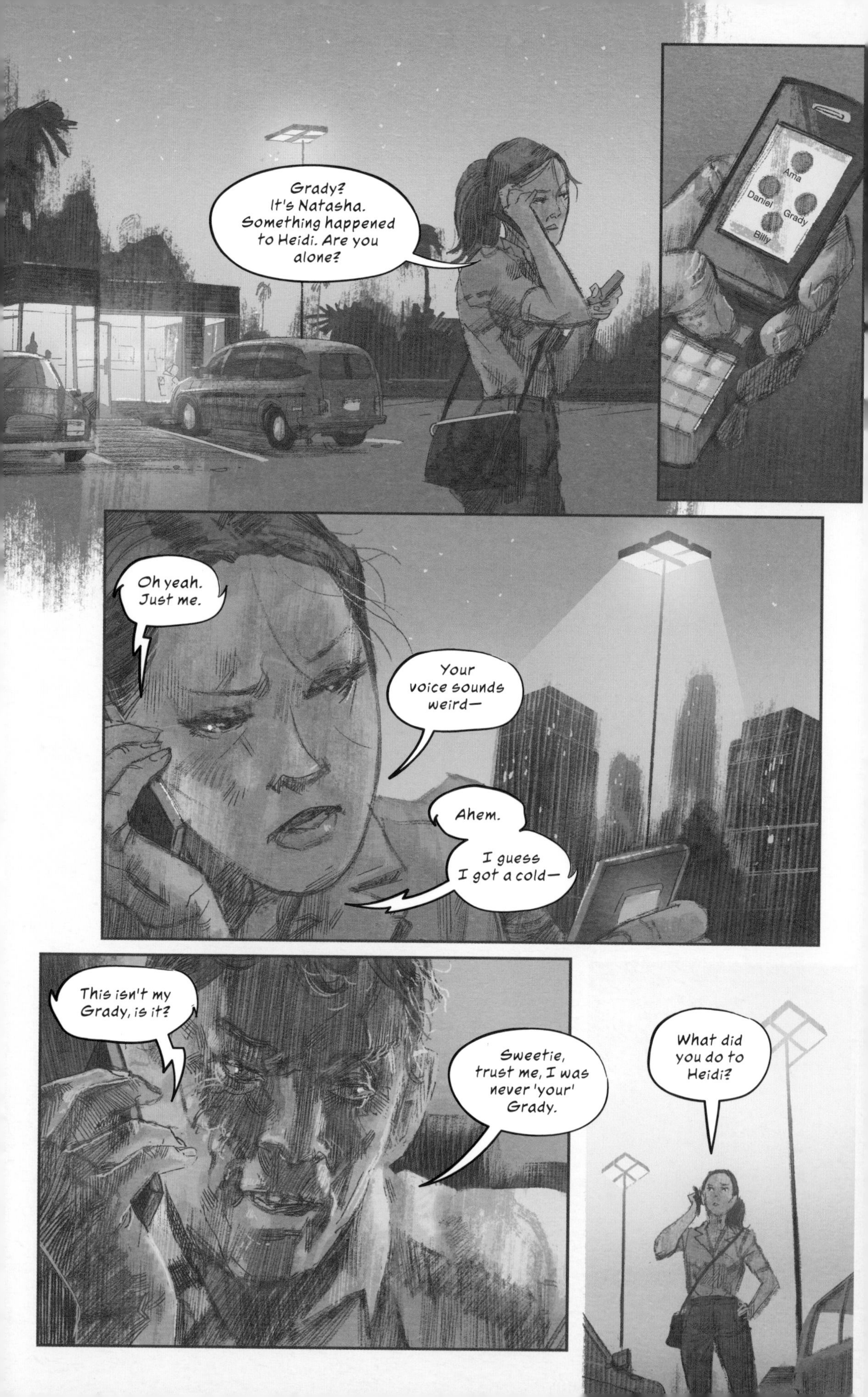

Grady? It's Natasha. Something happened to Heidi. Are you alone?
Ama
Daniel
Grady
Billy
Oh yeah. Just me.
Your voice sounds weird—
Ahem.
I guess I got a cold—
This isn't my Grady, is it?
Sweetie, trust me, I was never 'your' Grady.
What did you do to Heidi?

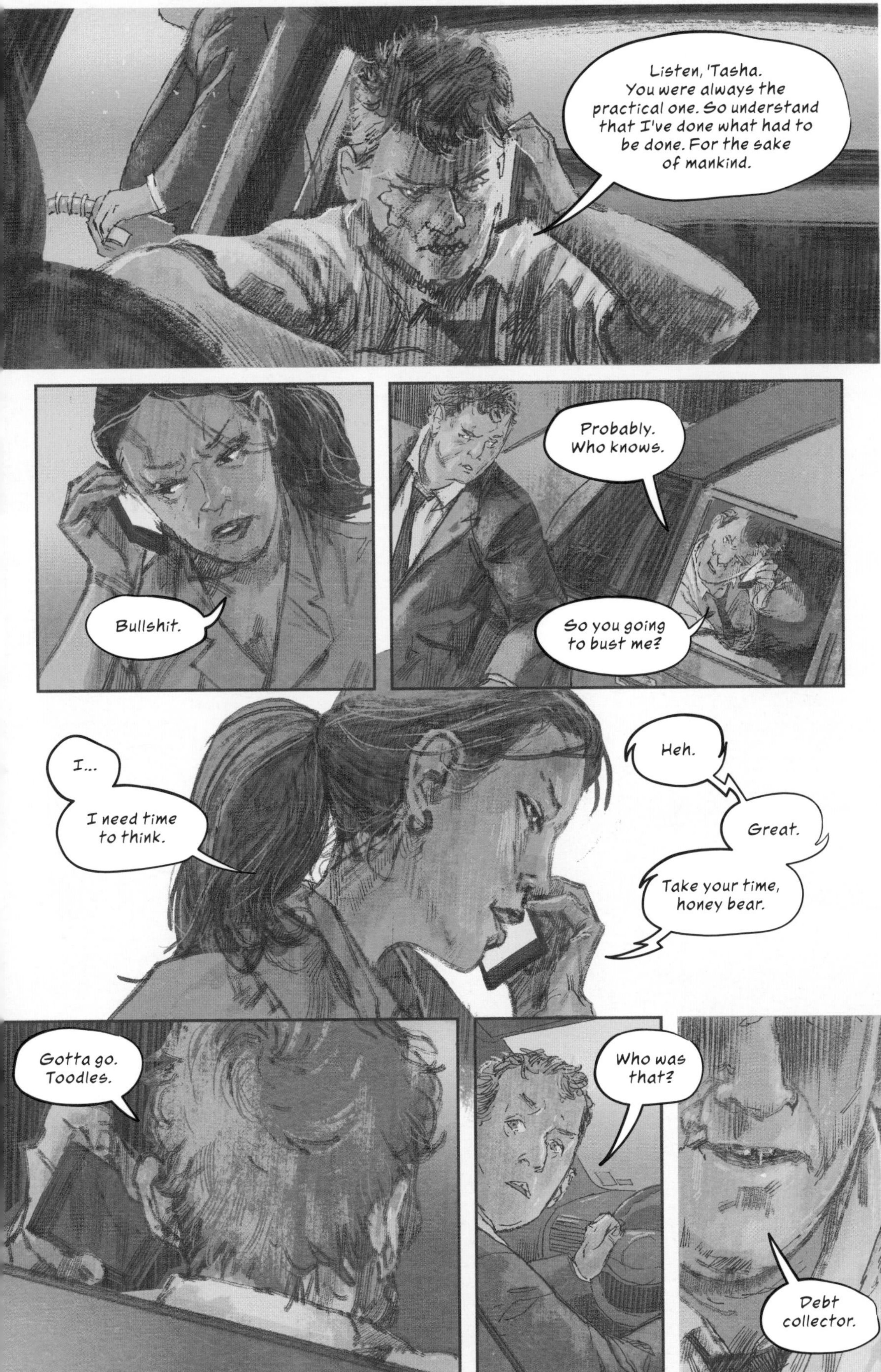
Listen, 'Tasha. You were always the practical one. So understand that I've done what had to be done. For the sake of mankind.
Bullshit.
Probably. Who knows.
So you going to bust me?
I...
I need time to think.
Heh.
Great.
Take your time, honey bear.
Gotta go. Toodles.
Who was that?
Debt collector.

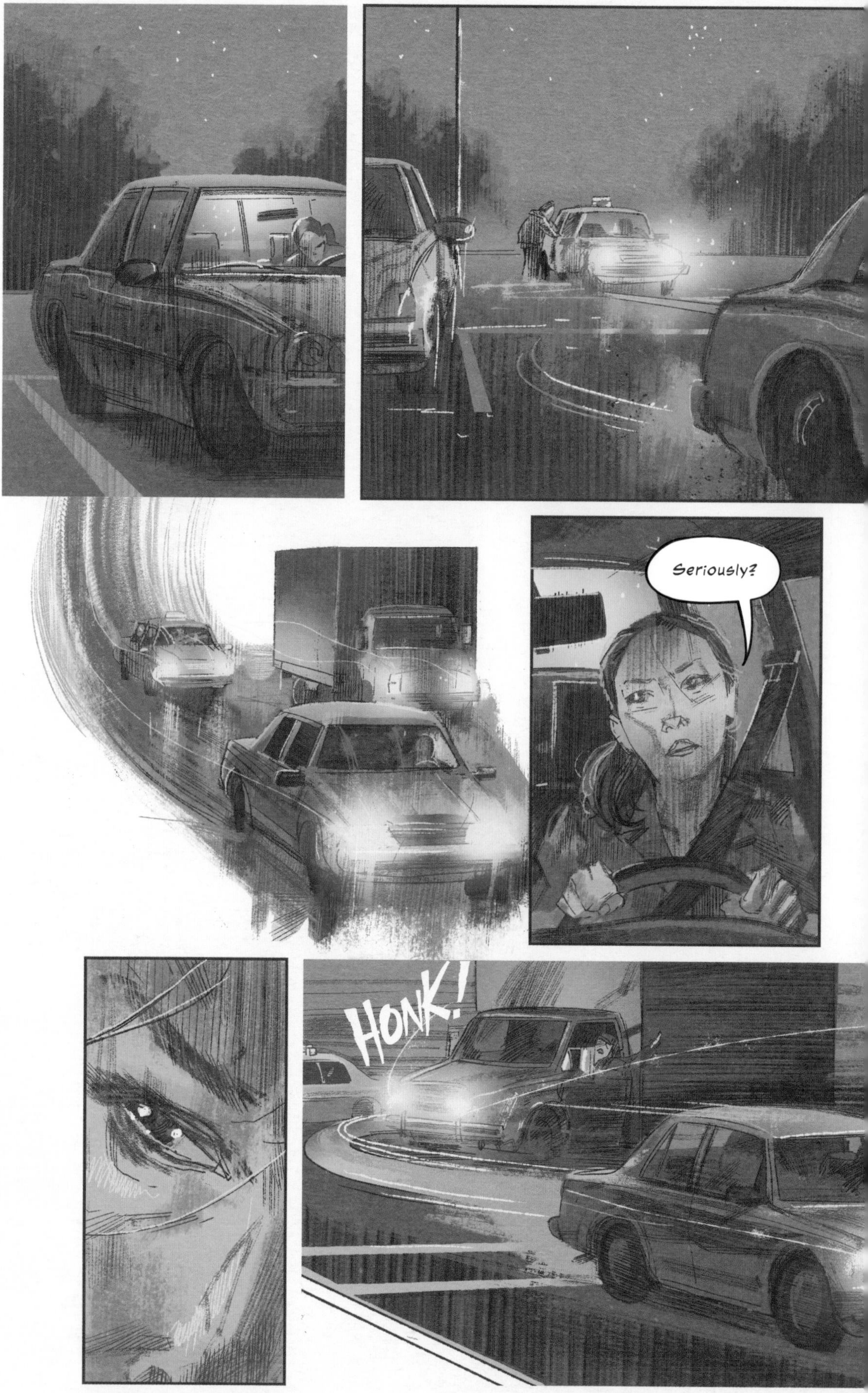
Seriously?
HONK!

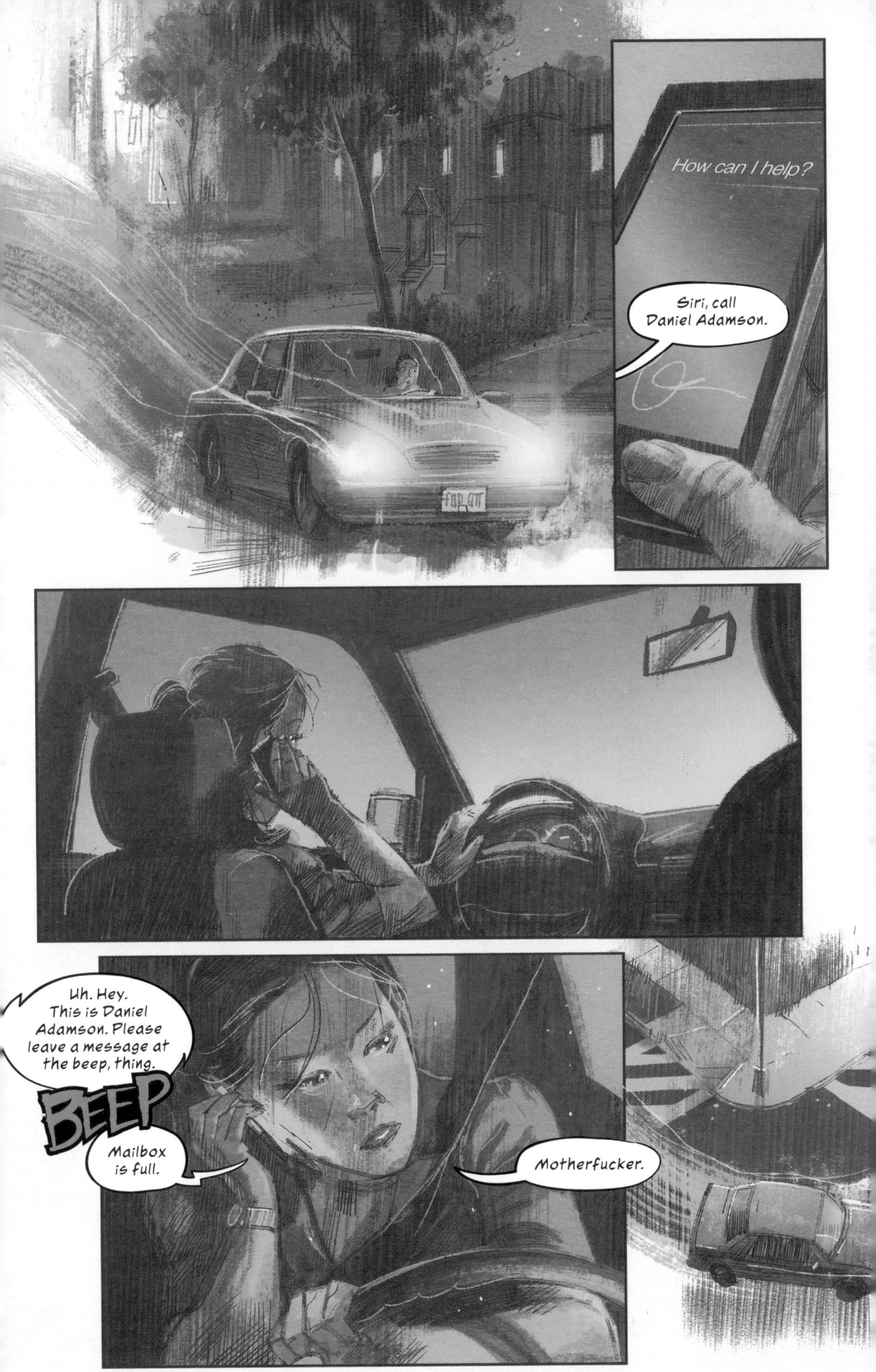
How can I help?
Siri, call Daniel Adamson.
Uh. Hey. This is Daniel Adamson. Please leave a message at the beep, thing.
BEEP
Mailbox is full.
Motherfucker.

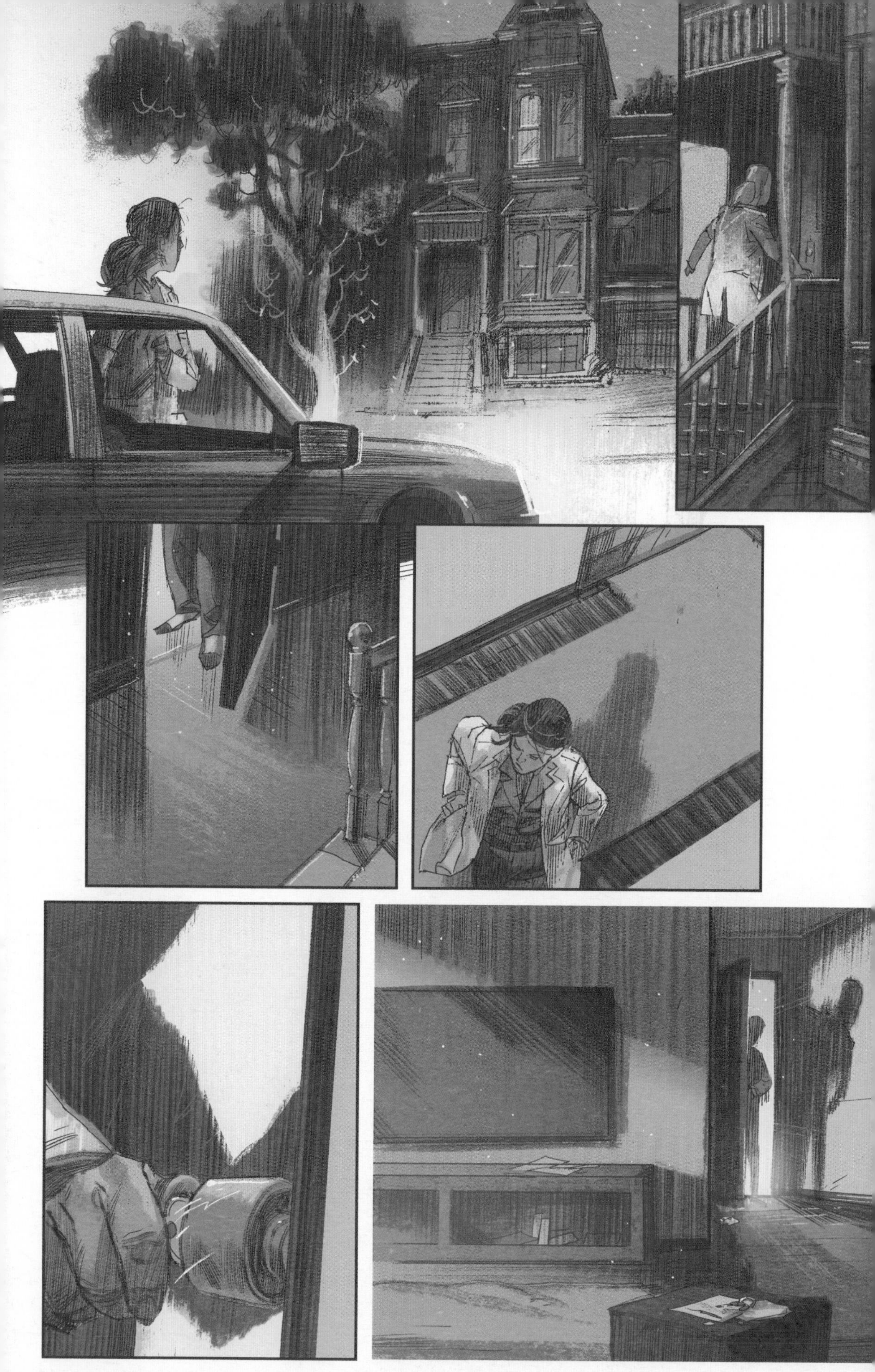

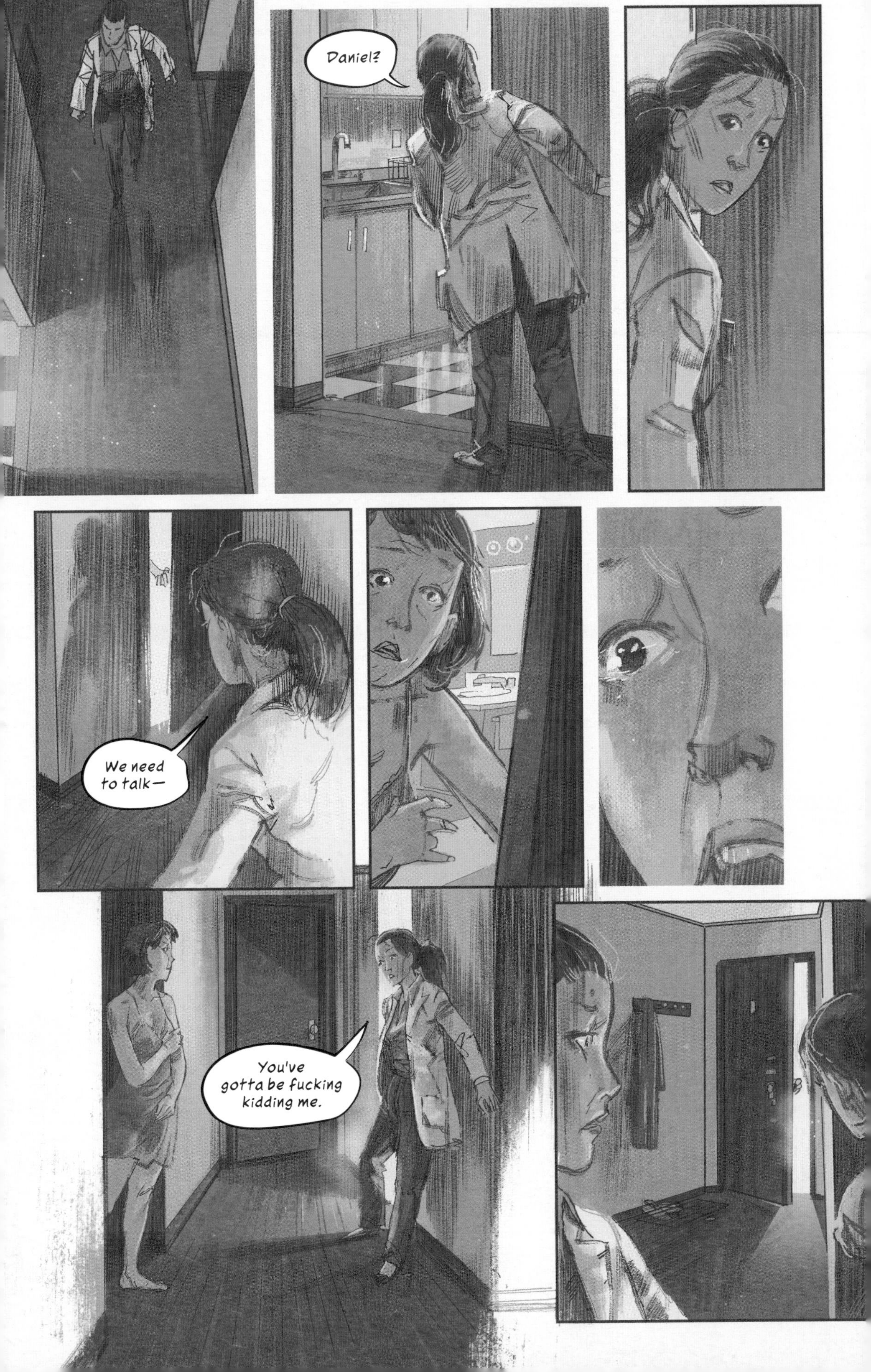
Daniel?
We need to talk—
You've gotta be fucking kidding me.

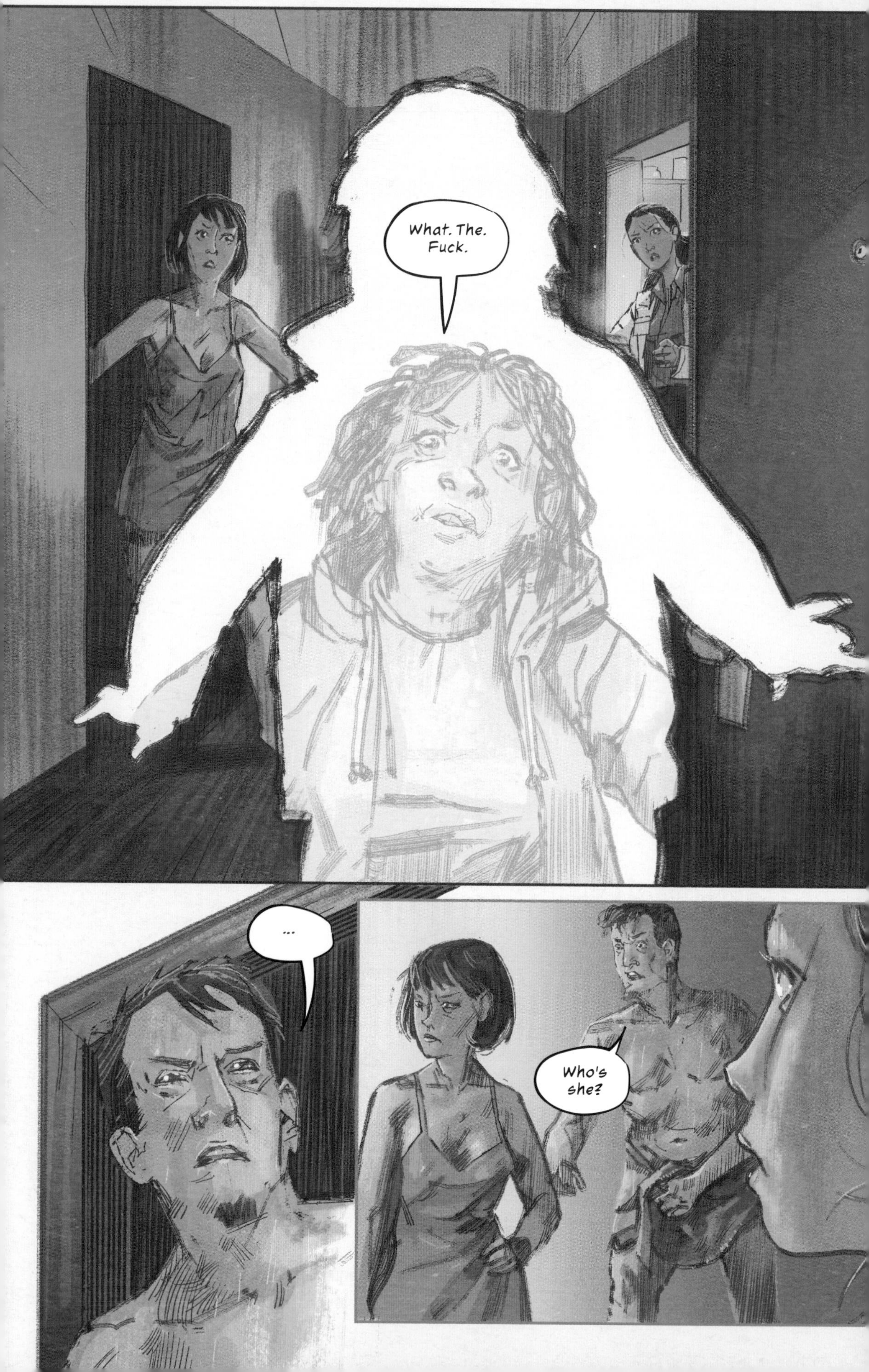
What. The. Fuck.
...
Who's she?

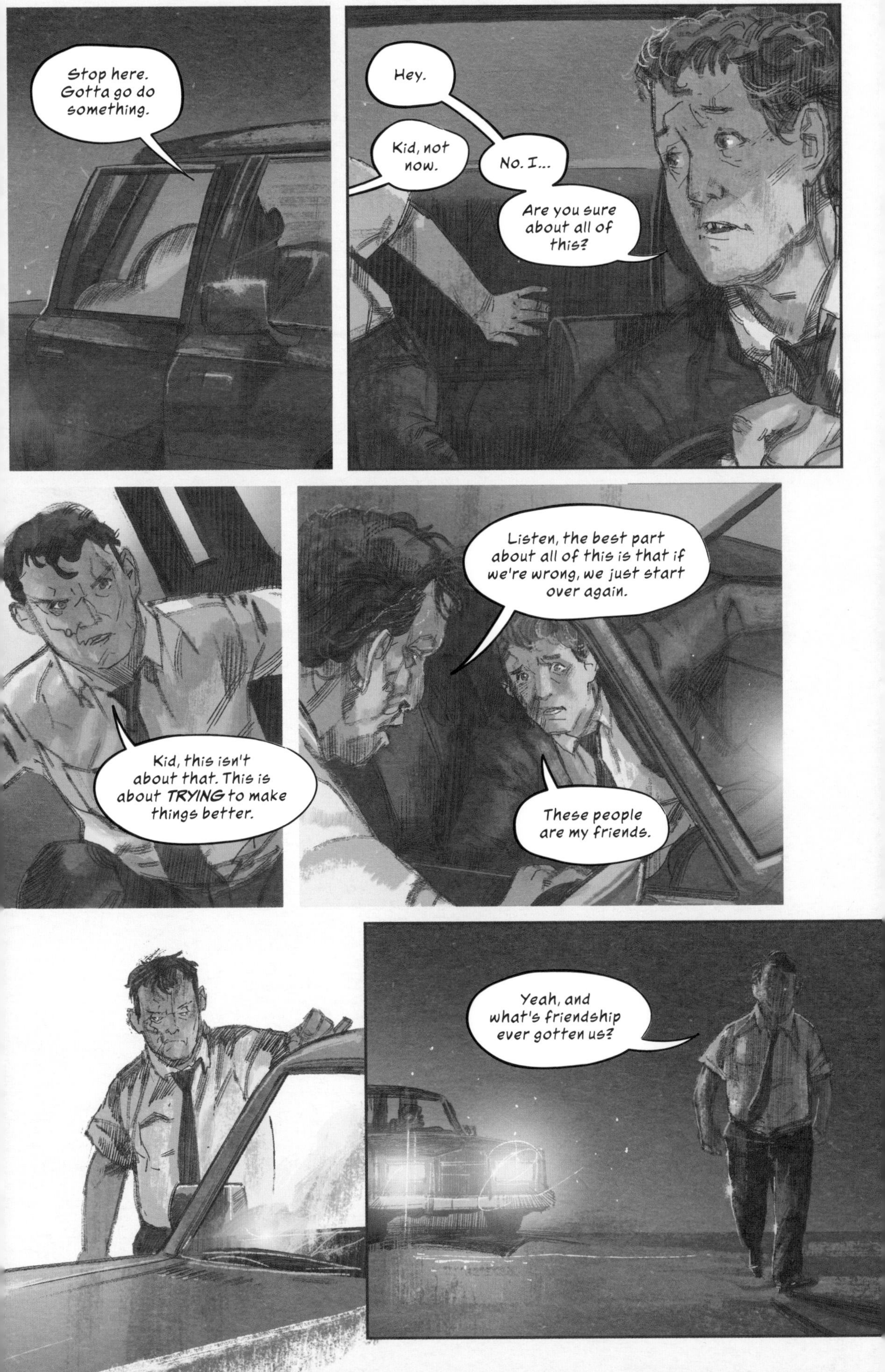
Stop here. Gotta go do something.
Hey.
Kid, not now.
No. I...
Are you sure about all of this?
Kid, this isn't about that. This is about TRYING to make things better.
Listen, the best part about all of this is that if we're wrong, we just start over again.
These people are my friends.
Yeah, and what's friendship ever gotten us?

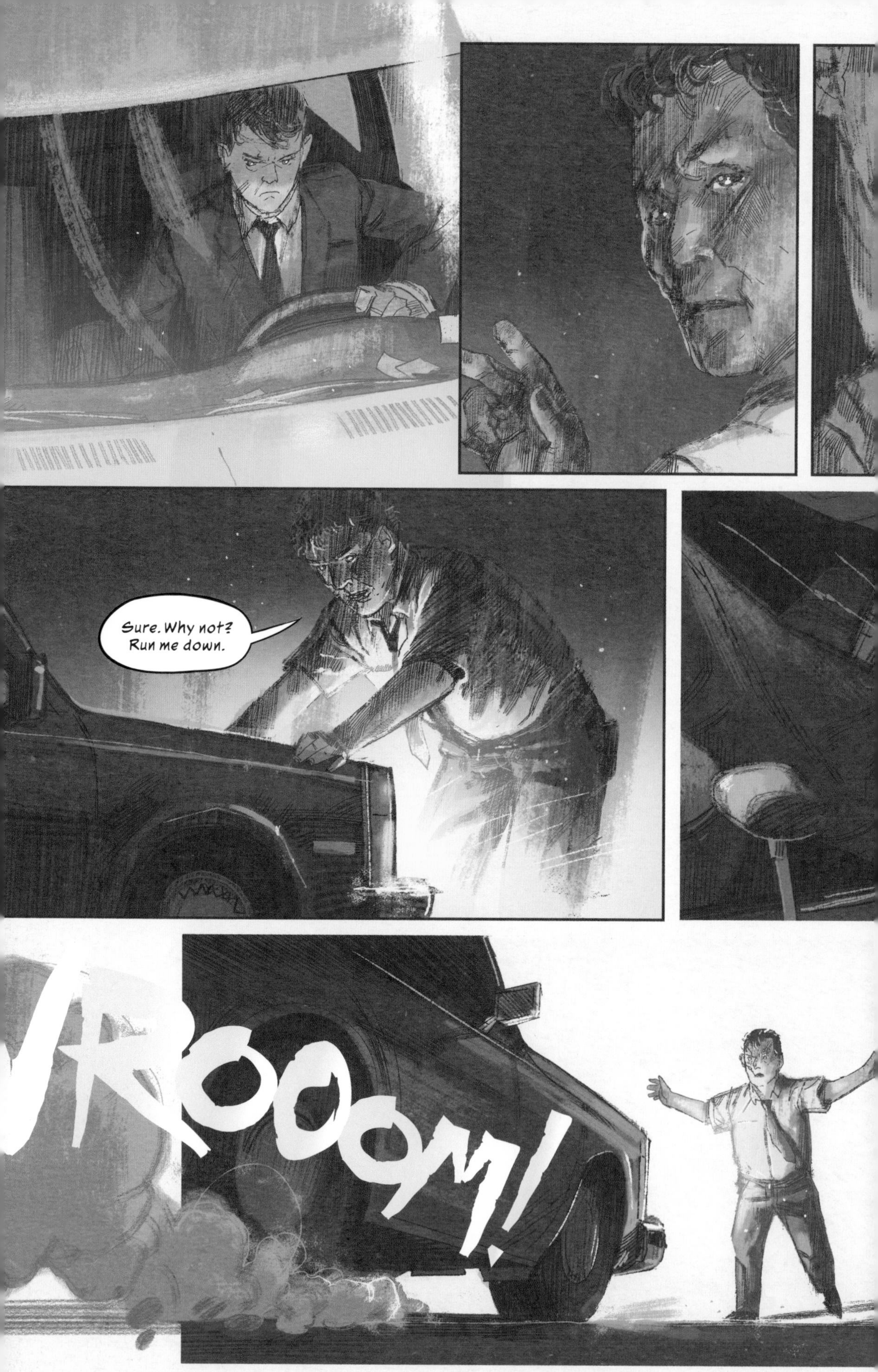
Sure. Why not?
Run me down.
VROOOM!

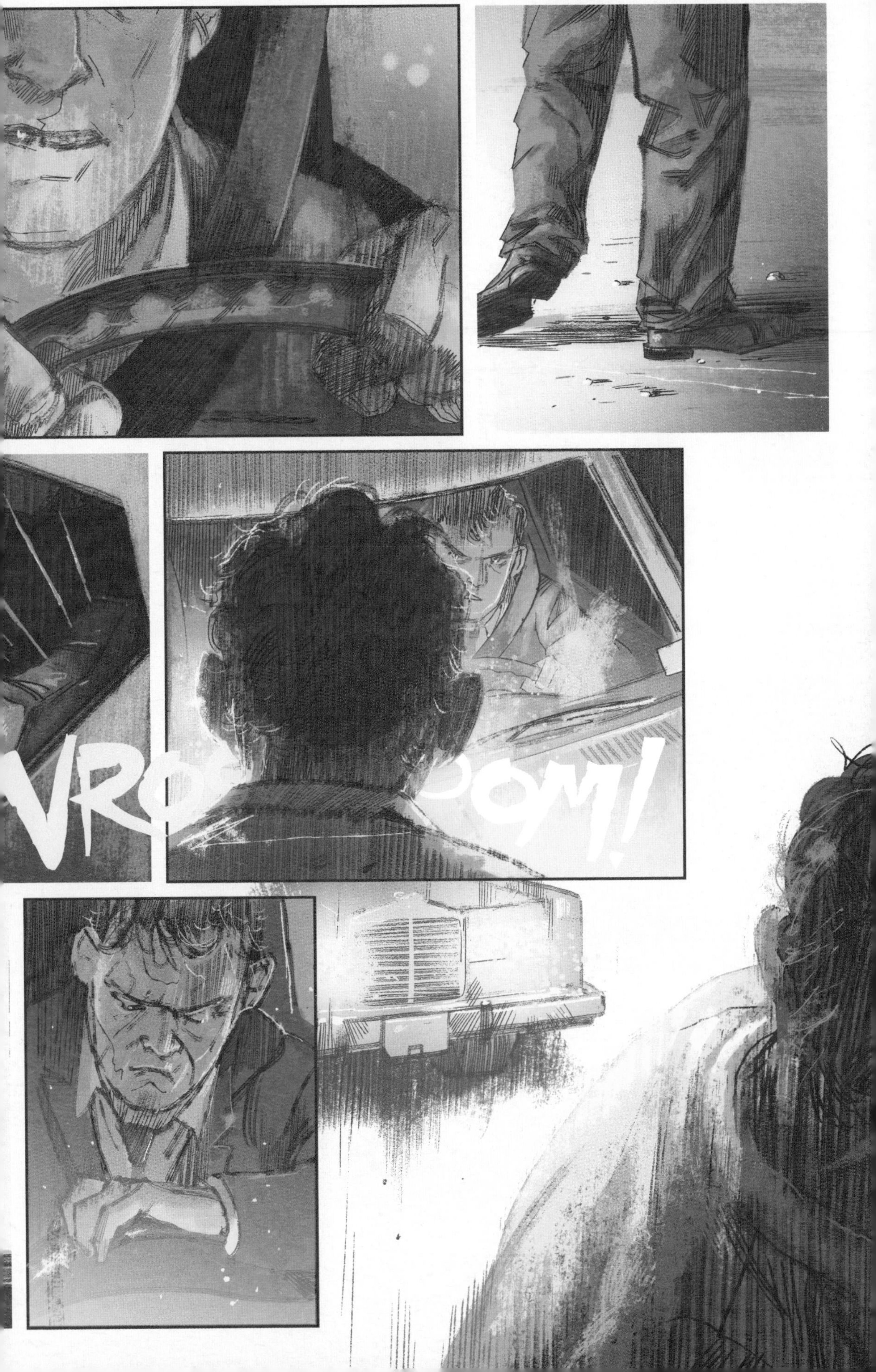
VRO
OOM!

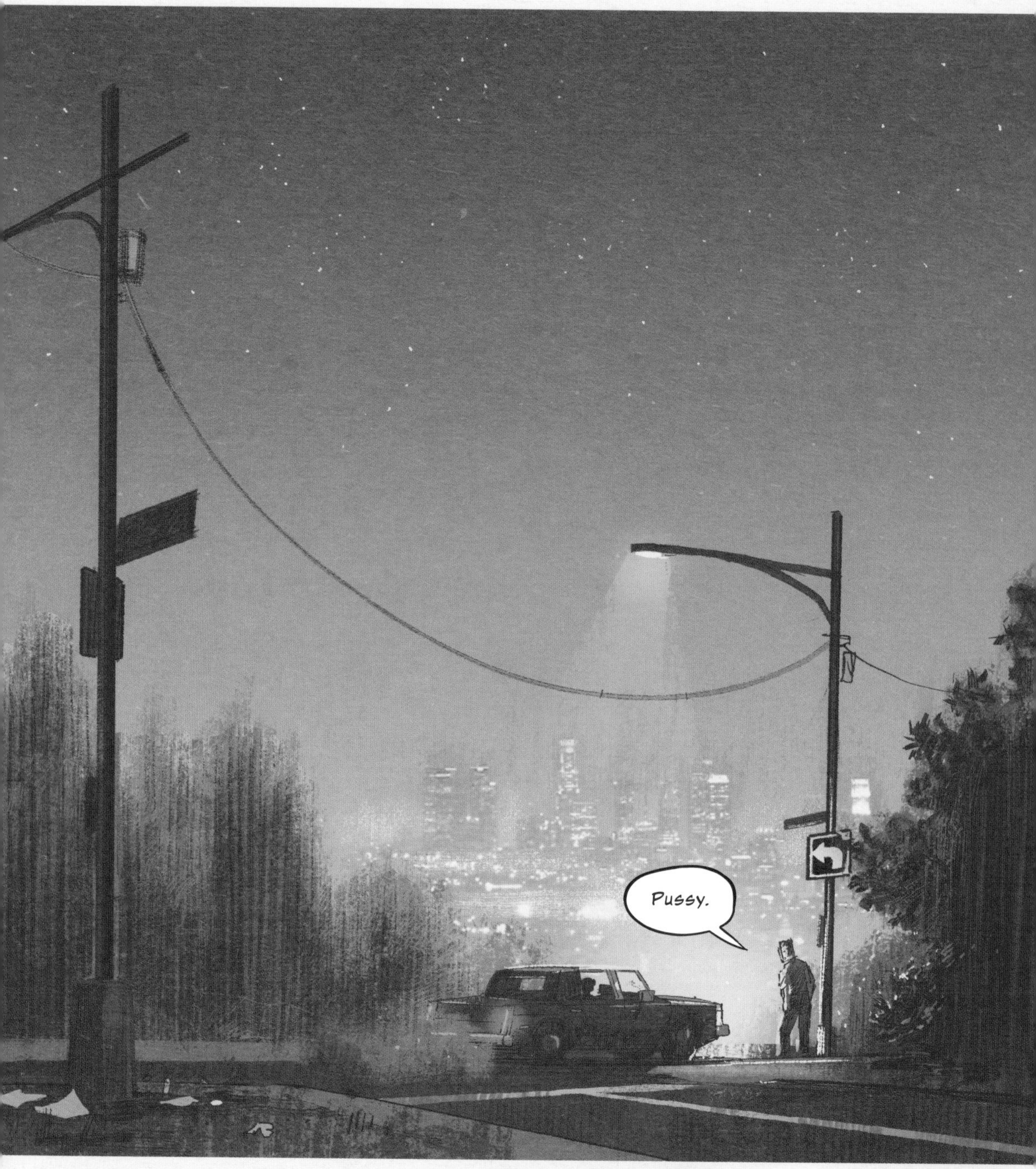
Pussy.

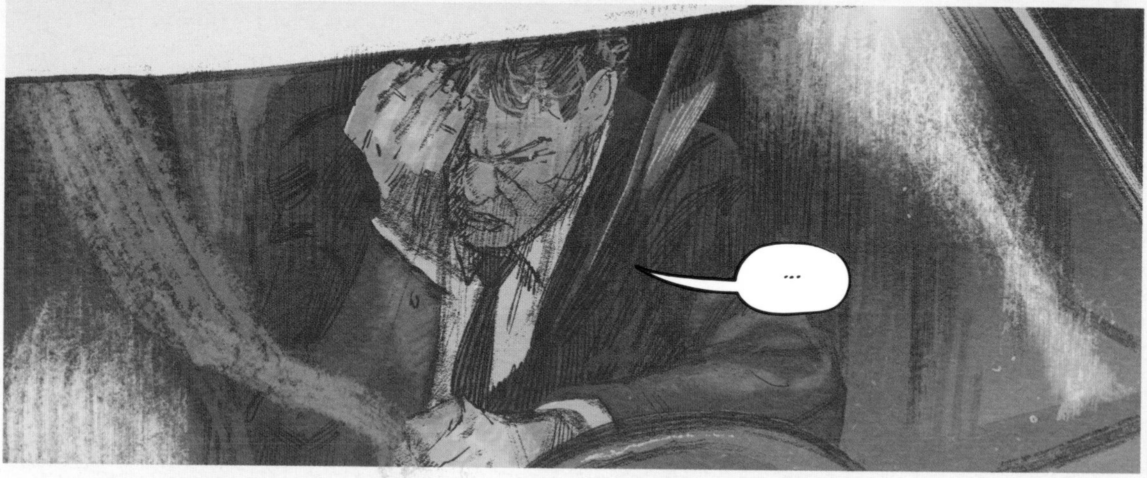
...

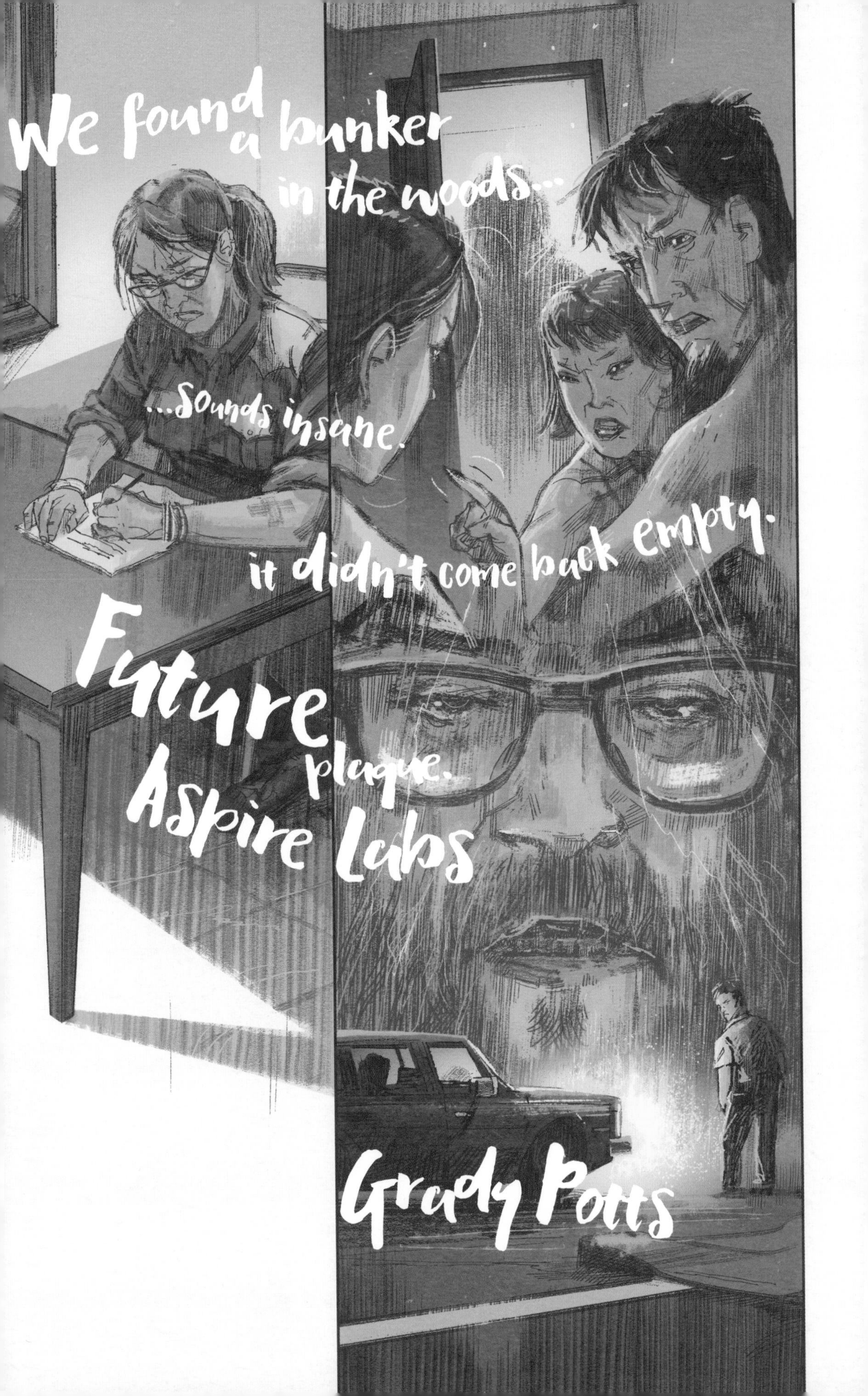
We found a bunker in the woods...
...sounds insane.
it didn't come back empty.
Future plaque.
Aspire Labs
Grady Potts

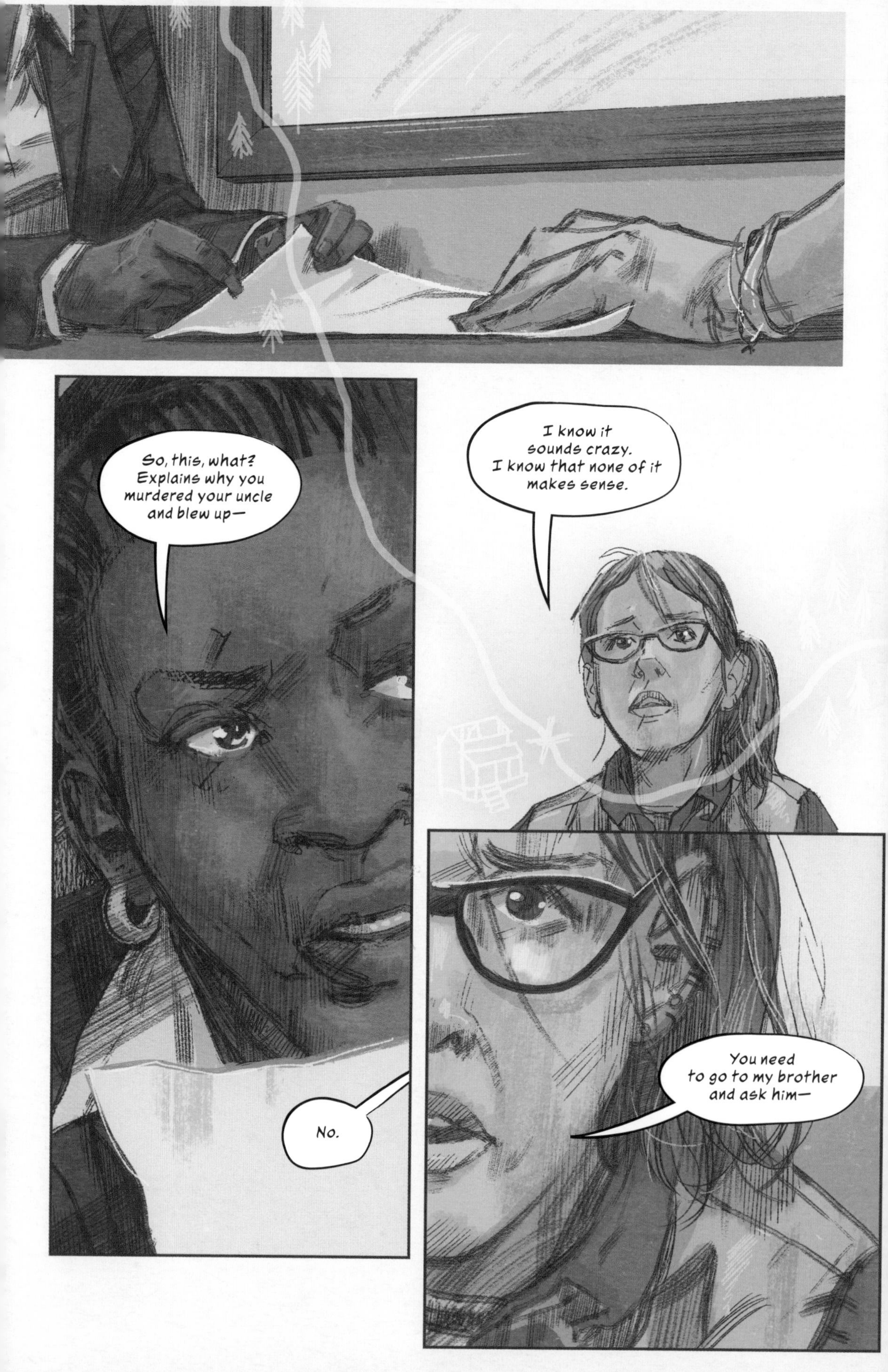

So, this, what? Explains why you murdered your uncle and blew up—
I know it sounds crazy. I know that none of it makes sense.
No.
You need to go to my brother and ask him—

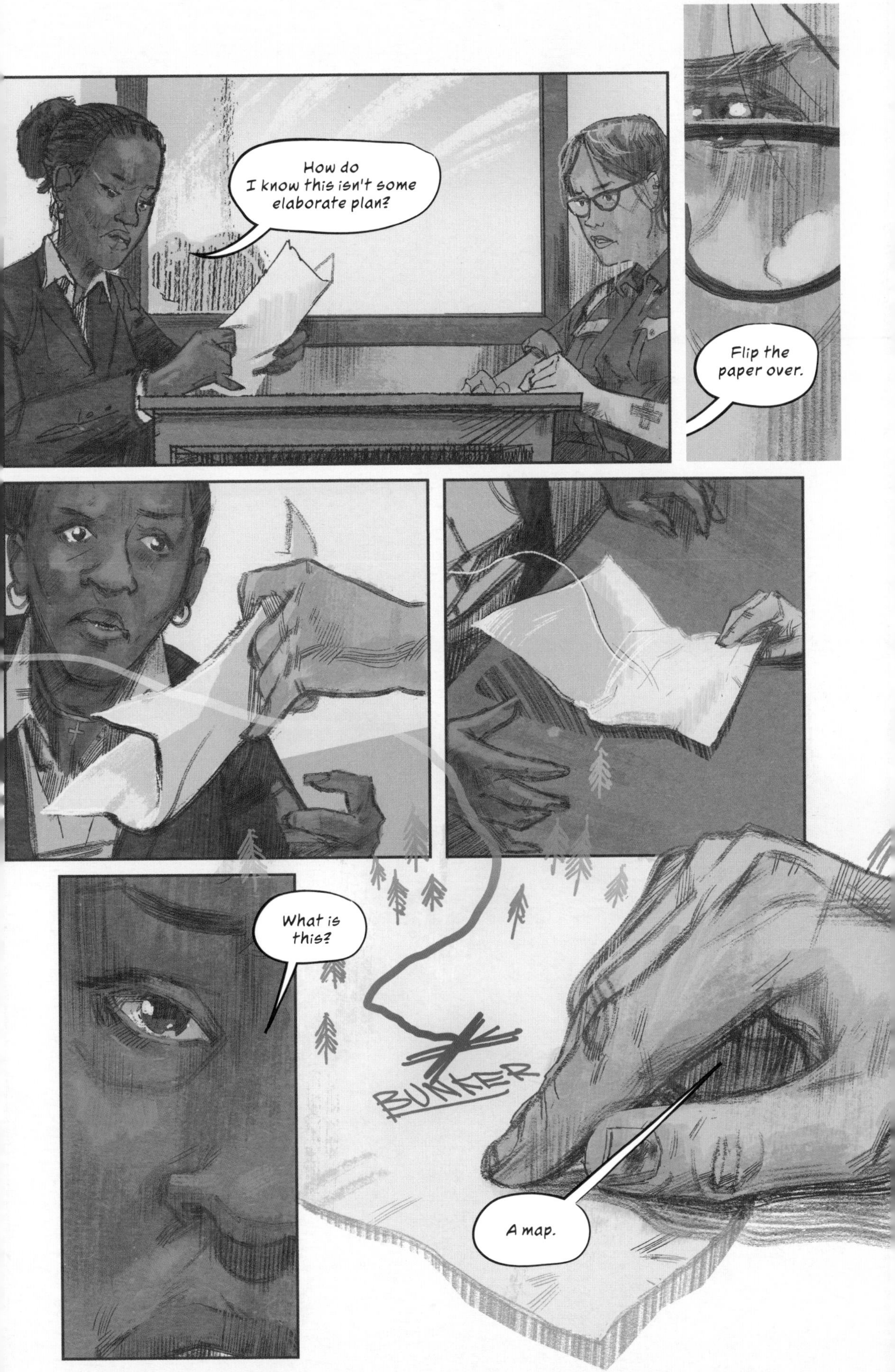
How do I know this isn't some elaborate plan?
Flip the paper over.
What is this?
BUNKER
A map.

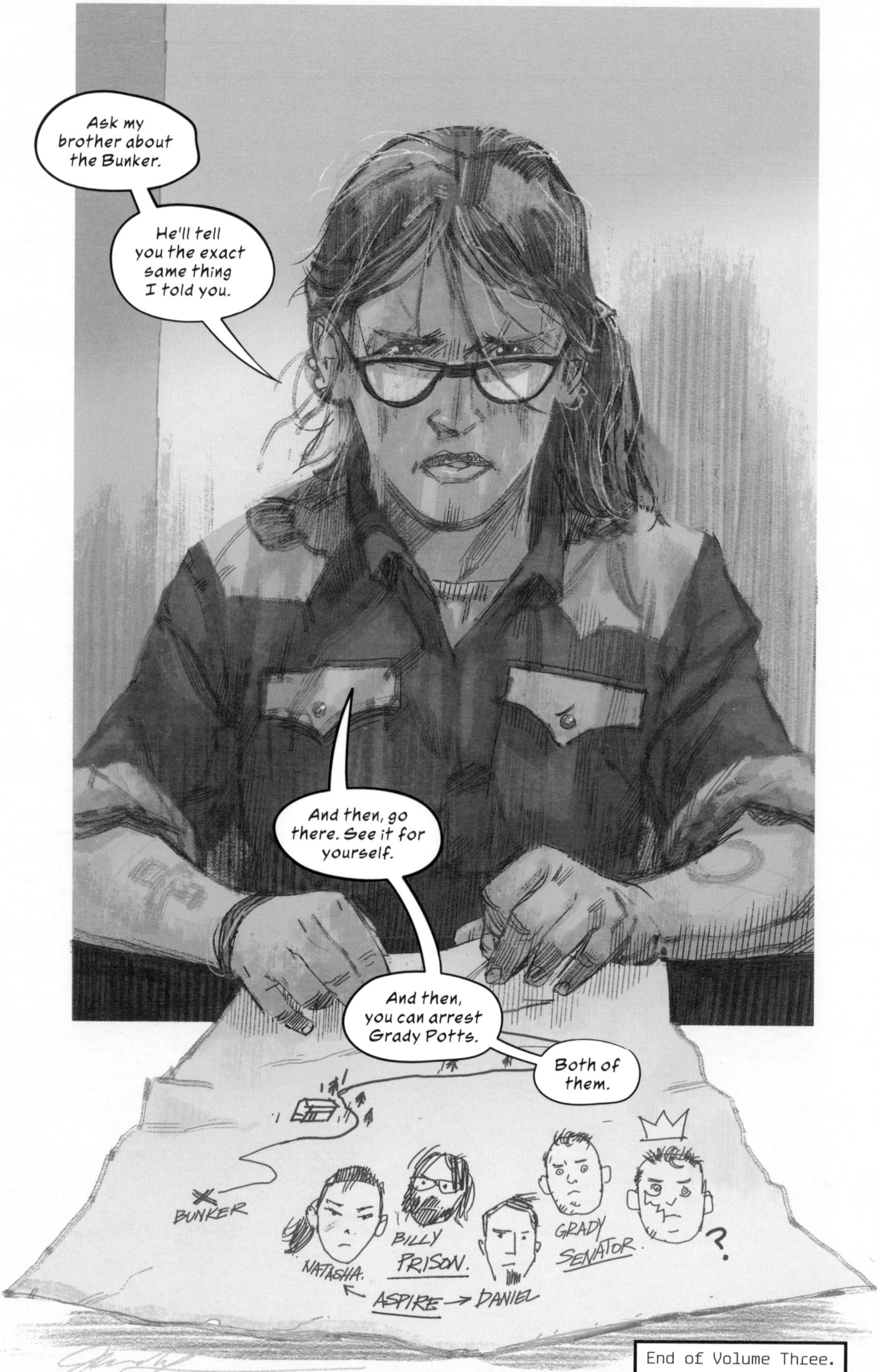

Ask my brother about the Bunker.
He'll tell you the exact same thing I told you.
And then, go there. See it for yourself.
And then, you can arrest Grady Potts.
Both of them.
BUNKER
BILLY
PRISON.
NATASHA.
GRADY
SENATOR
?
ASPIRE
DANIEL
2015

End of Volume Three.

CHAPTER
14

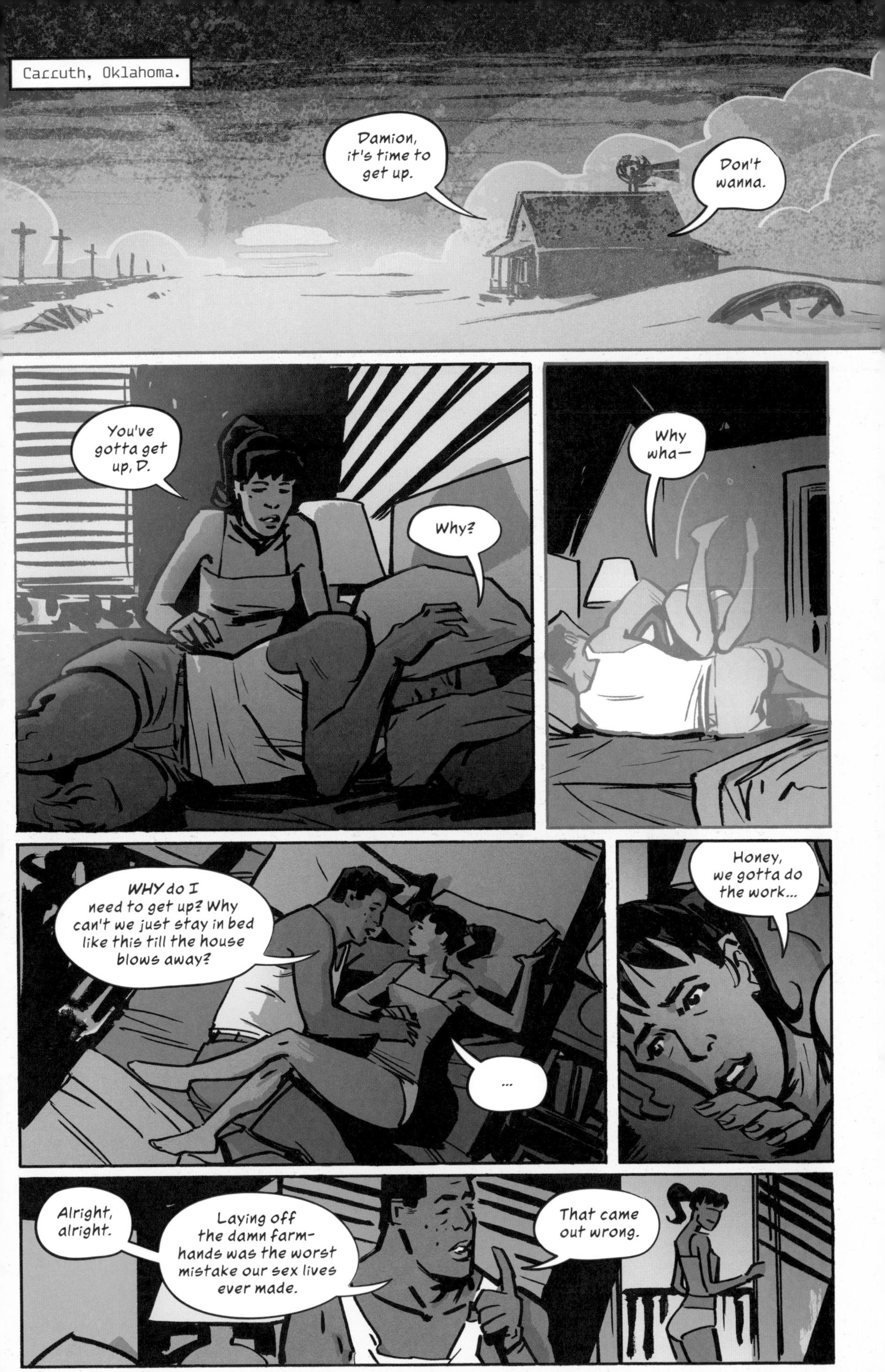
Carruth, Oklahoma.
Damion, it's time to get up.
Don't wanna.
You've gotta get up, D.
Why?
Why wha—
WHY do I need to get up? Why can't we just stay in bed like this till the house blows away?
...
Honey, we gotta do the work...
Alright, alright.
Laying off the damn farm-hands was the worst mistake our sex lives ever made.
That came out wrong.

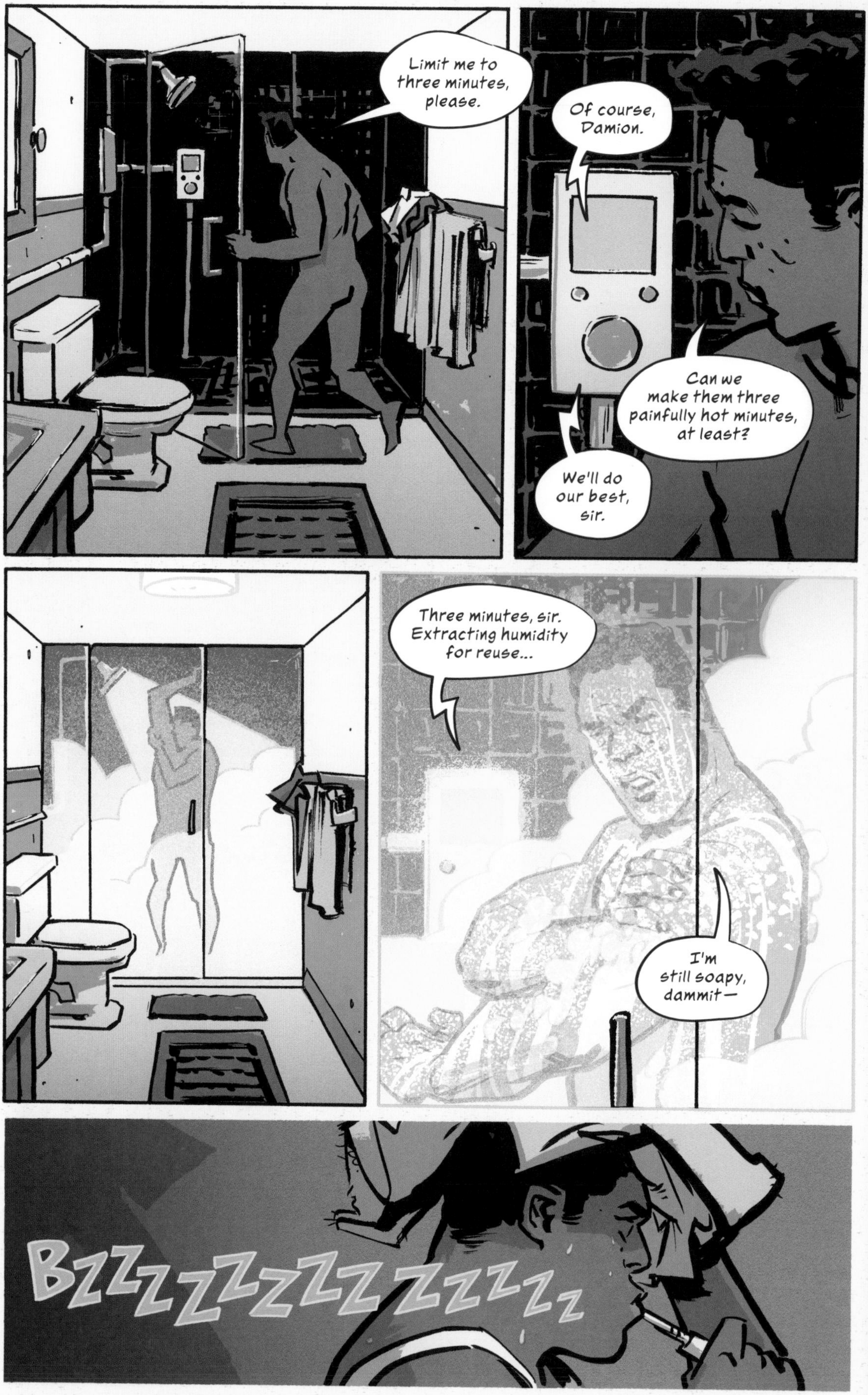
Limit me to three minutes, please.
Of course, Damion.
Can we make them three painfully hot minutes, at least?
We'll do our best, sir.
Three minutes, sir. Extracting humidity for reuse...
I'm still soapy, dammit—
BZZZZZZZZZZZZZZZ

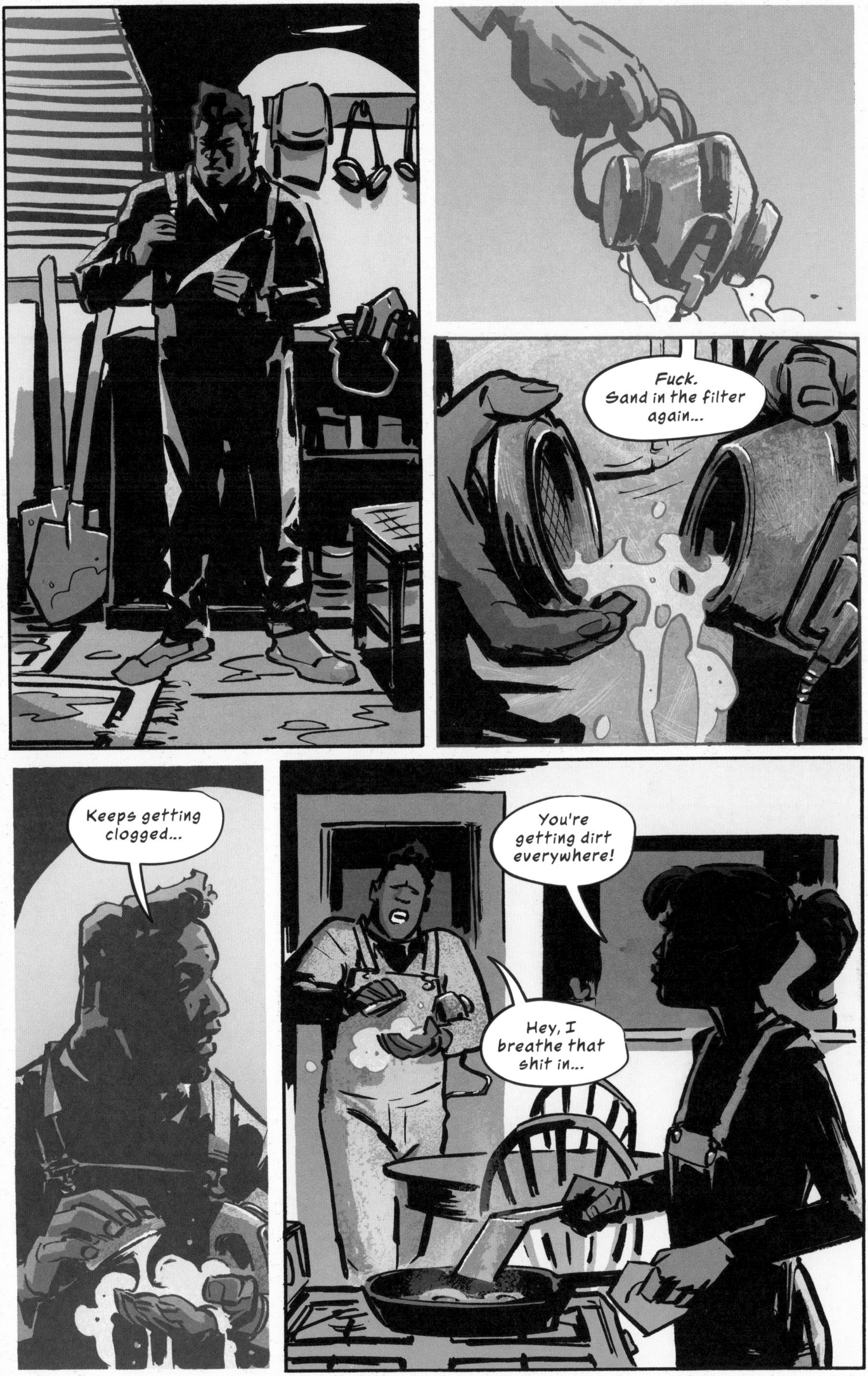
Fuck.
Sand in the filter again...
Keeps getting clogged...
You're getting dirt everywhere!
Hey, I breathe that shit in...

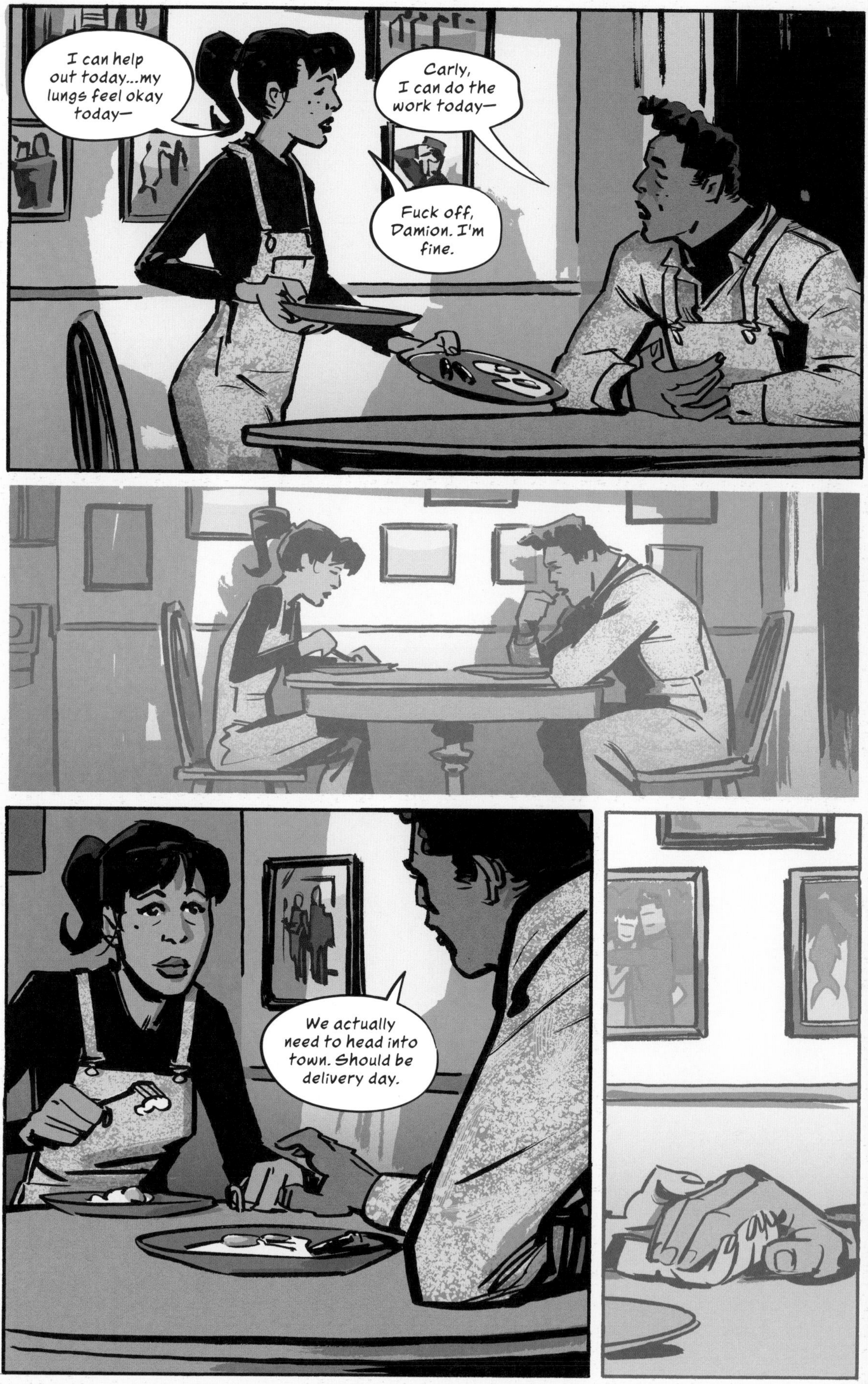
I can help out today...my lungs feel okay today—
Carly, I can do the work today—
Fuck off, Damion. I'm fine.
We actually need to head into town. Should be delivery day.

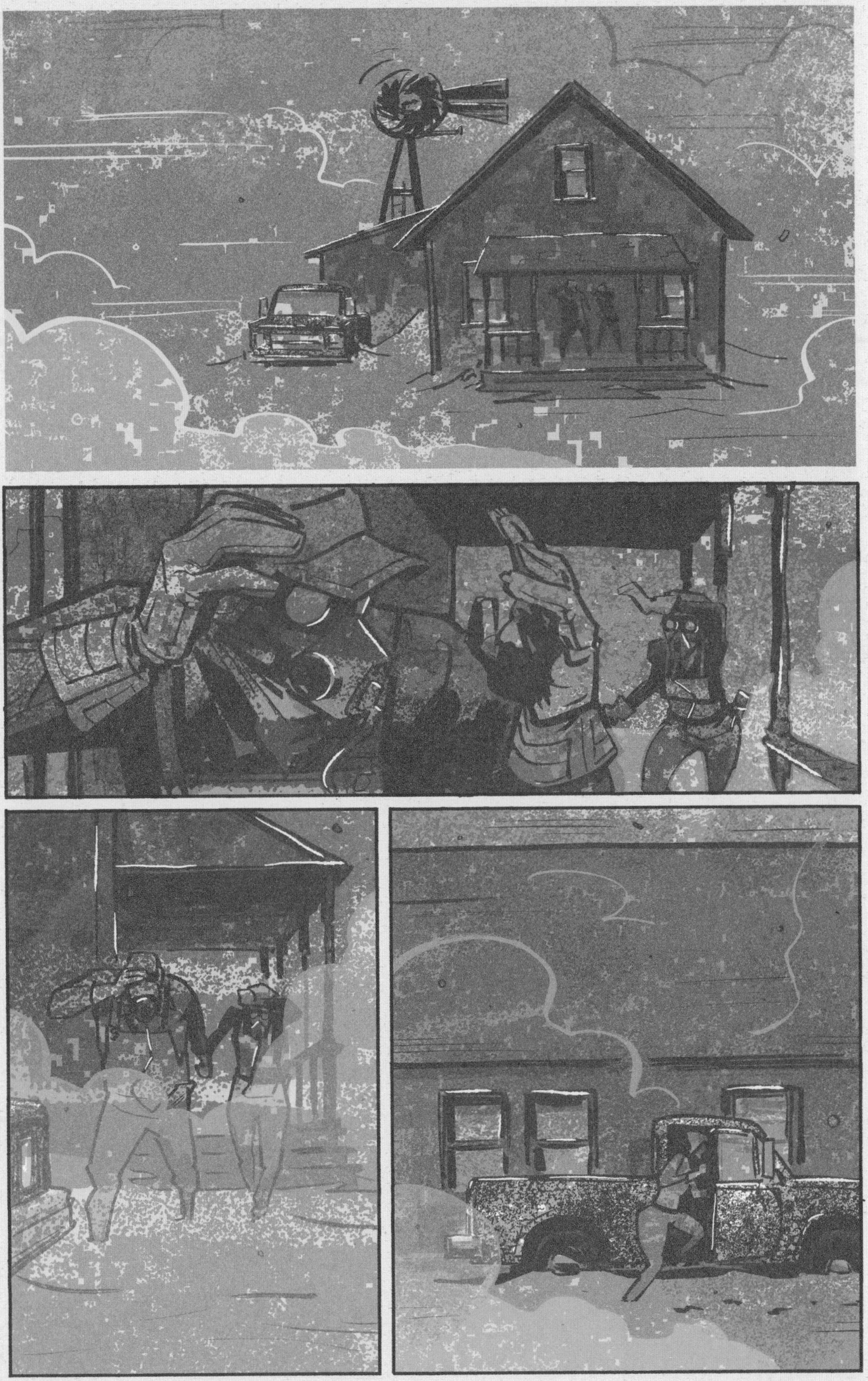

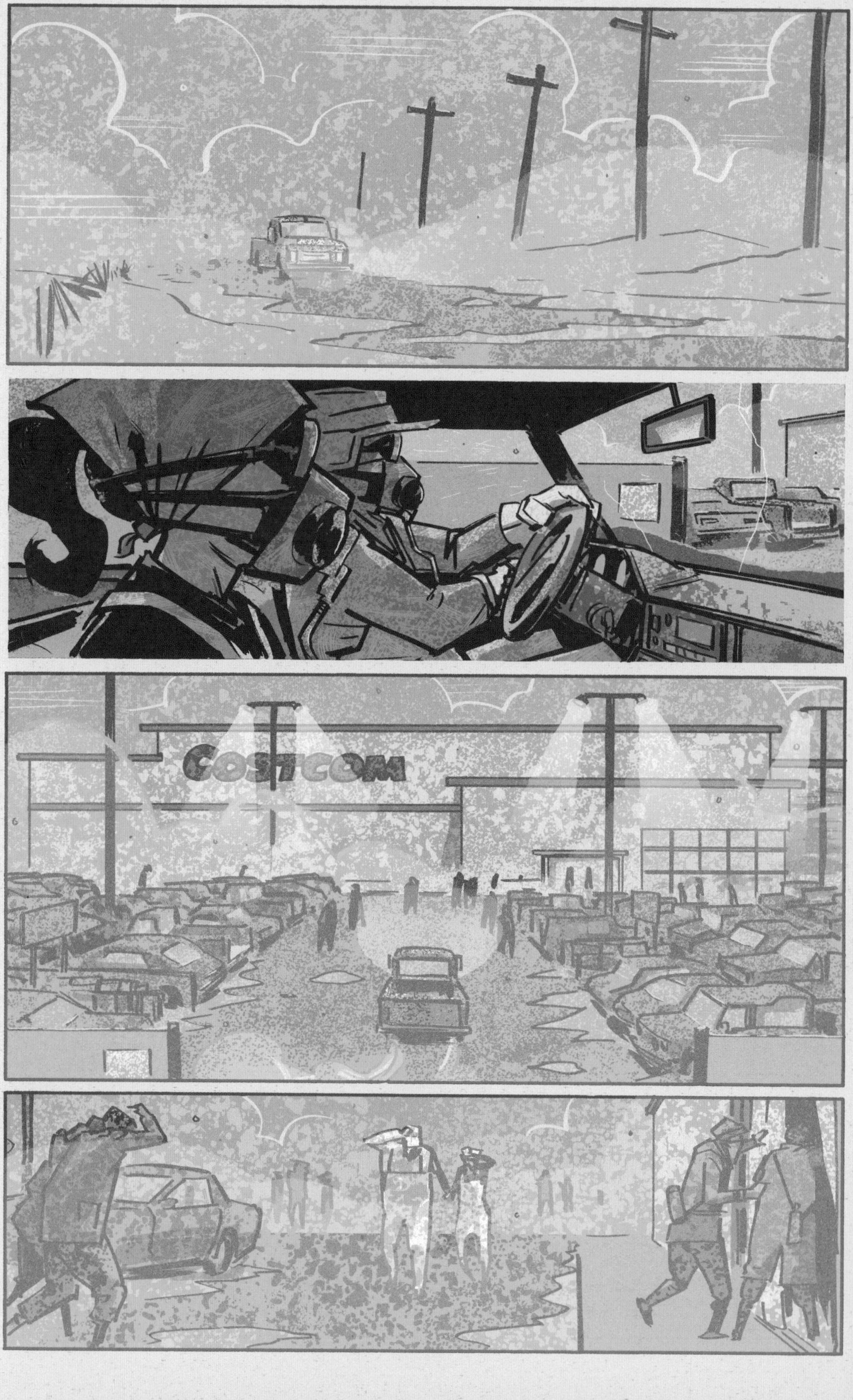
COSTCOM

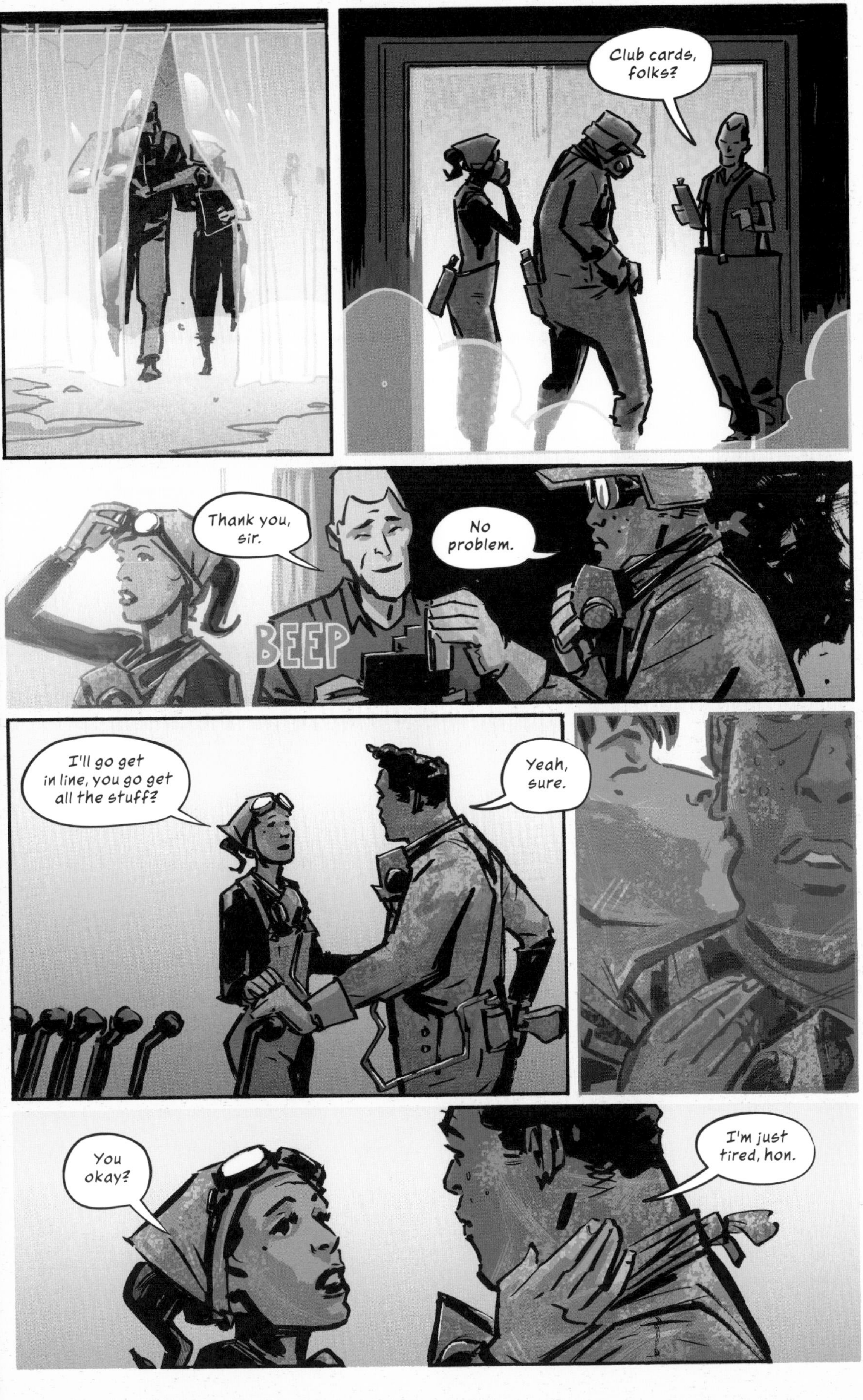
Club cards, folks?
Thank you, sir.
No problem.
BEEP
I'll go get in line, you go get all the stuff?
Yeah, sure.
You okay?
I'm just tired, hon.

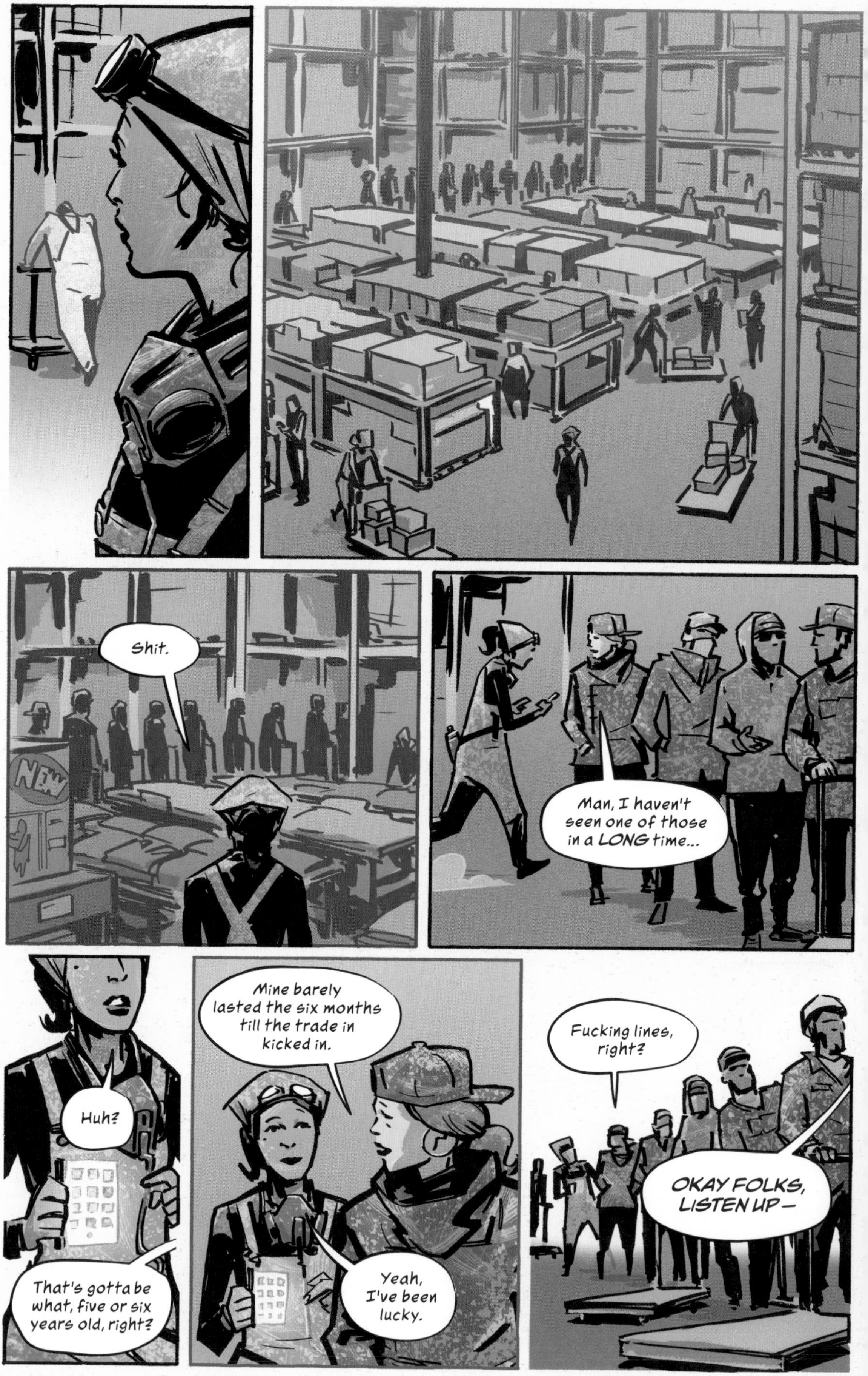
Shit.
Man, I haven't seen one of those in a LONG time...
Huh?
That's gotta be what, five or six years old, right?
Mine barely lasted the six months till the trade in kicked in.
Yeah, I've been lucky.
Fucking lines, right?
OKAY FOLKS, LISTEN UP—

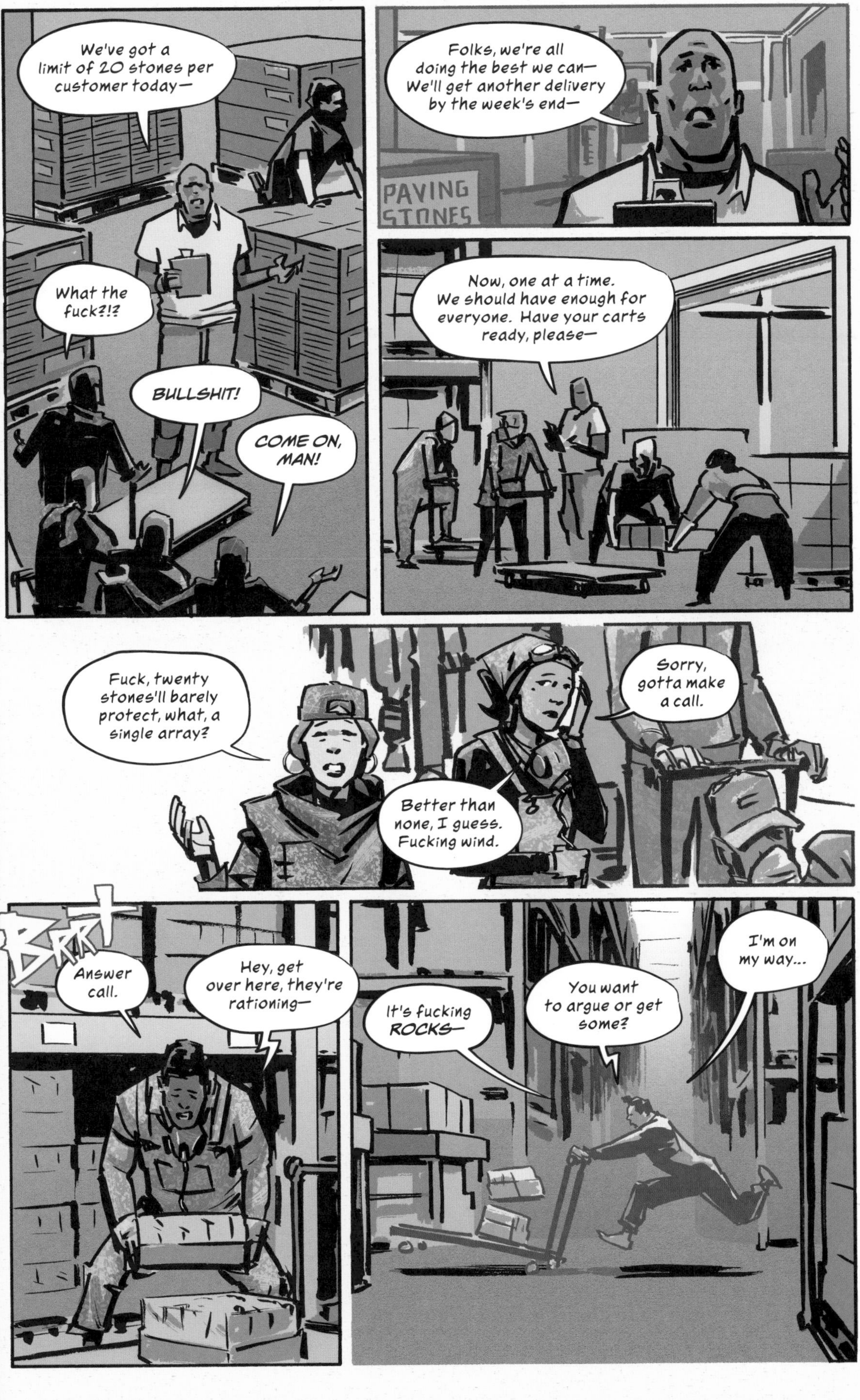
We've got a limit of 20 stones per customer today—
What the fuck?!?
BULLSHIT!
COME ON, MAN!
Folks, we're all doing the best we can— We'll get another delivery by the week's end—
PAVING STONES
Now, one at a time. We should have enough for everyone. Have your carts ready, please—
Fuck, twenty stones'll barely protect, what, a single array?
Better than none, I guess. Fucking wind.
Sorry, gotta make a call.
BRRRT
Answer call.
Hey, get over here, they're rationing—
It's fucking ROCKS—
You want to argue or get some?
I'm on my way...

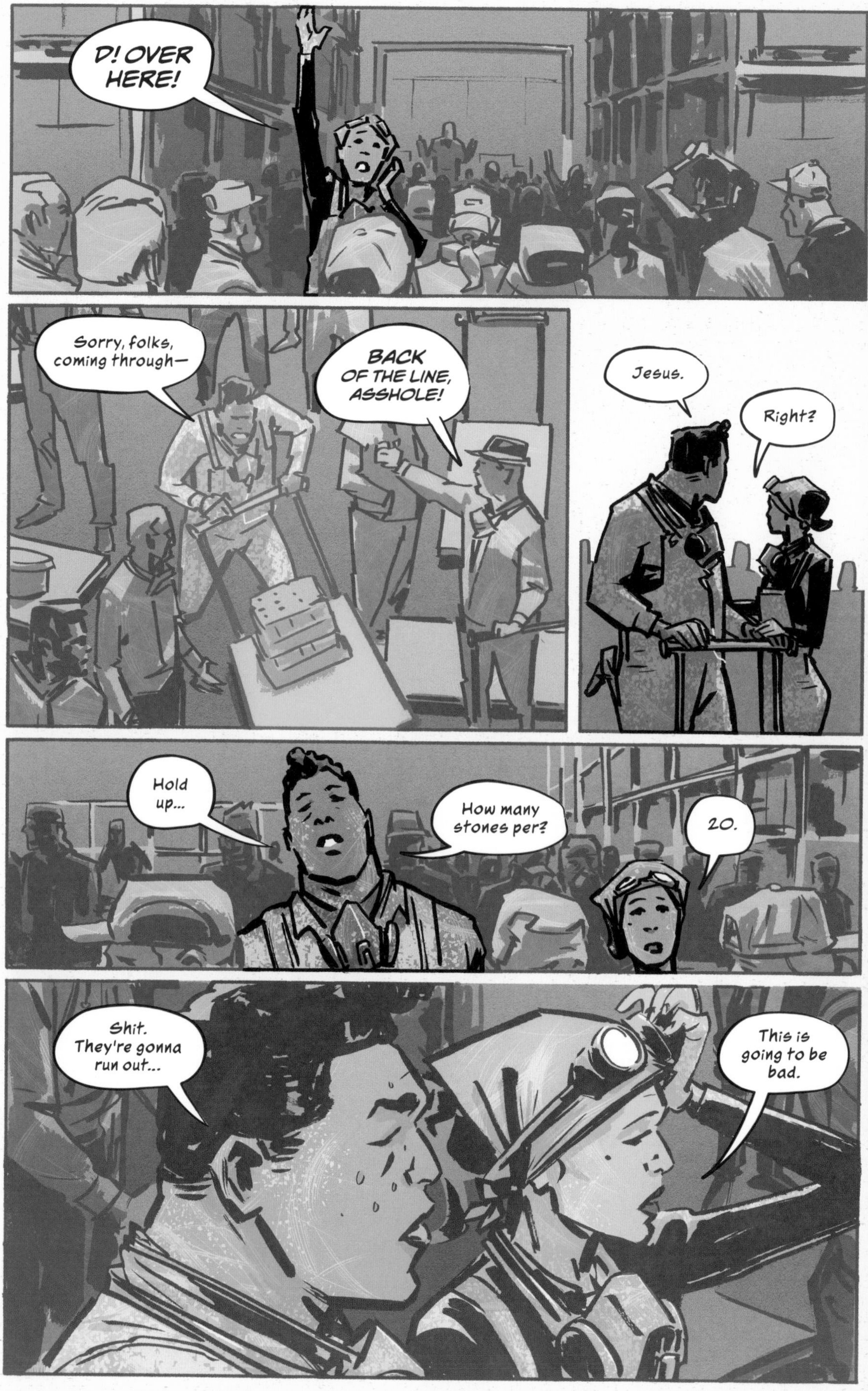
D! OVER HERE!
Sorry, folks, coming through—
BACK OF THE LINE, ASSHOLE!
Jesus.
Right?
Hold up...
How many stones per?
20.
Shit. They're gonna run out...
This is going to be bad.

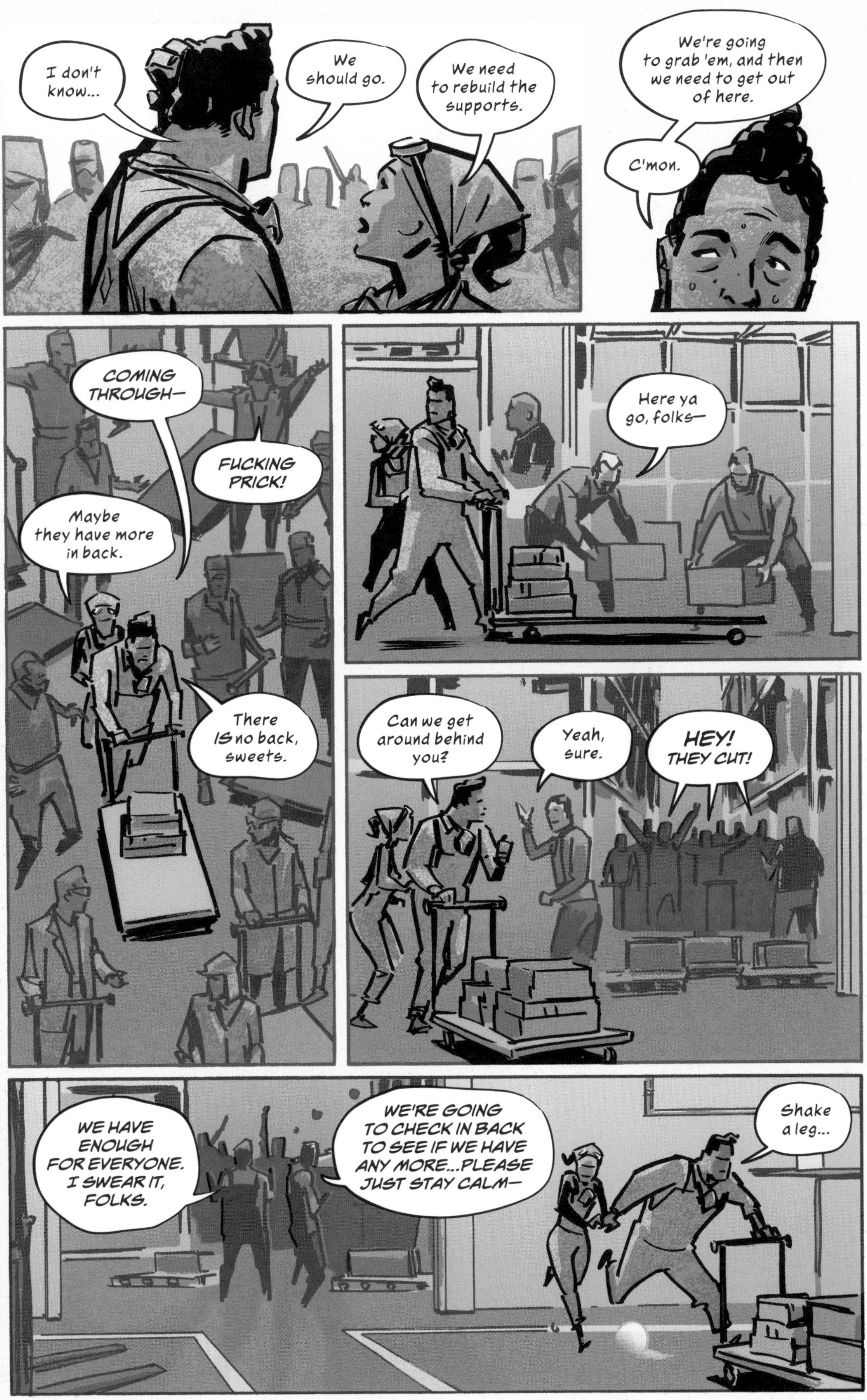
I don't know...
We should go.
We need to rebuild the supports.
We're going to grab 'em, and then we need to get out of here.
C'mon.
COMING THROUGH—
FUCKING PRICK!
Maybe they have more in back.
There IS no back, sweets.
Here ya go, folks—
Can we get around behind you?
Yeah, sure.
HEY! THEY CUT!
WE HAVE ENOUGH FOR EVERYONE. I SWEAR IT, FOLKS.
WE'RE GOING TO CHECK IN BACK TO SEE IF WE HAVE ANY MORE...PLEASE JUST STAY CALM—
Shake a leg...

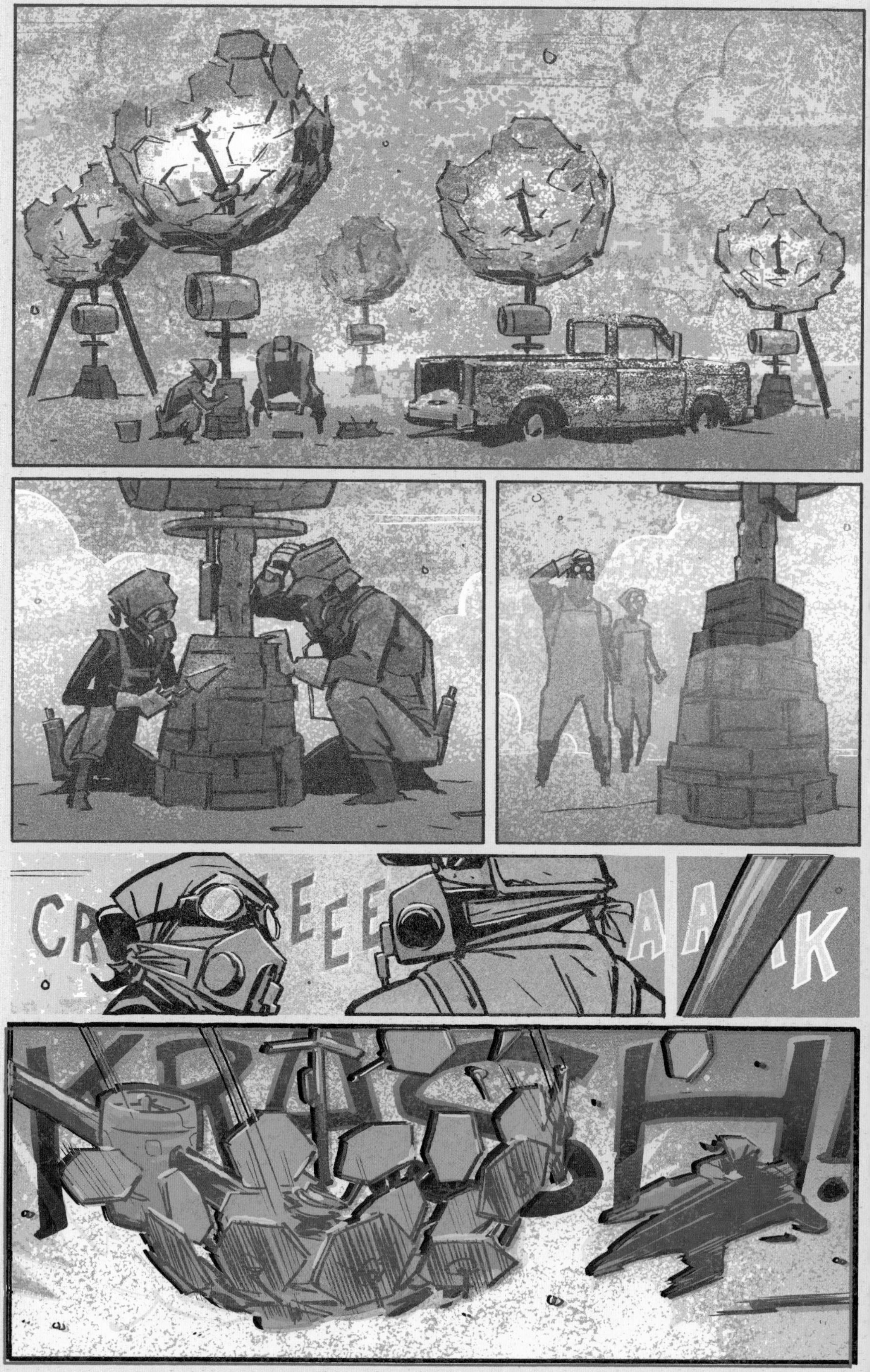
CR EEE AA K
KRA H!

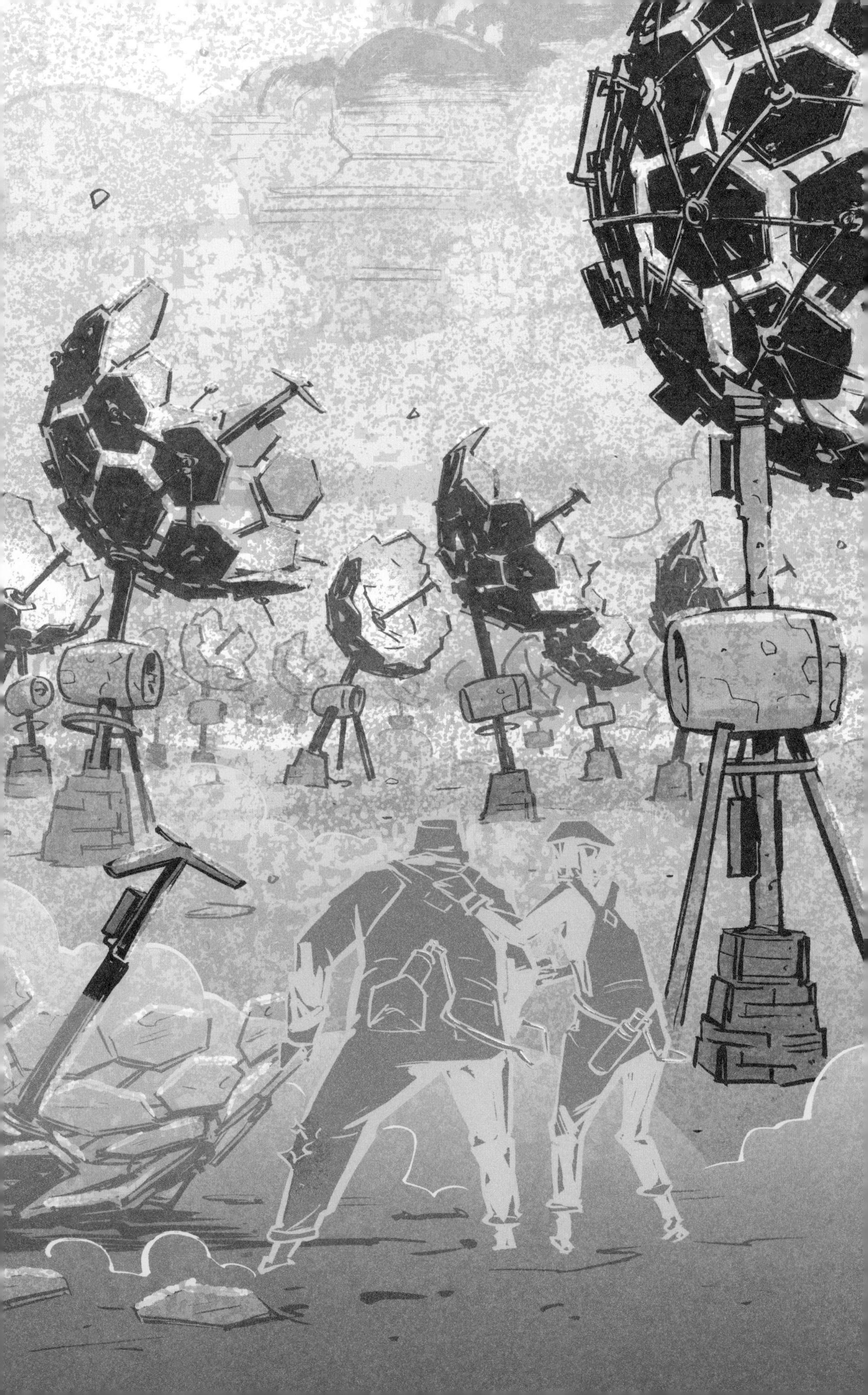

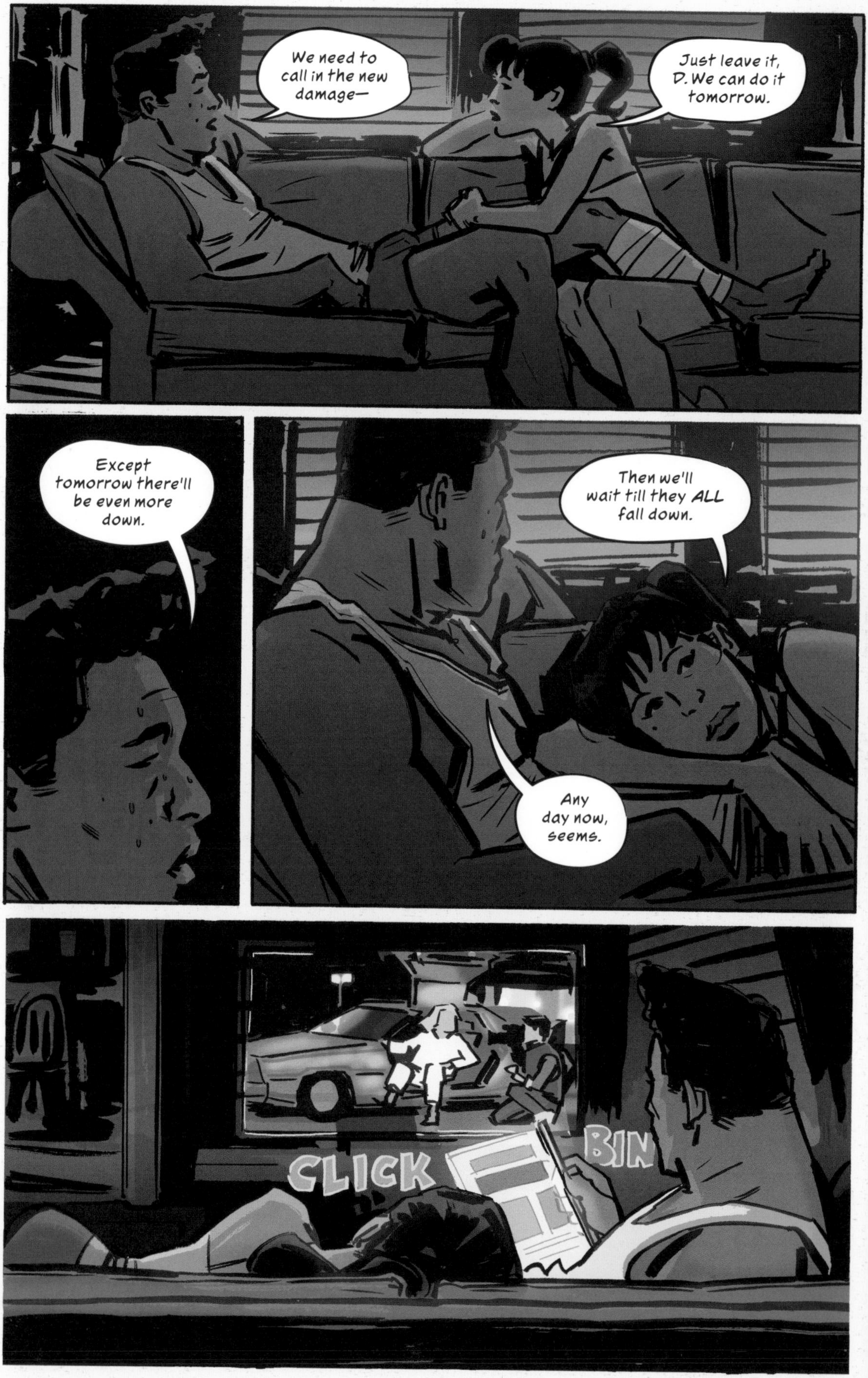
We need to call in the new damage—
Just leave it, D. We can do it tomorrow.
Except tomorrow there'll be even more down.
Then we'll wait till they ALL fall down.
Any day now, seems.
CLICK
BIN

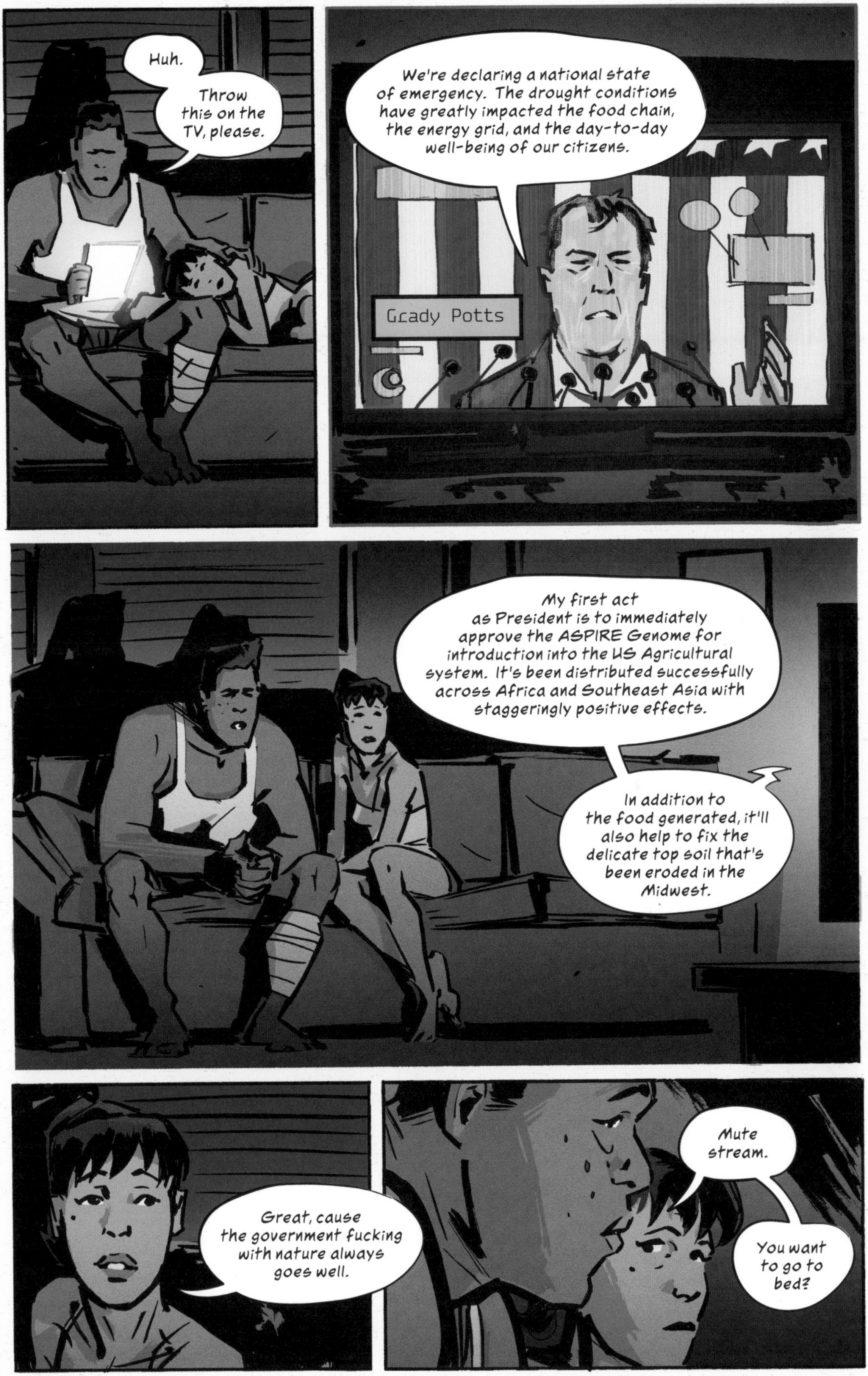
Huh.
Throw this on the TV, please.
We're declaring a national state of emergency. The drought conditions have greatly impacted the food chain, the energy grid, and the day-to-day well-being of our citizens.
Grady Potts
My first act as President is to immediately approve the ASPIRE Genome for introduction into the US Agricultural system. It's been distributed successfully across Africa and Southeast Asia with staggeringly positive effects.
In addition to the food generated, it'll also help to fix the delicate top soil that's been eroded in the Midwest.
Great, cause the government fucking with nature always goes well.
Mute stream.
You want to go to bed?

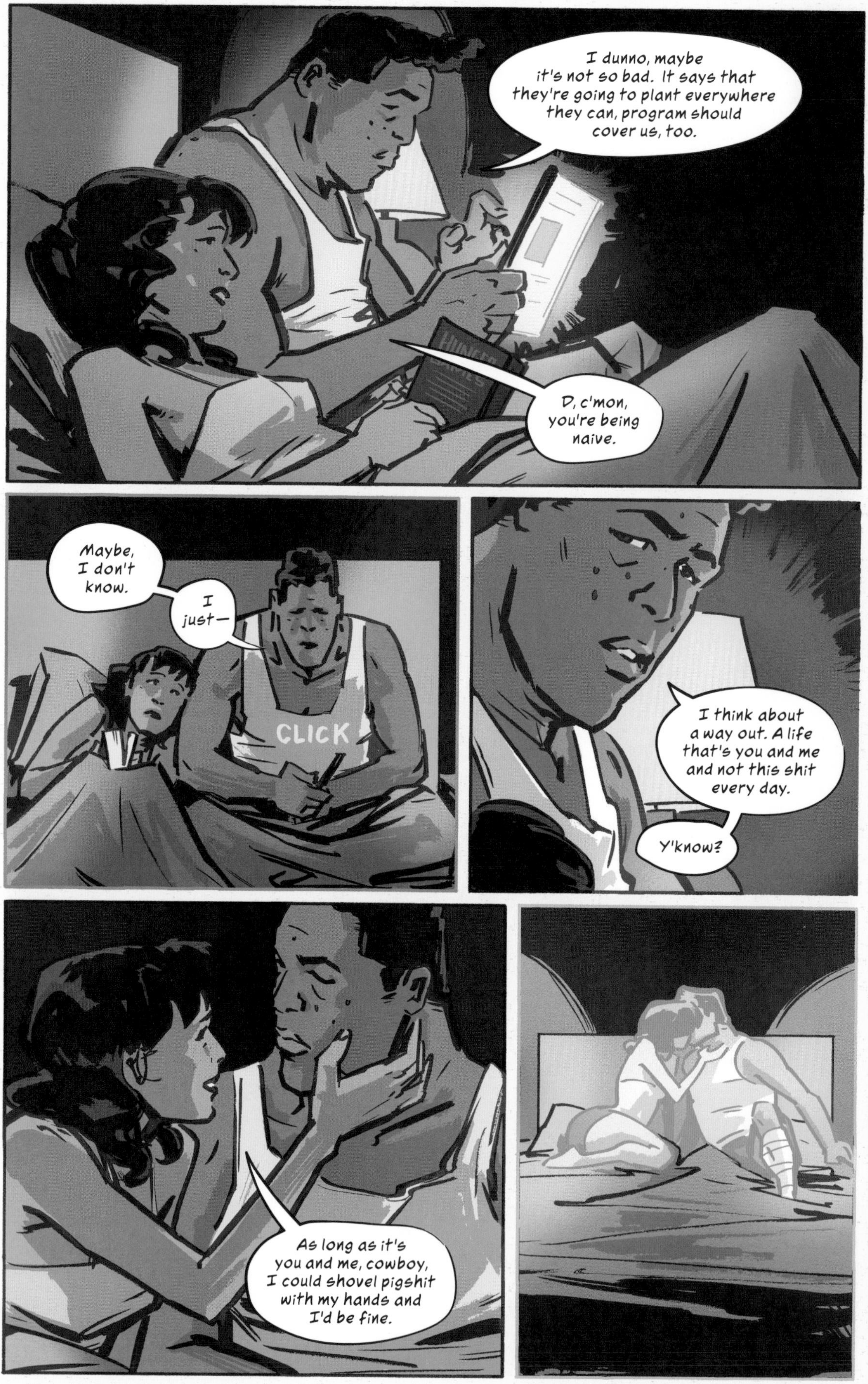
I dunno, maybe it's not so bad. It says that they're going to plant everywhere they can, program should cover us, too.
D, c'mon, you're being naive.
Maybe, I don't know.
I just—
CLICK
I think about a way out. A life that's you and me and not this shit every day.
Y'know?
As long as it's you and me, cowboy, I could shovel pigshit with my hands and I'd be fine.

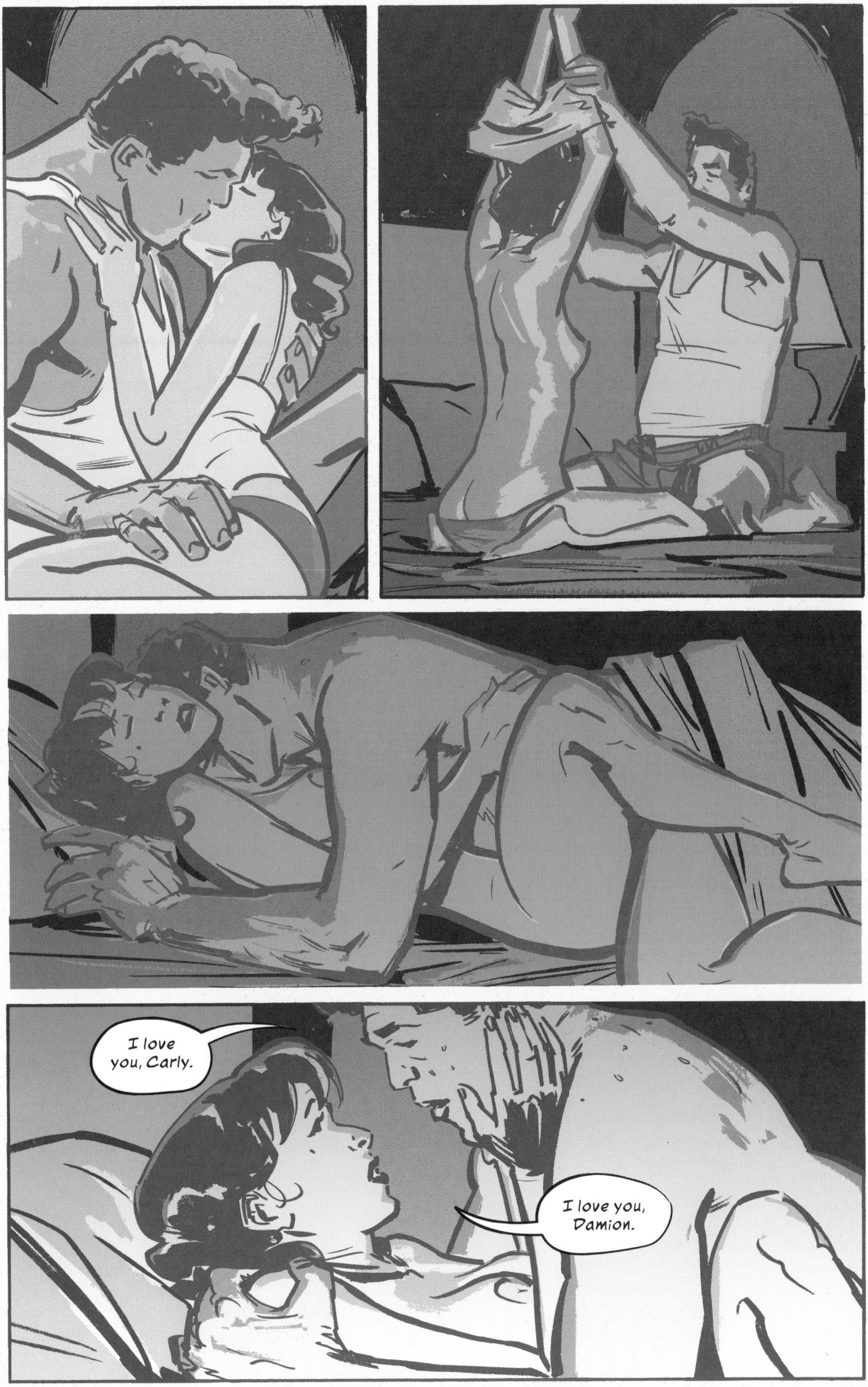
I love you, Carly.
I love you, Damion.

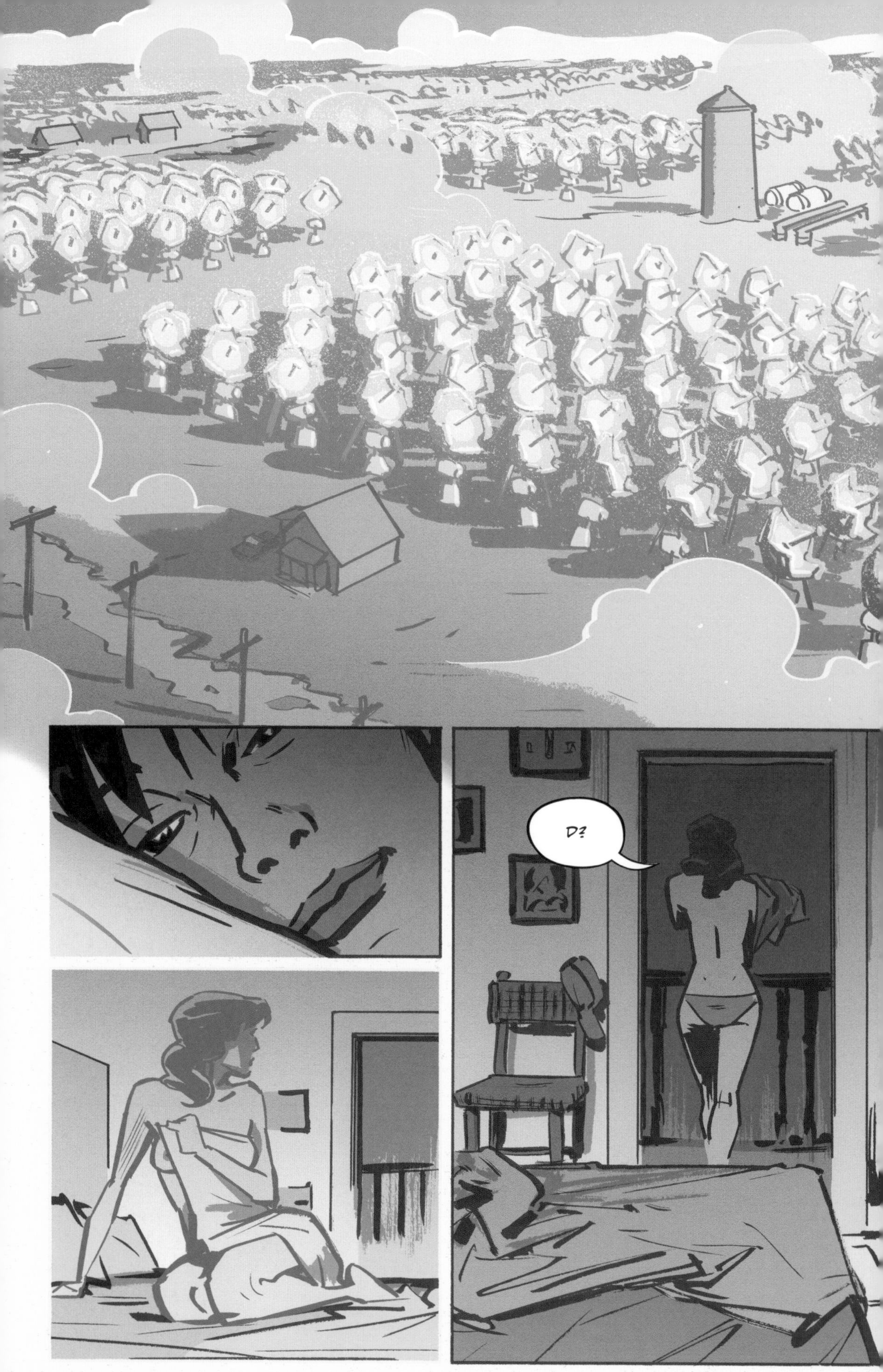
D?

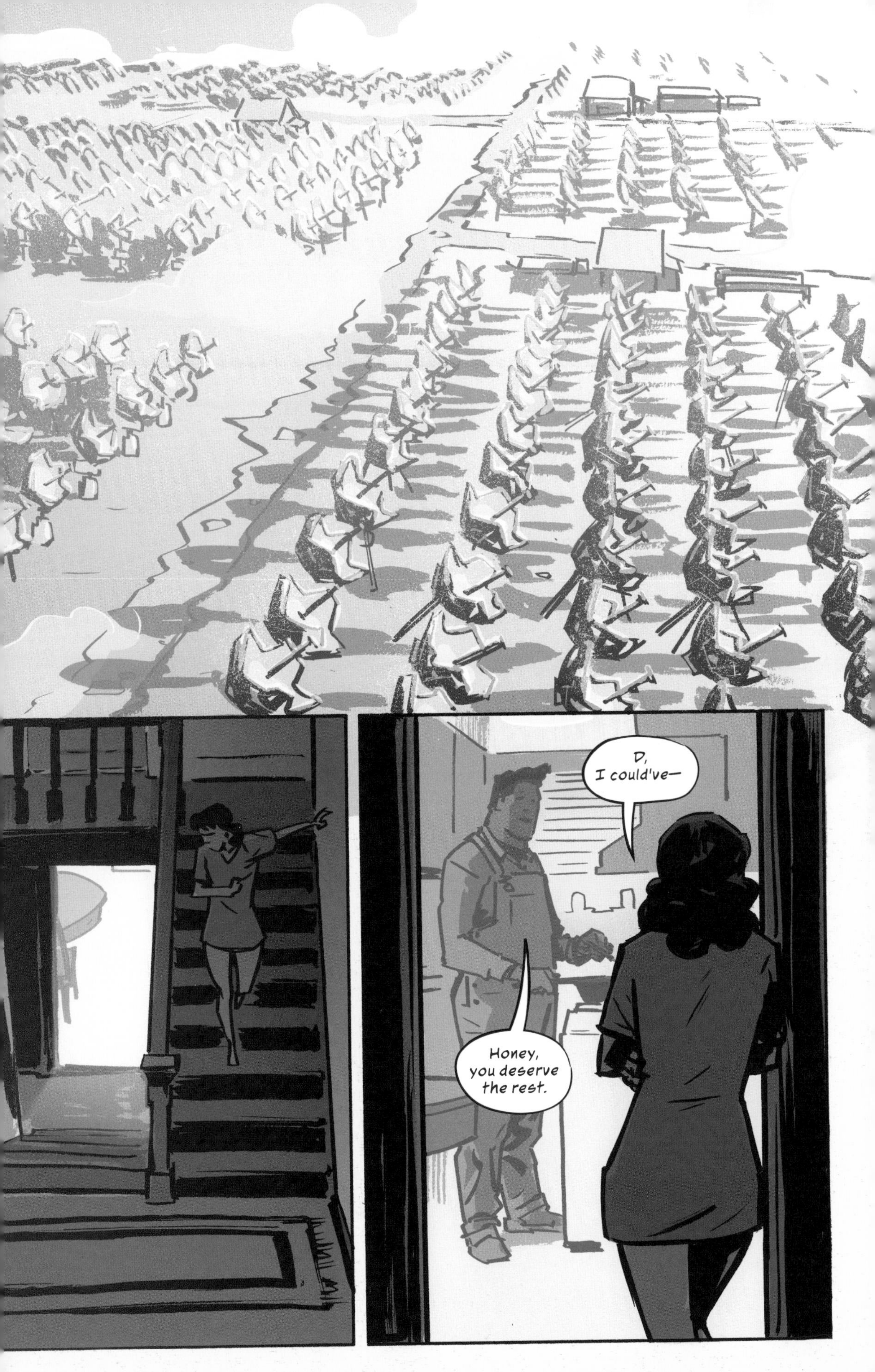
D, I could've—
Honey, you deserve the rest.

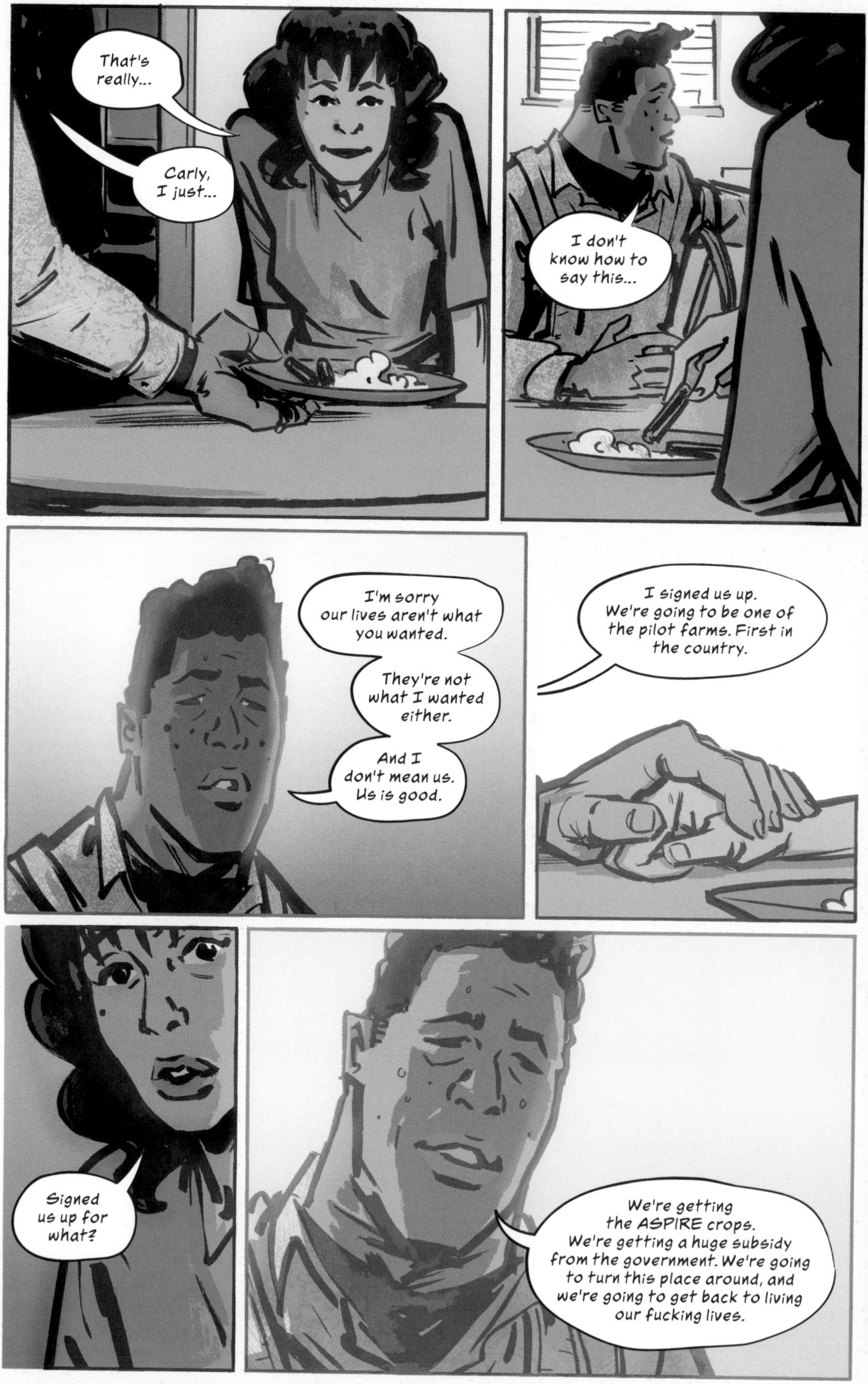
That's really...
Carly, I just...
I don't know how to say this...
I'm sorry our lives aren't what you wanted.
They're not what I wanted either.
And I don't mean us. Us is good.
I signed us up. We're going to be one of the pilot farms. First in the country.
Signed us up for what?
We're getting the ASPIRE crops. We're getting a huge subsidy from the government. We're going to turn this place around, and we're going to get back to living our fucking lives.

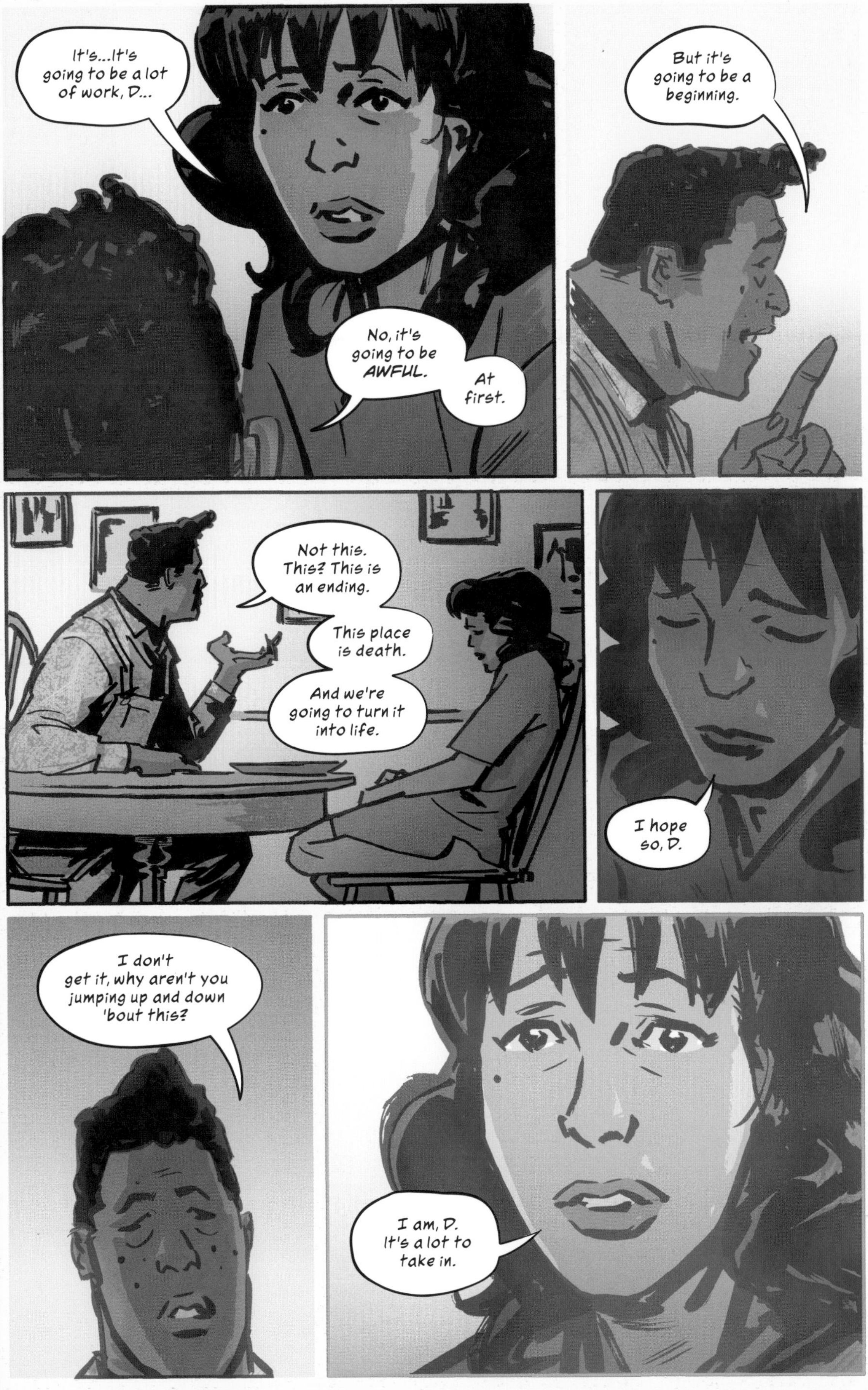
It's...It's going to be a lot of work, D...
No, it's going to be AWFUL.
At first.
But it's going to be a beginning.
Not this. This? This is an ending.
This place is death.
And we're going to turn it into life.
I hope so, D.
I don't get it, why aren't you jumping up and down 'bout this?
I am, D. It's a lot to take in.

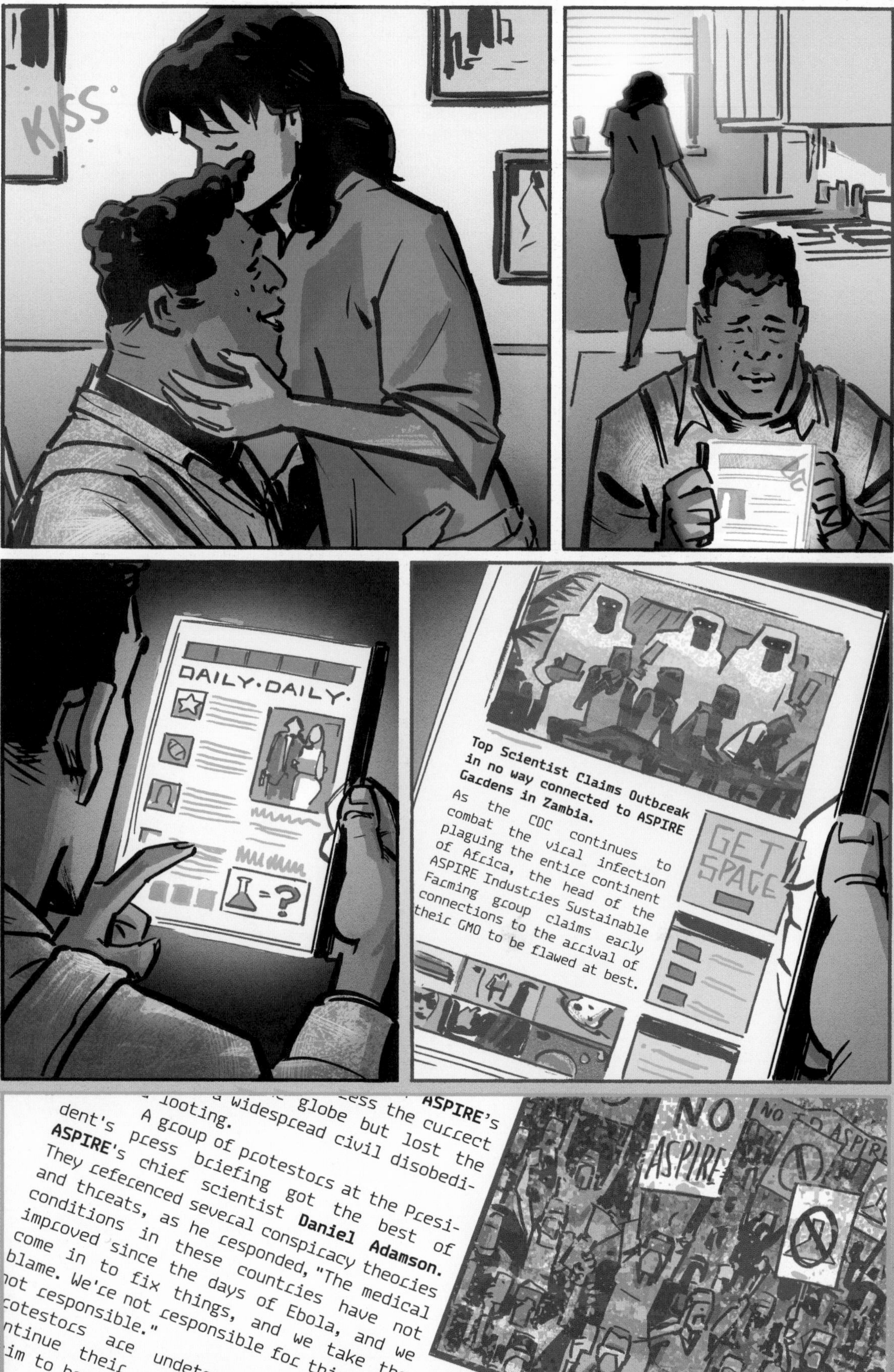
KISS
DAILY·DAILY·
=?
Top Scientist Claims Outbreak in no way connected to ASPIRE Gardens in Zambia.
As the CDC continues to combat the viral infection plaguing the entire continent of Africa, the head of the ASPIRE Industries Sustainable Farming group claims early connections to the arrival of their GMO to be flawed at best.
GET SPACE
ASPIRE's
globe but lost the current
widespread civil disobedi-
looting.
A group of protestors at the President's press briefing got the best of
ASPIRE's chief scientist Daniel Adamson.
They referenced several conspiracy theories
and threats, as he responded, "The medical
conditions in these countries have not
improved since the days of Ebola, and we
come in to fix things, and we take the
blame. We're not responsible for this. I am
not responsible."
protestors are undeterred and vow
continue their struggle for
to be basic human
NO ASPIRE
NO ASPIRE

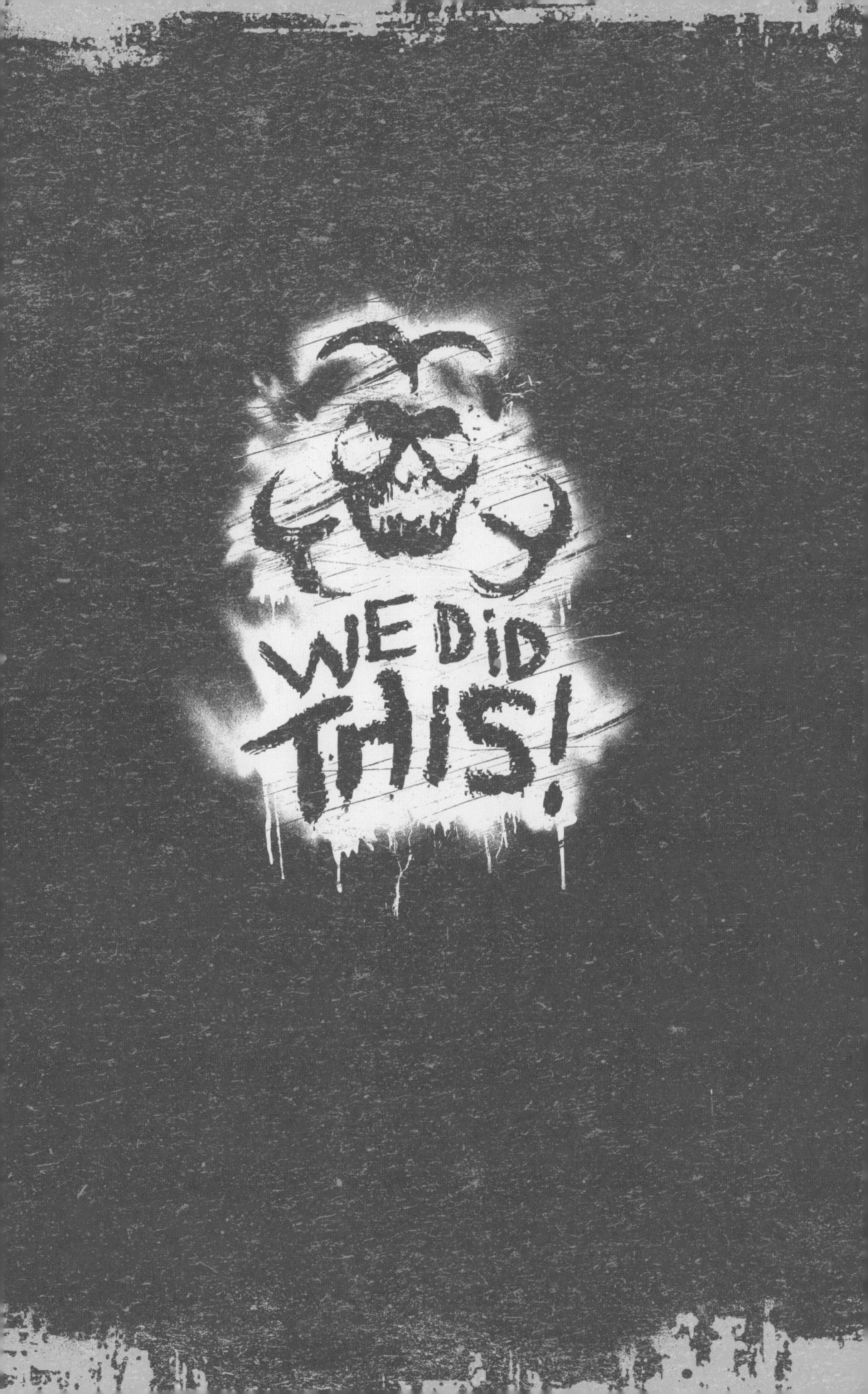
WE DID
THIS!

COVER GALLERY

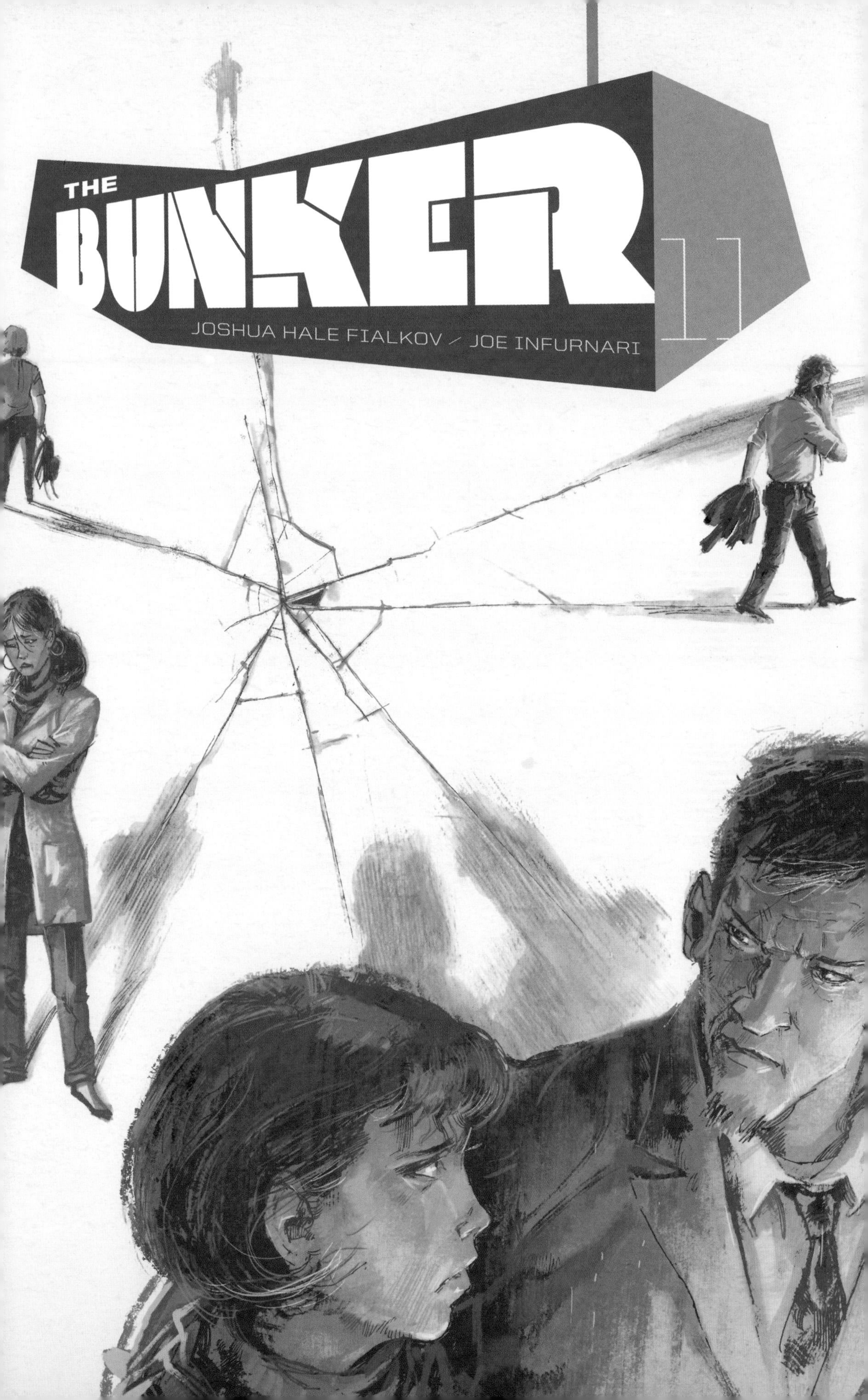
THE BUNKER
11
JOSHUA HALE FIALKOV / JOE INFURNARI

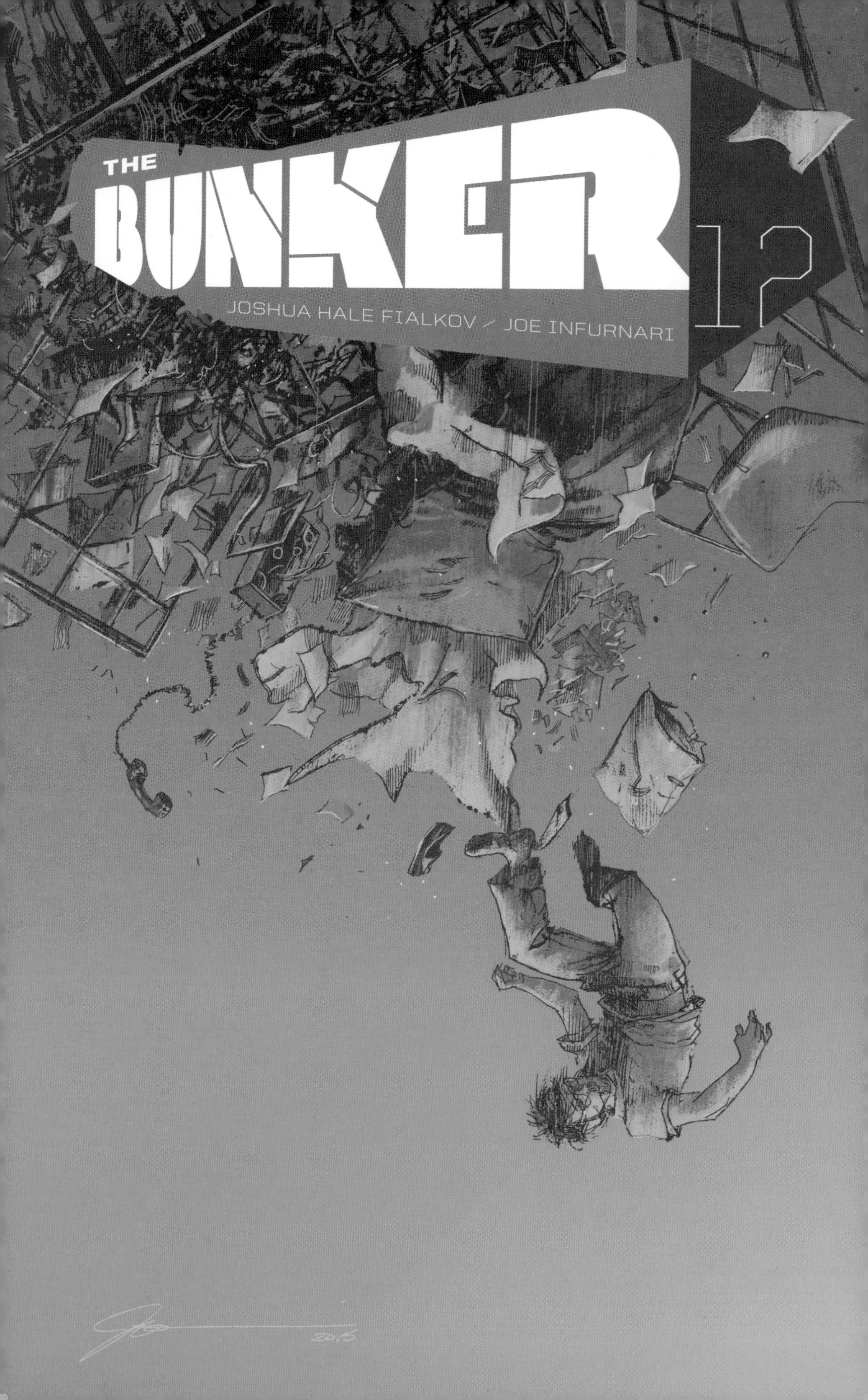
THE BUNKER
12
JOSHUA HALE FIALKOV / JOE INFURNARI
2015

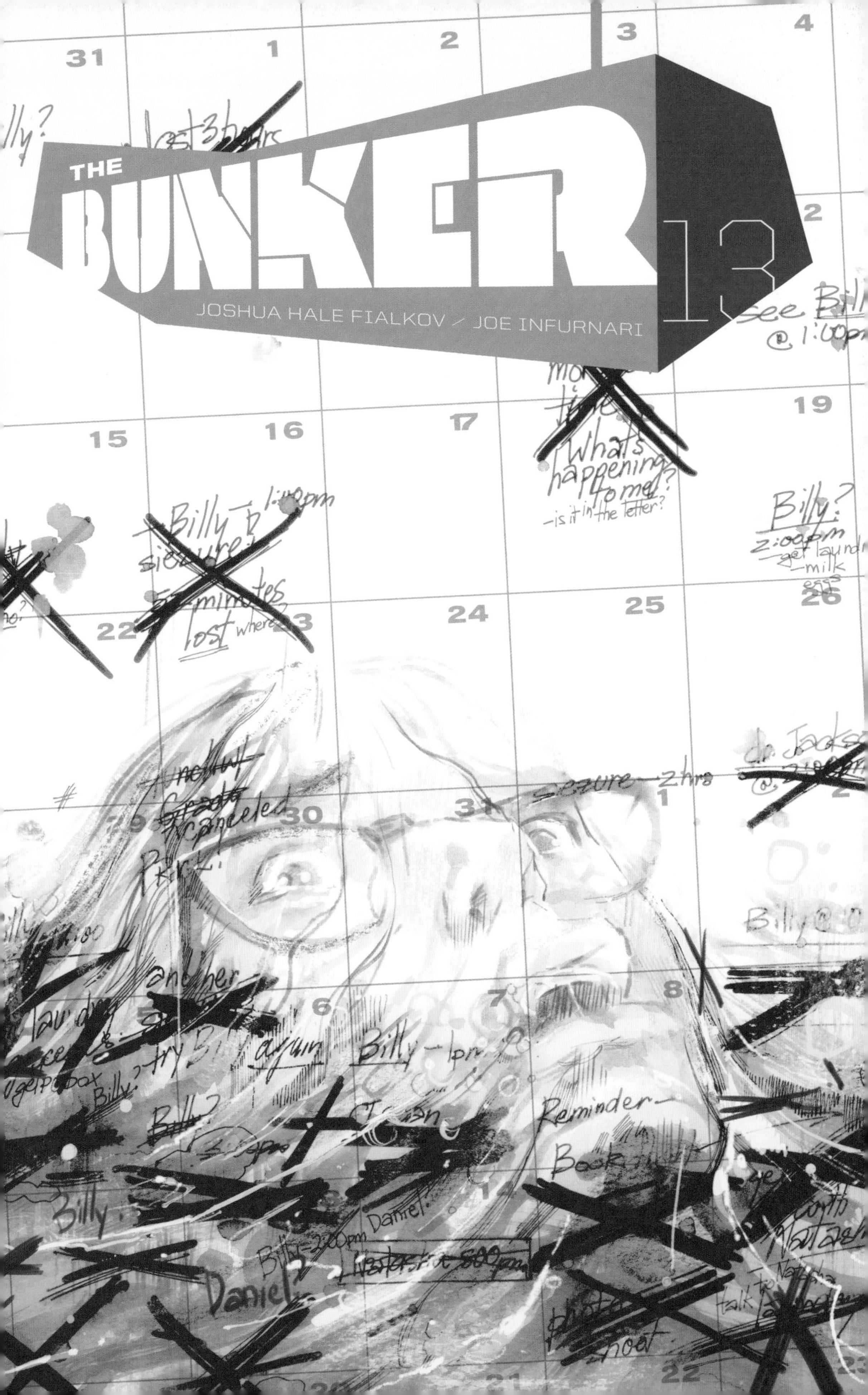
THE BUNKER
13
JOSHUA HALE FIALKOV / JOE INFURNARI
What's happening to me?
—is it in the letter?
Reminder—

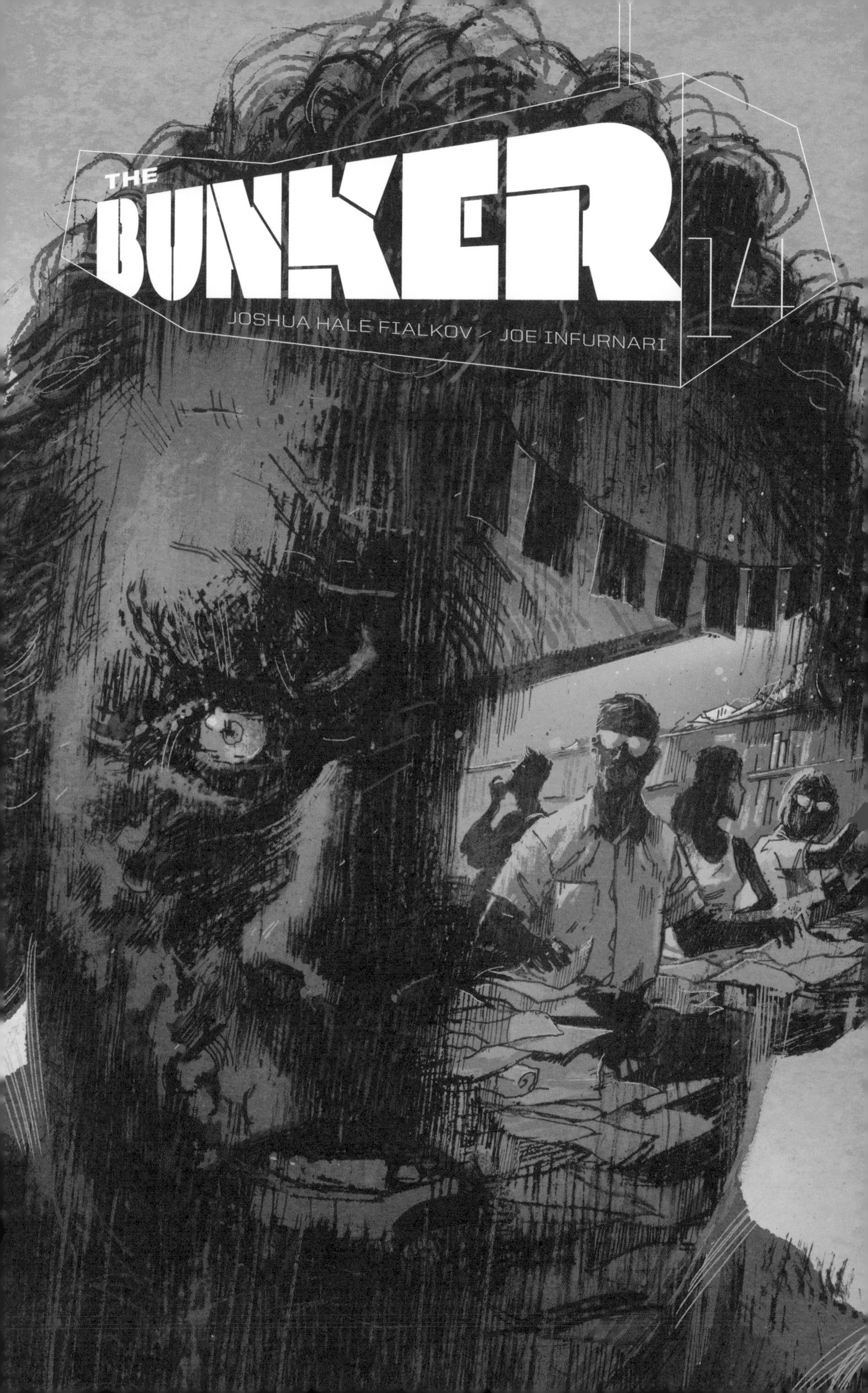
THE
BUNKER
14
JOSHUA HALE FIALKOV / JOE INFURNARI

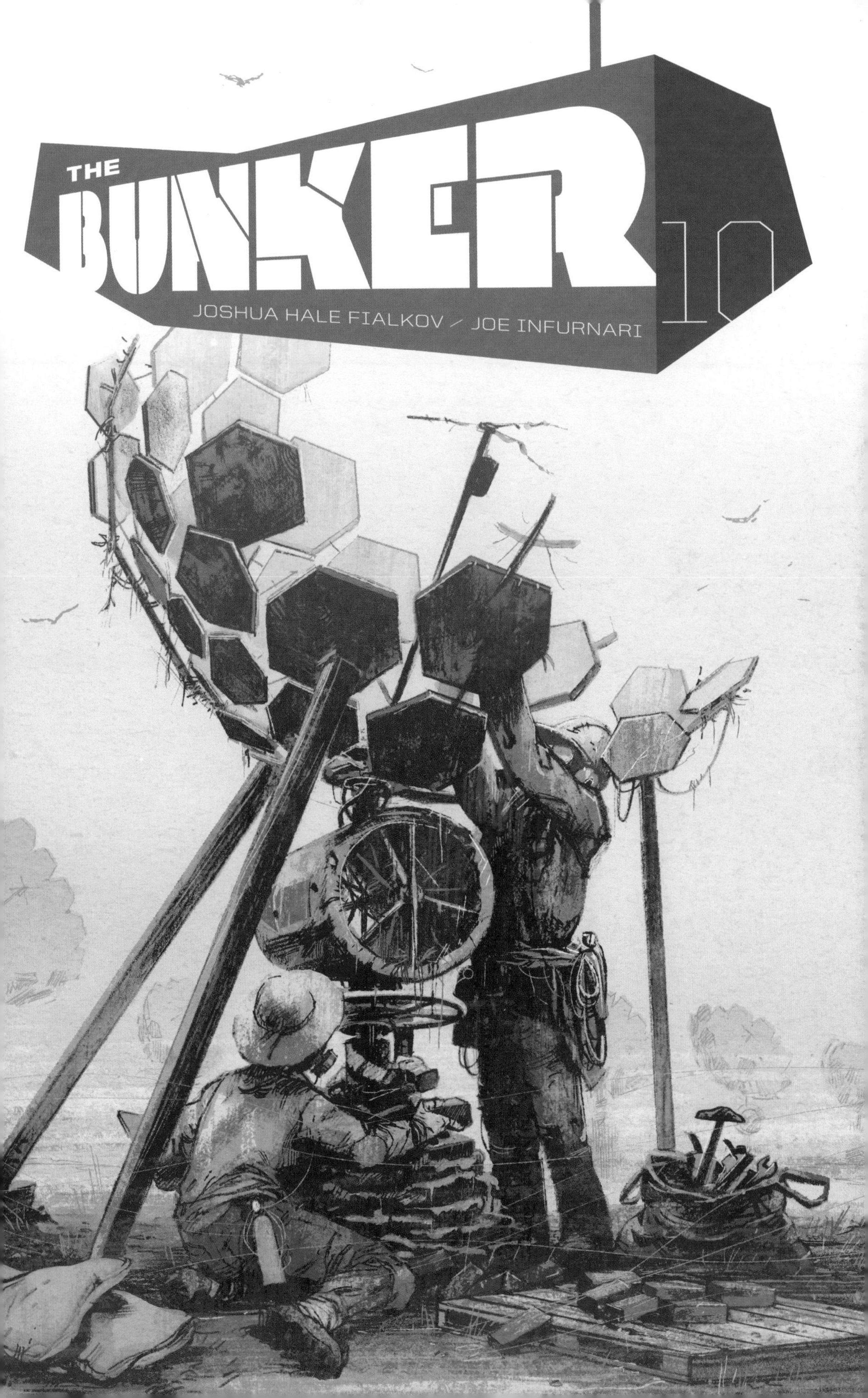
THE BUNKER
10
JOSHUA HALE FIALKOV / JOE INFURNARI

Photo by Heidi Ryder

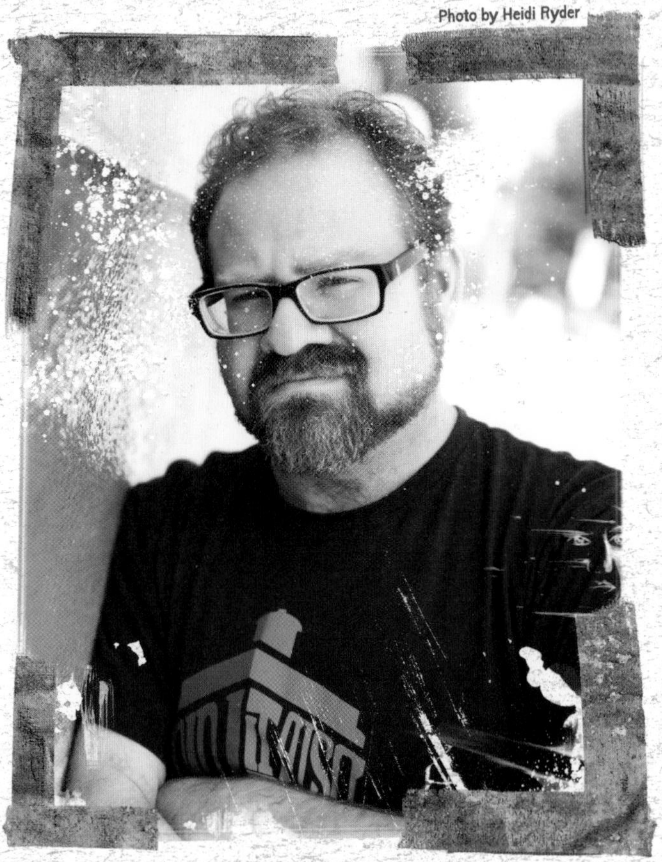

Joshua Hale Fialkov is the writer and co-creator of graphic novels including *Elk's Run*, *Tumor*, *The Life After*, *Punks*, and *Echoes*. He has written *The Ultimates* for Marvel and *I, Vampire* for DC Comics. He lives in Los Angeles with his wife, author Christina Rice, their daughter, who will remain anonymous (and adorable), their dogs Cole and Olaf, and a very pissed off cat named Smokey.

Photo by Seth Kushner

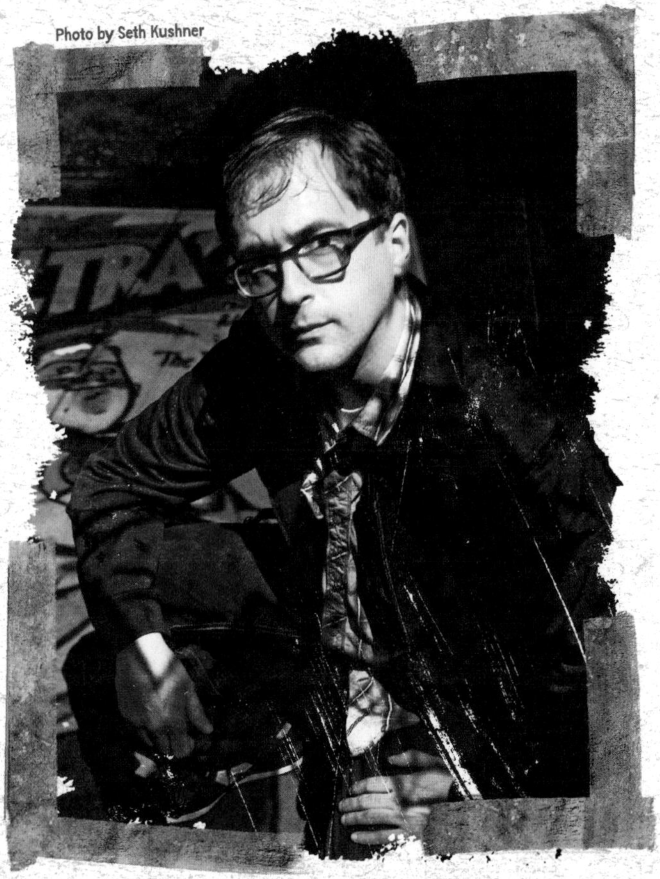
TRA

Being the singular genius behind the infamous *Time F#©ker*, Joe Infurnari's talents are uniquely suited to the vagaries of illustrating a time travel story. Whether tracing deadbeat dad DNA back to Paleolithic times or propping up a drawing pad in the midst of the apocalypse, Joe's upper lip remains stiff and his focus resolute. It's not all work and no play for Joe 'The Towering' Infurnari! Leisure time is lovingly spent with his new bride and their four crazy cats in a bunker of his own design.

Brahm Revel has spent the first half of his life in San Francisco and the second half in New York City. As a result, he has no idea what a moderately priced apartment is. In that time he's worked extensively in the film and animation industries, most notably sharing storyboarding duties for a time on *The Venture Bros*. In recent years he's turned his attention squarely to comics, recently writing and drawing the *Marvel Knights: X-Men* mini for Marvel Comics. He's probably best known (hopefully) for his creator owned series, *Guerillas*, from Oni Press, and he promises that "the new volumes are almost done and will be well worth the wait!" Currently, Brahm is *en résidence* at La Maison des Auteurs in Angoulême, France, eating baguettes and reminding everyone that his middle name is Jacques.

Jason Fischer has been flatting *The Bunker* since issue #3 and fully colored issue #10. He's been working on comics and art for several years and had the pleasure to work with Bryan Lee O'Malley on *Seconds* as a drawing assistant. Jason is currently working on a graphic novel for Oni Press while publishing mini comics. He lives in Portland, OR with his wife, Robin, and cat, Tigre.

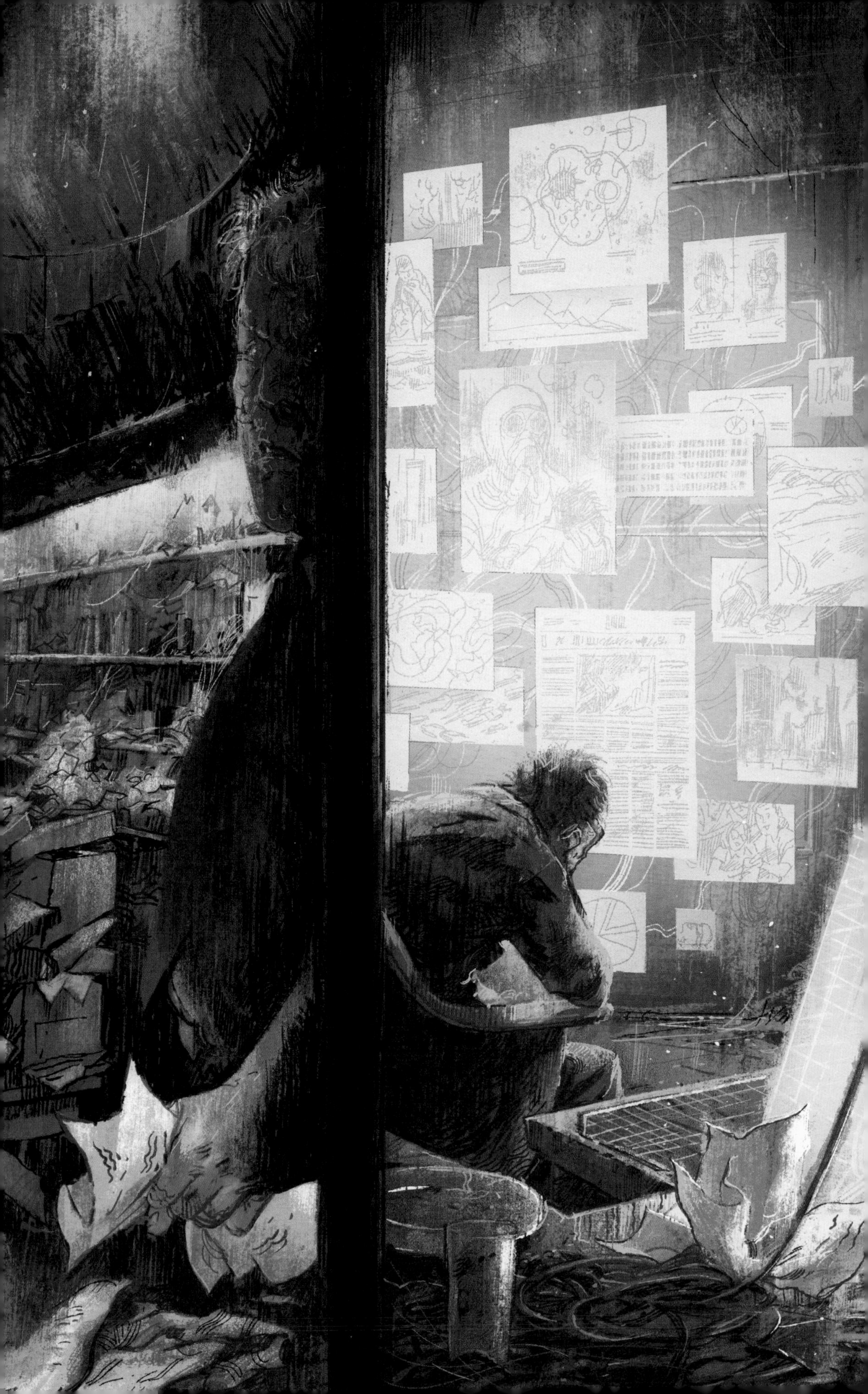

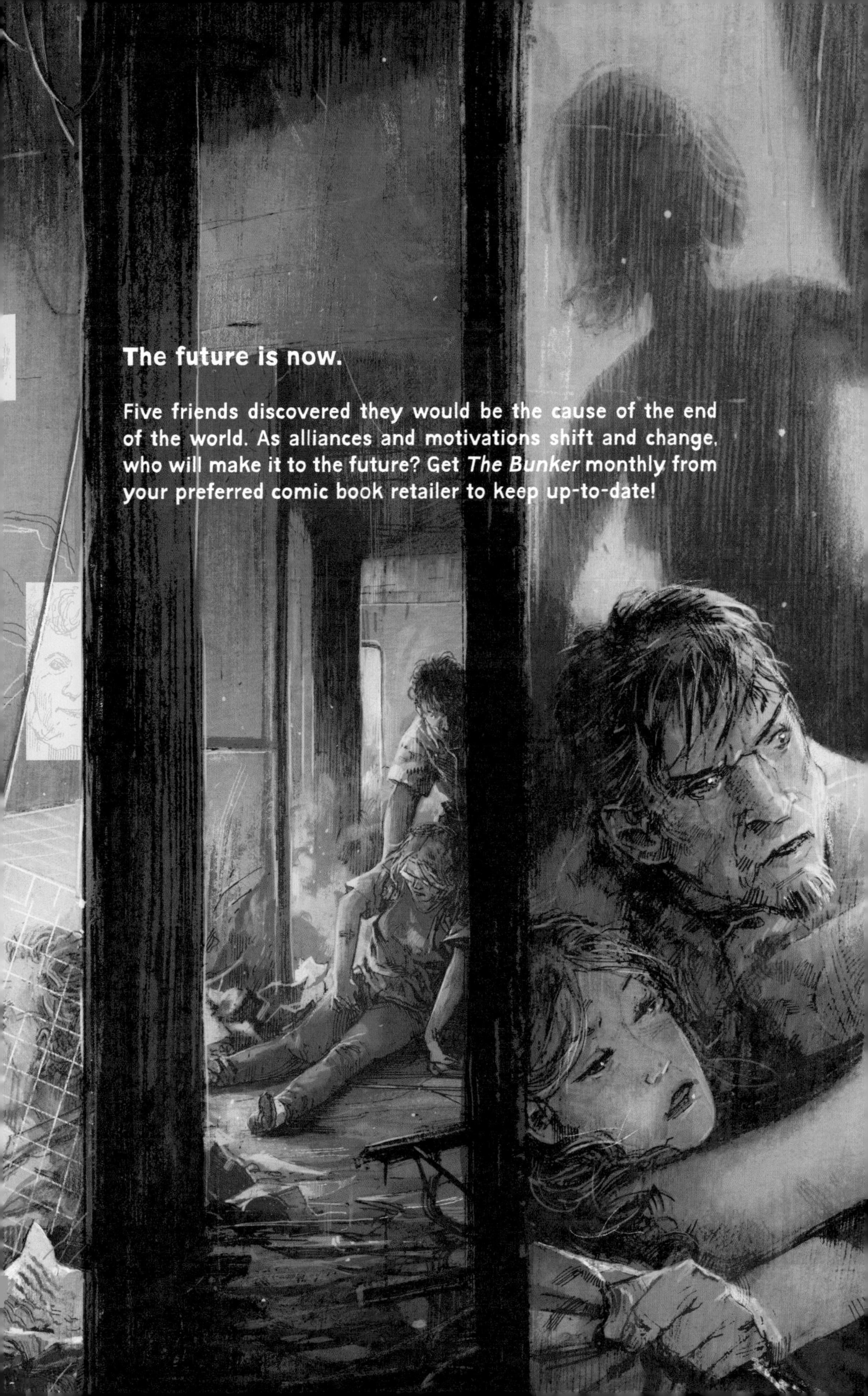

The future is now.

Five friends discovered they would be the cause of the end of the world. As alliances and motivations shift and change, who will make it to the future? Get *The Bunker* monthly from your preferred comic book retailer to keep up-to-date!

MORE FROM JOSHUA HALE FIALKOV AND ONI PRESS!

THE BUNKER
JOSHUA HALE FIALKOV | JOE INFURNARI
VOLUME 1

THE BUNKER
JOSHUA HALE FIALKOV | JOE INFURNARI
VOLUME 2

THE BUNKER VOL. 1:

By Joshua Hale Fialkov & Joe Infurnari
136 pages, softcover, full color interiors
ISBN 978-1-62010-164-3

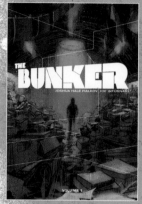

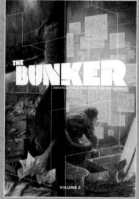

THE BUNKER VOL. 2:

By Joshua Hale Fialkov & Joe Infurnari
136 pages, softcover, full color interiors
ISBN 978-1-62010-210-7

THE LIFE AFTER
JOSHUA HALE FIALKOV • GABO
1
10/10

THE LIFE AFTER
JOSHUA HALE FIALKOV • GABO
2

THE LIFE AFTER VOL. 1:

By Joshua Hale Fialkov & Gabo
136 pages, softcover, full color interiors
ISBN 978-1-62010-214-5

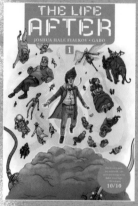

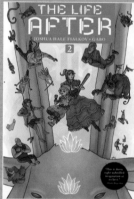

THE LIFE AFTER VOL. 2:

By Joshua Hale Fialkov & Gabo
144 pages, softcover, full color interiors
ISBN 978-1-62010-254-1

ELK'S RUN
A TALE OF SMALL TOWN HORROR
New York Times Best-Selling Authors
JOSHUA HALE
NOEL
SCOTT KEATING

LETTER 44
VOLUME 1: ESCAPE VELOCITY
01

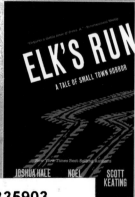

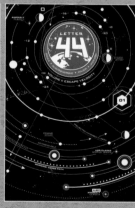

ELK'S RUN: 10TH ANNIVERSARY EDITION

By Joshua Hale Fialkov & Noel Tuazon
248 pages, hardcover, full color interiors
ISBN 978-1-62010-279-4

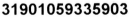

LETTER 44 VOL. 1: ESCAPE VELOCITY

By Charles Soule, Alberto Jiménez Alburquerque, Guy Major, & Dan Jackson
160 pages, softcover, full color interiors
ISBN 978-1-62010-133-9

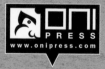

ONI PRESS
www.onipress.com

For more information on these and other fine Oni Press comic books and graphic novels visit onipress.com.
To find a comic specialty store in your area visit comicsphops.us.